THE WEALTH OF CHRISTIANS

THE WEALTH OF

CHRISTIANS

Redmond Mullin

ORBIS BOOKS
Maryknoll, New York 10545

The Catholic Foreign Mission Society of America (Maryknoll) recruits and trains people for overseas missionary service. Through Orbis Books Maryknoll aims to foster the international dialogue that is essential to mission. The books published, however, reflect the opinions of their authors and are not meant to represent the official position of the society.

Originally published by the Paternoster Press, Ltd., 3 Mount Radford Cresent, Exeter, Great Britain, copyright © 1983 by Redmond Mullin

U.S. edition 1984 by Orbis Books, Maryknoll, NY 10545

Typeset in Great Britain and printed and bound in the United States of America

---

Library of Congress Cataloging in Publication Data

Mullin, Redmond.
  The wealth of Christians.

  Bibliography: p.
  Includes index.
  1. Wealth—Religious aspects—Christianity.
  2. Economics—Religious aspects—Christianity. I. Title.
BR115.W4M77 1984   261.8'5   84-7262
ISBN 0-88344-709-6 (pbk.)

CONTENTS

For Caedmon and Gregory

Foreword and Acknowledgements

I am conscious of a great debt to those who, for no other reason than generosity, advised and guided me in my researches for this book, and to those in my household who have patiently endured me while it was written. There are some to whom I give exceptional thanks. Rabbi Nachum L. Rabinovitch, until recently the principal of Jews' College in London, gave my request for comment on the manuscript a detailed and careful response. Fredman Ashe Lincoln, Q.C., remarkable for his christian as for his jewish studies, gave me early, invaluable guidance. My old friend and former fellow student, Rev. Dr. Anthony Meredith, S.J., read and commented on the M.S. with characteristic scholarship and kindness. Beyond these there is a small throng who should be acknowledged, but only a few can be named: John Glaser for obtaining materials from Salt Lake City; Graham MacNamee; Kay Holmes-Siedle and Jose Westgeest for some supplementary research; Peter Levi; Nicholas Toke-Nichols for ancestral letters, and my editor Peter Cousins. Liz Parkinson, as I have come to expect, worked with amazing speed, accuracy, cheerfulness and interpretative skill in typing the manuscript. Michael Walsh was as usual enormously helpful, both in locating sources and in making available the great resources of the Heythrop library. Finally, above all, my wife Carol must have my thanks as well as my love. She has quite enough to do, coping with us all, but my writing is always the occasion for chaos and upset routines, about which she is uncomplaining. She made time between cooking, washing clothes and faces, nose-wiping, brewing, mending clothes and knees, tidying, comforting and encouraging husband and children, maintaining house and garden, responding to questions and cries, letter-writing, creating pots and drawings, to do the index for me.

A comment needs to be made on the sources quoted in the notes. Since I run a business as well as writing, the sources must usually be those that are to hand. Therefore a few rather odd editions are cited, which I would not ideally have chosen.

REDMOND MULLIN
Tunbridge Wells

Introduction

This extended essay is based on a simple observation, and on a growing anxiety. Most Christians today live in societies which have effectively ceased to be christian, and which promote values subversive of Christianity. My particular concern here is with economic behaviour and attitudes; with the ways Christians earn, own and dispose of their wealth. Although, as I shall argue, the organization of both labour and industry, as well as private attitudes to philanthropy and to property rights, have roots in christian teachings and practices, their christian forms have become disfigured. Yet no effective, christian alternative has emerged either to capitalist or to marxist systems.

Our context for living a christian life today is remarkably similar to that of Christians under the pagan, roman emperors. There are strong and positive secular ethics of economic and social behaviour, on which Christians draw with benefit, but the secular ethic of our modern society cannot be adopted whole and unchanged; like the christian communities described by Tertullian, Christians today form part of the state, but they should form an awkward part of it. Their outlook and behaviour ought to be distinctive. The issue is not of manners, but of justice. At a time when economic institutions and attitudes inherited from the eighteenth and nineteenth centuries are increasingly discredited, when the financially disadvantaged at home are again making conspicuous the divisions in our society, and when mortal poverty in a large section of the world is becoming a threat as well as an accusation, cosy concepts of charity appear fatuously inadequate. Christian responsibility must be to seek responses that are adequate, and will need to include the use of the organs of the state to achieve this; but the solution must be of Christ, not of Marx or of

Milton Friedman with the cross stuck as a brooch on their lapels. The christian response must also be profoundly disturbing.

This is a period of special opportunity, perhaps more positive than any since the early centuries after Christ, or at least since the Reformation. The reason is that the links between church and state and the commercial establishment, which were an expression of mutual solidarity, and which positioned the churches as part of the civil establishment and culture, are now being rapidly weakened. The separation should give the churches a new freedom to assert their integrity, and to work and live out a distinctly christian ethic in their economic lives.

Effective initiative or leadership in any movement to reform christian, economic teaching and behaviour is more likely to come from self-motivated laity rather than from clergy, who have demonstrated little ability to instigate the kind of change that is required. However, my argument is not for the construction of a christian secularism or humanism. The contents of any christian ethical teaching, it will be demonstrated, can be matched, at least in principle, by atheistic thinkers. What I am talking about is a work of grace, a true conversion, in which Christians' realization of the Incarnation will include their economic behaviour and all dealings, in business or out of it, with their neighbour.

Because the initiative to be taken must be radically revolutionary in Christians' lives, and must be carried through with the aim of being effective in our real, historical society, it will work through a variety of channels, including those of traditional, organized charity. The latter cannot be enough. If justice rather than benevolence is the objective, 'charity' may block apter solutions; but routine charity can prepare the way for just economic behaviour. Therefore the ways Christians have organized and financed their charity is relevant to this study.

My method will be to survey a range of christian and some relevant non-christian teachings on wealth, poverty, charity and the economic life, to establish the origins of our own prejudices and practices and to explore a variety of related, pertinent themes. These include attitudes to wealth and poverty, the use of goods, the conduct of business, the treatment of the poor, fundraising, philanthropy and relations between church and state.

I have handled the materials as follows: first, I have surveyed greek, roman and jewish teachings, to illustrate Christianity's debt to them and to demonstrate the kind of economic ethic which can be developed quite independently of Christ. Next, I look at the New Testament. To show the character of christian teaching and practice in a pagan society, I deal separately with developments up to the collapse of the roman empire under barbarian assault. I then deal with the main themes topic by topic, drawing on materials from the middle ages to the nineteenth century, to review how Christians thought and behaved and to show the scale of our pagan society's debt to previous forms of Christianity. This section also shows how sound christian teachings on wealth have tended to corrupt themselves, generating the injustices we confront today. Finally, I look at what is happening now, evaluating the effects of both radical christian and marxist thinking. For some readers, it may be more satisfactory to read my last chapter first, because it shows where apparently random lines in my survey are leading.

The purpose is to travel observantly, but not to enjoy the views. The terminus contains conclusions. We are at such a special moment in the evolution of Christianity that current wisdom is not enough; we need to be aware of Christianity's whole store, not out of curiosity but because the established churches have tended to distort or hide their own radical foundations and the more embarrassing consequences of their uncompromised doctrines. This is by no means the best of all possible surveys, but it may help Christians who, like myself, have become anxiously conscious of the churches' failures to respond adequately to the demands of our situation. I am a businessman, not a theologian, and I undertook this journey to emerge with some examples and insights that may help myself and a few others in a similar situation to talk to each other.

One very clear conclusion from my survey has to be that there is no single, coherent christian doctrine on wealth. To take a matching pair of examples, medieval teachings on christian poverty and post-reformation teachings on christian stewardship contradict each other. They led to very unchristian, practical conclusions; but the truth they combine to represent seems to rest in their contradiction and in the tension this creates. At a time when the anti-christian force of attitudes deriving from christian stewardship has resolved itself into vicious, capitalist dogma, while christian radicalism has resolved itself into equally vicious, socialist dogma, it is important to survey the whole. If truth is in the tension, christian truth today must commit us, in our contemporaries' eyes, towards a daft-seeming poverty. The conclusion is complex; as I will show (pp.175-179), some of the practical propositions to be derived from my survey are mutually incompatible, although they make up a reasonable summary of the teachings discussed in the chapters that follow.

My conclusion is firm. The experience of foregoing Christians belongs to us, and we are required to use it, despite its complexity; but our conclusion needs to be simple and practical. This is the theme at the end of this book. The wisdom we assimilate becomes part of us, and its christian conclusion expresses total, all-demanding simplicity. From the manifold of christian teaching and experience, the reality of the single, incarnate Christ must be expressed through each of us, in our own, present time.

Part One: Origins

1

Greek and Roman Teaching on Wealth, Poverty and Relief

Celsus, a pagan critic of Christianity, perhaps writing between AD 177 and 180, made two remarks which focus major themes for my book. They concerned the originality of the Gospel's ethical teaching and the poverty of Christ. He complained, said Origen, against 'our *ethical teaching* on the grounds that it *is commonplace and in comparison with the other philosophers contains no teaching that is impressive or new.'* He also mocked Christ's birth-story, partly on the grounds of class and riches: *'Then was the mother of Jesus beautiful?'* Celsus asked, *'And because she was beautiful did God have sexual intercourse with her, although by nature He cannot love a corruptible body? It is not likely that God would have fallen in love with her since she was neither wealthy nor of royal birth; for nobody knew her, not even her neighbours'.*[1] About AD 197, the christian Tertullian cited the unbeliever's argument that 'The (non-christian) philosophers present and promote these same values: innocence, justice, patience, temperance, modesty' but, he continues, they are rightly called philosophers, not Christians.[2] There clearly is a difference, but what is it? Far from being surprised that much of Christ's teaching was anticipated by earlier, pagan writers, my understanding of the Incarnation makes me expect this. The world transfigured by Christ is a reality, not a disembodied fantasy. I begin by inspecting some early teachings on wealth, unaffected by the New Testament, without making detailed claims about influences from one writer to another.

Wealth and Poverty

To Aristotle (384-322 BC), wealth is a prerequisite for noble enterprise and the liberal man must have money to practise liberality; possessing wealth is a condition for virtuous action. There is no crude suggestion that virtue increases in proportion to increases in wealth: 'A competence is enough to enable a man to behave in a virtuous manner.' With wealth as with all else, moderation is what is required; in acquiring it, holding it and disposing of it.[3] This implies the same kind of detachment which was strongly urged by the stoic philosophers about the time of Christ. Cicero (106-43 BC) argued that 'There is nothing more typical of a narrow, little mind than love of riches; no greater integrity and nobility than to despise money if one has none and to devote it to well-doing and generosity if one does.'[4] Seneca (5 BC-AD 65), claimed as a brother by some early christian writers,[5] regarded it as shameful to be bankrupt and did not approve of throwing money away, but also argued that a man should be prepared to face both death and poverty.[6] Wealth is here conceived as an indifferent good, certainly to be desired, but not obsessively; avarice must not master the man. Seneca writes in a letter: 'What difference does it make how much there is laid away in a man's safe or in his barns, how many head of stock he grazes or how much capital he puts out at interest, if he is always after what is another's and only counts what he has yet to get, never what he has already. You ask what is the proper limit to a person's wealth? First, having what is essential; and second, having what is enough.'[7]

This leads on to a balancing view in the literature, found for example in the cynic Diogenes (324 BC): 'The love of money he declared to be the mother-city of all evils.'[8] Even here it is avarice, rather than wealth itself, which appears as the evil; it is the greedy man rather than the wealthy man as such who is reproached. The jewish philosopher Philo (20 BC), a rough contemporary of both Seneca and Christ, imagines an interlocutor complaining: 'You call those rich who are utterly destitute ... You call those poor who are lapped round with silver and gold ... .' Elsewhere he writes: 'The bad man has a multitude of incumbrances, such as love of money or reputation and pleasure, while the good man has none at all.'[9] It is a man's inward virtue and self-discipline which are important in this tradition. The cyrenaic philosopher Aristippus (435-350 BC) had taught: 'It is not abstinence from pleasures that is best, but mastery over them without ever being worsted.'[10] When avarice erupted into Seneca's Golden Age, where all goods had been equally divided, it 'brought in poverty, by coveting a lot of possessions losing all that it had.'[11]

The principal greek and latin literature was addressed to a social and intellectual élite, not to the poor and humble. There was disdain for the business of earning money; a large income from landed estates was socially and philosophically desirable. The scale of a commercial activity could make it acceptable for a gentleman. Aristotle disapproved of men living off immoral earnings and of usurers lending small sums at extortionate interest; Seneca called usury 'vile', Cicero 'dishonourable';[12] yet Cicero's friend Atticus lent money out on a vast scale, at rates of interest as high as 47%. Cicero wrote: 'Trade, if on a small scale, is to be regarded as sordid; but if it is on a large scale, importing quantities of goods from all quarters and honestly distributing them, it is less deserving of contempt.'[13] At the same time, debtors were most savagely treated, facing ruin, prison and the enslavement of their families from their roman creditors.

Neither poverty nor the poor were held up as such for admiration; the Stoic should be able to meet poverty with indifference, but is not encouraged to seek it. Indeed, the words for 'the poor' need to be treated carefully in this literature: 'They were applied, in particular, to the vast majority of the people in any city-state who, having no claim to the income of a large estate, lacked that degree of leisure and independence regarded as essential to the life of a gentleman'.[14] As we shall see in a moment, 'the poor' as recipients of a wealthy man's benevolence would primarily be unfortunate members of his own class. It is stated by Aristotle that there are some who '*ought* to be poor', and Cicero says that amongst the unfortunate there will be some 'who deserve misfortune'.[15] These same writers are contemptuous of the mass of the labouring urban poor: Aristotle refers to 'the utter vulgarity of the herd of men', Cicero to 'the filthy scum of the city'.[16] These were the people whom the Guardians in Plato's *Republic* were to preserve from wealth and poverty, because: 'One produces luxury and idleness and a desire for novelty, the other meanness and bad workmanship and the desire for revolution as well.' Below the class of urban labourers were the destitute, and the beggars whom Plato would exclude from his ideal Republic because, where there are beggars, you find thieves, pick-pockets, and other criminals. In a well regulated state, no worthwhile citizen should fall into beggary.[17] As we shall see, though, Seneca expresses a different attitude: that all men, slaves included, are brothers.[18]

Against this must be set an apparently contradictory, equally ancient tradition; it creates the kind of tension between the endorsement and repudiation of private wealth which was to tug at christian societies after the first century. Plato (427-348/7 BC) said it was obvious 'That love of money and adequate self-discipline in its citizens are two things that can't co-exist in any society; one or the other must be neglected.'[19] Seneca associated Plato's master Socrates with Diogenes as the kind of men 'beyond any kind of covetousness, who are scarcely touched by what people normally want; to whom even good fortune has nothing to offer'.[20] If Antisthenes, devoted to Socrates and founder of the cynic school, pushed his master's negative practices towards excess, Diogenes carried them the full way. His dialogue and style of life were a deliberate contradiction of current values in material and intellectual life. He lived in the open, took to a tub for a time, masturbated in public, begged for alms, rolled his tub in hot sand in Summer and embraced icy statues in Winter, accustoming himself to hardship and emulating the freedom of a mouse which runs about, 'not looking for a place to lie down in, not afraid of the dark, not seeking any of the things which are considered to be dainties'. Personal independence and freedom was the objective of this austerity, which was paraded with pride: 'And one day when Plato had invited to his house friends coming from Dionysius, Diogenes trampled upon his carpets and said "I trample upon Plato's vainglory." Plato's reply was, "How much pride you expose to view, Diogenes, by seeming not to be proud." ' Diogenes persuaded his pupil Crates 'to give up his fields to sheep pasture, and throw into the sea any money he had'; and Crates was to declare 'Ignominy and Poverty ... to be his country, which Fortune could never take captive'.[21]

This was not the only model for voluntary poverty. If the

Cynics resemble the christian Stylites in spectacular self-deprivation, the pythagorean communities come closer to some other early christian patterns. The objective of these communities, of their poverty and austerities, was spiritual. The first community, at Croton in South Italy, was established not long after 550 BC. Pythagoras' disciples kept silence for five years, attending lectures, then took an examination which admitted them to his house and company. They 'put all their possessions into one common stock', but these were kept in trust during the five years. The novices could reclaim them if they failed their examination; otherwise, they went into the pool. Because of the pythagorean belief in metempsychosis, the killing and eating of animals were, apparently, forbidden.[22]

There was therefore a precedent for voluntary poverty and asceticism, even if the more accepted view encouraged a moderate enjoyment of natural pleasures. This is the view of Aristotle and of Epicurus, who wrote: 'And since pleasure is our first and native good, for that reason we do not choose every pleasure whatsoever, but oft-times pass over many pleasures when a greater annoyance ensues from them.' Moderation was the aim even of this philosopher who, according to the poet Lucretius (about 55 BC), 'made the good things in life shine out' and was 'discoverer of natural things'.[23]

Relief

Not everyone, however, had the choice to abstain from or enjoy the good things. The unemployed, disabled soldiers and other handicapped people, disaster victims, the starving or indigent, prisoners, virgins requiring dowries and widows needing support, the shipwrecked, children, orphans of the war dead, the sick, strangers and travellers are amongst those identified in the literature as needing help. There were also the great objects of civic benevolence: temples, public baths and other buildings, games and feasts, corn doles. Part of the need was, from time to time, dealt with officially. Doctors and teachers might receive tax reliefs in return for free services in the towns. The temple clinics devoted to Asclepios apparently made allowance for some poorer patients. Many temples and their priests were given tax exemptions, for which Christians competed during the late roman empire.[24] The tyrant Pisistratus about 600 BC boasted to Solon: 'Every citizen pays a tithe of his property, not to me but to a fund for defraying the cost of the public sacrifices or any other charges on the State or the expenditure on any war which may come upon us.'[25] To prevent subversion, there were doles and circuses in Rome and other cities, the initiative sitting on the borderline between official duty and ostentatious, power-seeking expenditure. There were mutual benefit associations set up by workmen and traders to help them through difficult periods.[26] Cicero even anticipated the spirit of eighteenth century North America, remarking on the instinct of people in civilized societies to join together in coping with calamities.[27]

Although there were no charitable institutions as we know them, there was some organized fundraising. A committee was set up to organize charity sales and fundraising for the temple of Athena at Lindos in the first century; donors' names could be commemorated on any still uninscribed bases of statues or on special plaques.[28] Beggars were active despite disapproval. Indeed, Diogenes practised begging as an art. He once begged alms of a statue and, when asked why he did so, replied: 'To get practice in being refused'. His formula was: 'If you have already given to anyone else, give to me also; if not, begin with me.'[29] More potently, giving of various kinds was expected of a public man, and was encouraged by social pressures.

A contrast with christian literature is the explicitness of selfish as against altruistic motivations in many greek and roman analyses of giving. There were many Victorians as proud and obsessed with the material survival of their names as the Greek of AD 161-9 whose bequest in perpetuity of oil for use in the baths to the citizens, non-citizens and slaves of Gytheion was to be commemorated in the most public spots in the city: 'And I wish my gift and favour bestowed upon the gymnasium on the stated conditions to be published on three marble pillars; of these, one should be set up in the market before my house, and one should be erected in the *Caesareum*, set close by the gates of the temple, and one in the gymnasium, so that both to the citizens of Gytheion, and the non-citizens, my philanthropic and kindly act may be clear and well-known to all.'[30] The Victorian might not have been quite so frank; and a medieval ancestor would certainly have added a request for prayers for his soul. The Man of Gytheion's action was consonant with much current theoretical teaching, though. 'Honour', wrote Aristotle, 'is the meed of goodness and beneficence.' Cicero mentions the gratitude of a man 'poor and unassuming but also honest' as a reward for kindness; and although Seneca adds that we should not be made more reluctant to do good by 'the mob of the ungrateful', he describes ingratitude as a vice and a disgrace.[31]

It is because giving is recognized as personally and socially important that there is such clear discussion in the ancient literature of ways to determine how much should be given, to whom and in what manner. Aristotle says of the liberal man: 'He will give in the right way, which means giving to the right persons to the right amount at the right time.' It is ignoble to 'enrich people who *ought* to be poor'. Cicero and Seneca agree that a kindly-intended action can harm the recipient, so that one should not make gifts carelessly. Giving can also be harmful to the donor; nobody should ruin himself financially through kindness. Seneca declares that if judgement is withdrawn, charity vanishes.[32]

Cicero's rules for philanthropy are precise:

(1) Because there is no liberality without justice, a gift must not be from ill-gotten resources, and should be arranged to help friends and harm nobody.

(2) The gift should not exceed the donor's means or jeopardise his family's security. It seems, he writes, that many people make ostentatious gifts because they want to be regarded as generous, rather than from good-will.

(3) Finally, there should be a careful selection of beneficiary, in terms of his foregoing usefulness and of his character, attitude, connections and compatibility in relation to the donor.[33]

There is a very clear distinction between deserving and undeserving poor, and a preference for kin and social equals. However, these attitudes are not unqualified. A stranger can be a proper object of charity, especially but not exclusively in terms of hospitality; and Diogenes Laertius tells two related stories of Aristotle giving alms to a bad and a dishonest man, and justifying the acts by saying: 'It was the man and not his character that I pitied' and: 'It was not the man that I assisted, but humanity.'[34] This raises yet again the question of motivation, but before dealing with that subject a comment must be made on the recommended manner for making a gift, which obviously reflects the donor's attitude. Seneca says we should not shame a man in need by forcing him to ask for help; we should anticipate the need, prevent the request. The object should be to give the recipient pleasure. The faces of those giving and receiving gifts should be cheerful; the philosopher, like the Lord, prefers a cheerful giver. Above all, the gift should not be made insultingly.[35]

In considering the motives attributed to donors, certain important distinctions must be made. Firstly, a slice of bread or small coin handed out in the street is not the kind of gift Aristotle, Cicero and Seneca are concerned with; such token gestures are taken for granted and discounted precisely because of their triviality.[36] My interest is primarily in 'liberality', which is concerned with fairly significant, material support for the needy, but which is unlike 'prodigality' in that it preserves the mean between tight-fistedness and an imprudent and random scattering of excessive sums to anyone indiscriminately. Both 'prodigality' and 'liberality' are to be distinguished from 'lordliness' or 'magnificence', which has to be associated with pride in necessarily spectacular public expenditure, and which is concerned with great matters and large sums of money. 'Liberality' is not always expected to attract honour to the donor. As we have seen, honour is admitted as a motive, and gifts may be made expecting an equal return.[37] Neither motive needs to be present, though. Seneca's definition of a benefit requires a degree of disinterest in the donor: 'It is a well-intentioned initiative giving and taking joy from the deed of giving whatever is involved freely and willingly', with the object of helping and pleasing the recipient.[38] While Cicero is sceptical of many benefactors' motives, reckoning they too often seek recognition for their acts, he emphasizes the virtue of spontaneous kindness.[39] Aristotle distinguishes between the creditor, who wants the debtor to live so that his debt can be paid, and the benefactor, who 'has a sincere kindness and affection for the man he has assisted', even if there is no return he can expect.[40]

In Seneca, the brotherhood of all men is a major motive: 'All men have the same source and the same origin; nobody is greater than any other, except the man of higher moral character who is more inclined to good action ... Heaven is the single parent of us all ... .' This leads to a balance: 'He is best who gives readily, makes no demands, is happy if a return is made, but genuinely forgets what he provided, and who accepts the return in the spirit of a beneficiary.'; 'I look for no return from a good deed, no pleasure, no glory; satisfied to have given pleasure to someone, I give only to do what is my duty.'[41]

Given such an attitude, it is not surprising to find Seneca recommending wholly anonymous gifts in certain circumstances. Arcesilaus had a friend who was ashamed of his poverty. The poor man became ill, and lacked the necessities for life. To save his feelings, Arcesilaus secretly put a purse under his friend's pillow 'so that this man who was so impractically shameful could discover what he required, rather than be given it'. The principle here is that, if notice of the gift will offend, the donor must make the gift unnoticed, 'since it is amongst the first rules and is essential that no one should be humiliated by a gift or reminded of it.' In such a situation, no honour or return for the donor is possible.[42]

On a higher level still, Euripides had described a pagan ideal of stewardship: 'We are but stewards of the gifts of heaven. Possessions are not ours to call our own.' Enunciating the theme of the Imitation of God that was also influential in christian and jewish teaching, Seneca declared: 'We must follow the example of the gods.'[43]

Finally, the radical Diogenes, also anticipating later christian trends, claimed assistance as a right: 'Being short of money, he told his friends that he applied to them not for alms, but for repayment of his due.'[44]

It would not be difficult to assemble a small anthology of events and phrases which anticipate the New Testament. That one should be a cheerful giver, that rain falls equally on the good and the wicked, that it is more blessed to give than to receive are all part of a common stock of proverbial wisdom. But there are underlying contrasts with aspects of Chris-

tianity, despite the fact that Cicero and Seneca in particular
were to have a potent influence on early patristic writers. The
contrast between the attitudes of Zeno and Jesus towards their
rich young men is dramatic; there is little love or respect for
the poor in this story and Zeno has no regret at the young man's
departure: 'A Rhodian, who was handsome and rich, but nothing more, insisted on joining his class; but so unwelcome was
this pupil, that first of all Zeno made him sit on the benches
that were dusty, that he might soil his cloak, and then he
assigned him to the place where the beggars sat, that he might
rub shoulders with their rags; so at last the young man went
away.'[45]

2

Jewish teaching at the time of Christ

Although roman authors had the strongest external influence on many of the christian writers who developed the church's teaching on wealth, poverty and relief between the second and fifth centuries AD, the tradition in which Christ and his earliest followers grew up was, of course, jewish. In this section I shall look at some aspects of jewish teaching and practice, using a number of sources later than AD 100, since most reflect attitudes and patterns of behaviour with which Christ and members of the primitive church would have been familiar. For jewish writers of the time, the birth and death of Christ were not special dates, and made little difference to the development of their teaching. There was an acceleration and adaptation of conservative jewish teaching after the destruction of the Jerusalem temple in AD 70, and the division between Jew and Christian was fairly advanced by the time a formal curse on the Christians had been adopted by the synagogues at the end of the first century AD.[1] Even after this date, however, there were friendly exchanges between the two communities.

A reason for this division is a fundamental feature of Judaism, which also helps us understand one point of differentiation between Christianity and greek or roman cults and teaching. The Jews were conscious of their destiny as the chosen people and family of God. Their history was framed in terms of their discourses and relationships with God, and their ordinary lives were organized in response to these perceived realities and in expectation of the coming Messiah. According to Ezra, the Jew was to 'Separate from the Gentile but not from Israel'.[2] Everyone within the community, simply because of membership, deserved special care. It was a grave matter that the early Christians cut themselves off from normal association with the jewish community and that they claimed Jesus as

Messiah. The rabbi Hillel, who lived a little before Christ, was apparently criticizing the essene communities when he advised: 'Sever not thyself from the congregation.'[3] Stronger criticism was deserved by the Christians. But they in their turn came to see themselves as separated from jewish as from pagan society by God's special election and friendship.

Within the jewish community as a whole and its individual congregations the handling of wealth, support of religious functions and care of the needy were carefully regulated. There was no disapprobation of wealth or earnings; Rabbi Judah (known simply as 'Rabbi', who edited the *Mishnah* late in the second century) was admired for his alleged riches. On the other hand, what God has given he can also take away, so that the enjoyment of wealth is not to be taken self-indulgently for granted: 'He who fulfils *Torah* when he is poor will fulfil it in the end when he is rich. And he who makes void the *Torah* when he is rich will in the end make it void when he is poor.' God is prepared to give or withold riches in response to good or bad behaviour. Tithes, a device which we shall see much abused and misunderstood over the centuries, were partly a practical levy, partly a method for redistributing wealth in favour of the poor, but were also 'a fence for riches', protecting the observant against the glamour of wealth or its abuse.[4]

Legislation

Taxes and tithes for the support of temple or priests were not regarded as charity. The Heave offering (a portion of the harvest) was to be eaten only by the priests. Every competent adult male was to pay a half-shekel annually to the temple. Additionally, there were three tithes: the first was for the Levite, who was in his turn to give a tithe of the tithe to the priest; the second was to be consumed in Jerusalem, unless a corresponding sum of money were sent to Jerusalem (this tithe was in part a form of relief for the poor in the city); the third tithe was for the poor, and replaced the Levitical tithe in the third and sixth years of each seven-year cycle. All this and more was expected of an observant Jew. There were some more general provisions for the poor: 'These are things for which no measure is prescribed: *Peah* (literally, the corner of a field left unharvested for use by the poor), First-Fruits, the Festival Offering, deeds of loving-kindness and the study of the Law. These are things whose fruits a man enjoys in this world while the capital is laid up for him in the world to come: honouring father and mother, deeds of lovingkindness, making peace between a man and his fellow; and the study of the Law is equal to them all. *Peah* should be not less than one-sixtieth part (of the harvest). And although they have said that no measure is prescribed for *Peah*, it should ever accord with the size of the field and the number of the poor and the yield (of the harvest).' *Peah*, gleanings and forgotten sheaves, as the *Book of Ruth* illustrates, involve the labour of the poor in their own relief.[5]

It was the higher not the lower levels which had no measure. The rules were so exact they specified that corn falling into ant-holes before harvest belonged to the householder; after harvest, 'What lies uppermost (in the ant-holes) belongs to the poor, and what is beneath to the householder', although the Rabbi Meir said that, after harvest, they all belonged to the poor. Such provisions extended beyond grain to grapes, olives, dates and other crops. Further, any sheaf (within certain rules) abandoned in the field was a 'Forgotten Sheaf', and dedicated to the poor. Every seventh year, the land was to be left fallow, and its produce kept off the market; the whole community could regard any produce as their property. And, every seventh year, all debts were to be cancelled.[6]

There were abuses. Pilate diverted temple funds to build an aqueduct, causing an uproar; in Jerusalem, the powerful priests forcibly robbed the poor priests of their tithes; Jesus accused the pharisees of observing their tithes while neglecting justice.[7] However, since such resistance to tithes and other levies as well as their abuse will be recurrent themes, it is important to note how constructively the laws set out to deal with the problem that a degree of wealth is a requirement for any community but that, in justice, all members should have equitable access to it. And, looking well beyond the period of Christ, it is worth remembering what Maimonides was to write in the twelfth century: 'The practice of all these things

accustoms man to act liberally and to spend money unhesitat-
ingly to the glory of God.'[8]

Looked at this way, the elaborate provisions are a defence
against covetousness and a preparation for just-redistribution
or charity — but this view may force an anglo-saxon, christian
vocabulary on jewish teaching. There is less distance between
'charity', 'law', 'justice' or 'observance' in jewish than in most
christian teaching. Only partly because of the complexity of
the term and consequent difficulties with translating it,
tzedakah has been translated both as 'righteousness' and
'charity', although it generally approximates most closely to
'righteousness'. Today, *tsadik* is a 'righteous man'; *tsadaka*
means 'charity'. There is also the word *mitsva* which can mean
a command or a good deed.[9]

Beyond and superior to almsgiving are the *gemilut hasadim*,
acts of loving kindness, amongst 'the three things on which the
world standeth'. These are greater because they are concerned, not with money alone, but with personal service and
money; they reach not only the poor but the wealthy as well;
they affect the dead (by offering burial, for example) as well as
the living.[10] What I want to stress here is the assimilation of
duty, justice and obedience, which we associate with legal
observance, to spontaneity and love, which we usually associate with charity. I shall argue later that it is a fault of our
traditional attitudes that they too often dissociate concepts of
rights and justice from the concept of charity.

Fundraising

Three characteristics of jewish relief measures were the efficiency of their fundraising techniques, their fairness in the distribution of alms and their sensitivity towards recipient and
donor. At least by the end of the second century AD, a regular
system for collecting the Poor Fund, which was a form of community chest, had been perfected. It was laid down in the
Mishnah: 'The (Poor-) Fund is collected by two and distributed
by three.'[11] The two collectors, men of standing and respect in
the community, personally made house-to-house visits each
Friday, going to market, shops and homes and collecting both
money and gifts in kind. The sum expected of each contributor

was related to his means, and a pledge was acceptable if the contributor could not pay immediately. There were also daily house-to-house collections of food.[12] Another organized form of fundraising was directed to Jerusalem. Before the destruction of the Temple, the Jews of the *diaspora* had loyally sent up their annual offerings. The custom had revived, at the latest by the third century, when fundraisers, controlled by a rabbinical board, raised money for the central court in Jerusalem.[13] Fundraisers were not ill-regarded: the Rabbi Akiba said, 'It is a greater virtue to cause another to give than to give one's self.'[14]

Informal charity outside these systems was encouraged and there was some more occasional fundraising. The rabbis might make 'a collection of contributions for the maintenance of students'; and, despite the provision of food and clothing through the community chest, there was some mendicancy, although it was discouraged.[15] Sir Immanuel Jakobowitz, the U.K.'s chief rabbi, stresses in his *Journal of a Rabbi* that there is a constant reminder in jewish law 'to remember the wants of the needy and homeless in times of joy. ... Hence we make a special collection for the poor on Purim, giving them the proceeds of the *Machatzith Haskekel* contributions. Similarly, the *Seder* service, the happiest home celebration of the year, is the only occasion when we issue a statutory invitation to the hungry to join us in our festivities. And again, it is during *Pesach* when a special appeal for contributions to the poor is made — the *Ma'oth Chittin* campaign. Our joy is not to be complete or justified unless we share our privileges with the underprivileged.'[16] There has always been a potential crisis in certain forms of charity. The redemption of captives was 'the highest priority of communal needs.' Yet the *Mishnah* states: 'Captives should not be ransomed for more than their value as a precaution for the general good (Gittin 4, 6). Rabbi Nachum L. Rabinovitch comments: 'There was here a conflict of values — concern for the hapless captives who needed to be redeemed as against concern for others who might be captured if rapacity and greed were seen to be rewarded.'[17]

The Jews were, and are, a people. They have taken it for granted that all members should be cared for, and this fact is an ancient truism: querulously affirmed by the Emperor Julian in the fourth century when he wrote, 'No Jew ever has to beg,'[18]

and affirmed by the jewish historian Salo Barron: 'No Jew
seems ever to have died of hunger whilst living in a Jewish
community in the whole of history.'[19] All categories of the poor
were catered for: widows, orphans, the sick, the indigent, girls
without dowries, prisoners, travellers and strangers. Rabbi
Jakobowitz has commented on the distinction made in the
Torah between one's *neighbour,* who 'is independent of us, or
has something that we may want' and one's *brother,* who
'needs something from us or ... depends upon our support and
sympathy. ... To us the burden of true brotherhood is to claim
equality not with our equals or superiors, but with those
materially our inferiors. The acid test of brotherhood is how
far we are prepared to share what we have with others, enab-
ling them to *become* our equals as brothers.'[20]

Distribution

The jewish system for organized relief was highly sophisticated. To an extent, it was controlled and regulated. As we
have seen, three distributors for community chest resources
were prescribed by the *Mishnah,* and there were adminis-
trators of the funds, sometimes the rabbis. The Rabbi Jose ben
Halafta prayed to be given the job of fundraiser rather than dis-
tributor, because of the difficult choices required of the
latter.[21] They had to decide what each individual required and
how it should be provided, excluding for example from the
food dole anyone who had already begged food door-to-door,
and warning those who faked sickness or poverty that they
would in the end bring these conditions on themselves in
reality. They had to observe the priorities: 'A man must be
saved alive sooner than a woman, and his lost property must
be restored sooner than hers. A woman's nakedness must be
covered sooner than a man's, and she must be brought out of
captivity sooner than he.'[22] The trusteeship of funds had to be
observed, so that funds had to be spent as far as possible where
and on the conditions for which they were given; the objects
were variable only at the discretion of the approved adminis-
trators.[23] There were clear guidelines. The poor were to be
given enough food for the week and clothing was provided as

necessary, although beggars were to be fed automatically but be investigated if they wanted clothes as well.[24] The distributors had the compensation of privileged status in the community: 'All whose fathers are known to have held office as public officers or almoners may marry into the priestly stock and none need trace their descent.'[25]

The implicit distinction between deserving and undeserving poor does not seem to have been enforced too rigorously. There was encouragement for the poor not to become dependent on the community: 'Rather skin a carcass for pay in the public streets, than lie idly dependent on charity.'[26] Perhaps it was this respect for work and self-dependence that made many of the rabbis, like St. Paul, prefer to support themselves than depend on offerings. The *Pirke Aboth* (or Sayings of the Jewish Fathers) said:'Study of Torah along with worldly work is seemly ... And all Torah without work ends in failure and occasions sin.'[27] Against those who faked their needs, the threats were explicit, but were moral rather than legal: 'He who needs not, and takes, will not reach old age and die before he will really need help from others' and: 'He who binds rags on his eyes or on his loins, and says, "Give to the blind man" or "Give to the man who is smitten with boils", will end by having good cause to utter this cry.'[28] The existence of fraudulent candidates for charity was no excuse for witholding alms. Two rabbinic stories illustrate this point. 'One day R. Johanan and R. Simeon bar Lakish went to bathe in the public baths of Tiberias. They met a poor man who asked for charity. They said, "When we come back." When they returned, they found him dead. They said, "Since we showed him no charity when he was alive, let us attend to him now that he is dead." When they were laying him out for burial, they found a purse full of silver pieces upon him. Then they remembered what R. Abbahu had said, "We must show charity even to the deceivers, for if it were not for them a man might be asked for alms by a poor man, and might refuse and be punished." ' The second story tells that 'Samuel left his father, and halted by some huts of the poor. He heard them say: "Shall we eat today off vessels of gold or off silver?" He went back and told his father, who said, "It is incumbent on us to show gratitude to the deceivers amongst the poor." '[29]

The jewish approach to charity was conditioned by regard for the sensibilities of the poor. It was not enough to hand out a random dole; what was given and the way this was done should show consideration for the self-respect and accustomed life-style of the recipient. A gloss on the text: 'But thou shalt open thine hand wide unto (thy poor brother), and shalt surely lend him sufficient for his need, in that which he wanteth' (Deuteronomy 15:8) says: 'There are people who cause pain whether they give or no. Be thou not so: harden not thy heart.'[30] The text goes on to mention the example of the great Rabbi Hillel, who helped the son of a good but impoverished family, and gave him a horse to ride and a slave to run before him; and when the slave was not available, Hillel himself ran before the horse for three miles.[31]

It was in observance of the same basic principle that the Rabbis taught that it was better to make a loan than a gift, and attempt no recovery, because this would save the poor from shame; and the Chamber of Secrets in the Jerusalem Temple, where 'the poor of good family received support ... in secret', was partly designed to save their feelings.[32] In any case it was more constructive for society and the individual to set the poor man up in business or take him into partnership, so that he could support himself. 'He who gives alms — a blessing is upon him; he who lends is yet better, and he who gives a poor man money to trade with, and becomes a partner with him at half profits, is better than either.'[33]

Behind this was a respect for people and a kindness which extended beyond the jewish nation. Although prime consideration was to be given to a man's own family, the *Ger*, the stranger who is to be cared for, is explicitly not of the jewish faith.[34] The poor among the Gentiles were to benefit 'from gathering Gleanings, the Forgotten Sheaf and Peah (the unharvested portion of the crop) — in the interests of peace'. There is evidence in the following text that the breakdown between Christians and Jews was qualified: 'In a city where there are both Jews and Gentiles, the collectors of alms collect from Jews and from Gentiles; they feed the poor of both, visit the sick of both, bury both, comfort the mourners whether Jews or Gentiles, and they restore the lost goods of both — for the sake of peace.'[35]

Jewish kindness and consideration reached even to the animals. In a story from the *Aggadah,* Abraham asks Melchizedek how he came out of the ark. The great priest answers: 'By the charity we practised there.' Abraham says 'How could you practise charity in the ark? Were there any poor there? There was nobody but Noah and his sons. To whom could you show charity?' Melchizedek answers, 'To the tame and wild beasts and to the birds. We never slept, but we gave food now to this one now to that one, all through the night.' In the same spirit, Rabbi Judah taught: 'No one should sit down to his own meals, until seeing that all the animals dependent upon his care are provided for.'[36]

Motivation for Giving

It would be absurd to suppose that observation of the law was the sole effective cause of such wise, kindly teaching. We have seen that there was extensive legislation for the redistribution of wealth, support of religion and relief of the poor and, since salvation came through the law, these were matters for scrupulous study and observance. The effect could appear strange, for example in the conclusion that it was better to make one hundred small donations than one large one, because more acts of observance were involved;[37] that piece of casuistry appears freakish, though. Beyond the area of exact prescription were the acts for which no measure was set.

Outside the powerful motivations to observe both the prescriptions and encouragements of the law, there were attitudes and motivations too warm, compassionate and holy to admit an accusation of dry legalism. In a thoroughly practical way, it was thought better a man should act rightly for a lower reason than that he should not act rightly at all.[38] The *Torah* contained promises that the righteous would prosper materially. It was said that, by charity, a man could secure sons. Later jewish teaching, like Christ's, promised eternal rewards and treasure in heaven as rewards for charitable actions. When the wealthy Rabbi Tarphon, to buy a town or two, gave four thousand gold denarii to Rabbi Akiba, the latter handed the money out to the poor. Asked: 'Where are the

towns you bought me?' Akiba showed Tarphon the text: 'He
hath dispersed, he hath given to the needy; his righteousness
endureth for ever,' and exclaimed, 'This is the city I bought
you.' Pragmatically, one Rabbi advised: 'When a beggar
comes, hand him bread, so that the same may be done to your
children.'[39] Such lower motives were not held to be excellent.
A gloss on Deuteronomy 11:13 says: 'Should you say, I will
learn Torah that I may become rich, or that I may be called a
Rabbi, or that I may acquire a reward, the Scripture says "To
love the Lord your God" — whatever you do, do not do it
except for love.'[40] It was certainly not argued that the bare act
of giving was all that was required. Rabbi Elazer said: 'Almsgiving becomes increasingly perfect according to the amount
of love that is shown in it.' This was a love, as in stoic tradition,
which was to extend to all mankind, according to Hillel and
other teachers.[41] One basic principle behind this teaching was
the Imitation of God: this meant following his attributes who
clothed the naked (Adam and Eve), visited the sick (Abraham
at Mamre), comforted the mourner (Isaac after Abraham's
death) and buried the dead (Moses 'in a valley in the land of
Moab, over against Beth -peor').[42]

It was not the size of the gift that counted, but the means and
intention of the donor. When a woman brought a handful of
meal as an offering, the priest despised it; but he was told in a
dream: 'Despise her not; but reckon it as if she had offered
herself as a sacrifice.'[43] There was no question of giving in order
to attract honour. Secret charity was recommended and
provided for. Rabbi Eliazer said: 'Who gives charity in secret is
greater than Moses.' It was to cater for such gifts that there was
a Chamber of Secrets in the Temple where 'the devout used to
put their gifts in secret.'[44]

In all this, the Jews were practising a positive stewardship of
wealth. Rabbi Eleazar of Bartotha said: 'Give to Him of what is
His, for thou and thine are His; for thus in the case of David
Scripture says "For of thee cometh all, and of Thine own have
we given Thee." ' Rabbi Akiba interpreted the duty to love
God 'with all thy might' as meaning with 'all thy personal
possessions,' which were to be treated as a loan rather than an
outright gift. For this reason, it was laid down: 'Even the
beggar who is maintained by charity must himself practise

charity,' giving from the alms he had received.[45] A very special importance was given to charity in jewish teaching. The Rabbi Eliazer said that charity 'is greater than all' and 'more than sacrifices.'[46]

Wealth and Poverty

At this point it is useful to return to jewish attitudes regarding wealth and poverty. As wealth was not despised, nor was poverty considered positively desirable. There was no dominant argument that a man, to be perfect, should dispose of his property and give the proceeds to the poor. In supporting the chain of need which, in terms of priority, ran from family and kin to immediate neighbours to other Jews and so to gentile strangers, it was deemed wrong for a man to impoverish himself. There was a saying: 'Drain not the waters of thy well while other people may desire them.' One recommendation was that a man might give a fifth of his capital to the poor in the first year and after that the income on it; when Rabbi Jeshebab gave all his possessions to the poor, Rabbi Gamaliel rebuked him: 'Do you not know that the Rabbis have ordered that a man should not give more than a fifth?'[47] There were prescribed fasts, lavish expenditure was discouraged, but the Jews believed in a reasonable enjoyment of the good things: while 'He who increaseth in flesh' may but multiply 'food for the worms', it was a fault to shun pleasures and, on the Sabbath, even the poor man should enjoy some unusual luxury in food and drink. On the Sabbath, the community chest provided the indigent with three meals rather than the two which were customary at the time.[48] Real poverty was 'Worse ... in a man's house than fifty plagues;' poverty was the hardest of all afflictions in the world.[49]

Therefore, work was praiseworthy; the Jews of this period were not material aristocrats like the Romans, and there was honour rather than shame in productive labour. Rabbinic teaching was that: 'A man is obliged to teach his son a trade, and whoever does not teach his son a trade teaches him to become a robber.' Not all occupations were admired. Ass and camel drivers, sailors, bakers, shepherds, shopkeepers and

usurers were sometimes cited as being in undesirable occupations.[50] Certain commercial practices were discouraged.
Promotional offers — for example sweets for children and
price-cutting — were disapproved of by Rabbi Judah ben Ila'i,
though he was in a minority.[51]

The regulations which allowed the despised usurers to
charge interest only against gentiles created, according to one
account, a ban on dealings in futures, and permitted an
increase only when a man had improved profits by trafficking
in the produce lent to him. Where the borrower was a gentile,
the law was open: 'Money may be borrowed from gentiles on
usury and lent to them on usury, and the same applies to a
resident alien.'

Whatever the terms of a loan, there was a demand for kindness and justice. If a pledge had been given: 'You must restore
to him by day (i.e. early in the morning) the things he uses in
the day, and by night (i.e. before nightfall) the things he uses at
night: e.g. a blanket before night, an axe in the day.'[52]

This expresses a clear distinction: poverty was an affliction
to be avoided, but the poor were to be treated with loving kindness. The poor were the people of God, and would always be
there.[53] Poor and rich needed each other: 'He created poor and
rich, that one should be supported by the other.' Rabbi Joshua
even said: 'The poor man does more for the rich man than the
rich man for the poor man.'[54] To anyone with means, the *Pirke
Aboth* declared: 'Let the poor be thy household'.[55] Hospitality
should be ready, and even on the Sabbath alms could be given.
The man with means should not wait for the poor man to come
to him, but should seek the poor man out, and provide for him.

Evidently, this is a very summary account of early jewish
teaching and practice; and it omits a different strand. The
Rabbi Hillel was said to have given away half his daily earnings to study the law, although he was then poor; the Rabbi
Eleazar gave away all his great wealth, 'and journeyed from
town to town searching and expounding the law'; the Rabbi
Judah gave a high proportion of his riches to the poor.[56]

Essenes and Therapeutae

In comparison with the Therapeutae in Egypt or the Essenes,

these examples of voluntary poverty appear relatively unimpressive. Josephus presented the Essenes as a jewish community, who had 'no one city but everywhere have large colonies.'[57] Today, we associate them primarily with the ruins and caves in the bleached hills by the Dead Sea at Qumran, which may have been built on the site of the *City of Salt* referred to in Joshua XV, 62;[58] but the Essenes were apparently fairly widely scattered wherever there were jewish communities. Josephus said that they were 'contemptuous of wealth' and 'communists to perfection' so that none of them was 'found better off than the rest'. He described their unquestioning hospitality to visiting Essenes from other communities and stressed their discipline and asceticism.[59] This corresponds with the description from the graeco-jewish philosopher Philo who gave their 'defining standards' as: 'love of God, love of virtue, love of men'. He declared that: 'In no other community can we find the custom of sharing roof, life and board more firmly established in actual practice ... all the wages which they earn in the day's work they do not keep as their private property, but throw them into the common stock and allow the benefit thus accruing to be shared by those who wish to use it. The sick are not neglected because they cannot provide anything, but have the cost of their treatment lying ready in the common stock, so that they can meet expenses out of the greater wealth in full security. To the elder men too is given the respect and care which real children give to their parents, and they receive from countless hands and minds a full and generous maintenance for their latter years.'[60]

From the Dead Sea Scrolls, we know that, like the Pythagoreans, the novices surrendered their wealth by stages, and that (as with the professed fathers in christian religious orders such as the Jesuits) the most perfect disposed of their wealth more absolutely and exclusively than the rest. There were grades in the community, but the objective was that 'All those who fully devote themselves to this truth shall bring all their knowledge, powers and possessions into the community of God.' There was specific provision for those in want — 'the poor and needy, the aged sick and the homeless, the captive taken by a foreign people, the virgin with no near kin, the maid for whom no man cares ...'. The minimum requirement was that community-members should place two days earnings each month into the hands of the Guardian and Judges for distribution.[61]

The egyptian Therapeutae, who were mistakenly claimed as early Christians by the fourth century church historian Eusebius,[62] also lived in community, but were distinguished by Philo from the Essenes in that the latter were practical while the Therapeutae were contemplatives. They abandoned their property for divine contemplation, giving whatever they had to sons, daughters and kinsfolk (contrast Christ and St. Francis p.75) or, if they had no relations, to friends, surrendering 'the blind wealth to those who are still blind in mind'. Then they fled 'without a backward glance' leaving 'their brothers, their children, their wives, their parents' and all their kinsfolk and friends, retiring to deserted parts of the country. They lived in 'frugal contentment', like the Essenes who shared food and clothing abundantly, without expensive luxury as 'lovers of frugality'.[63]

There was, however, another aspect to the essene life: its fierce, even vindictive exclusivity. The outsiders, the 'men of the Pit', 'the lot of Satan', wallowing in wicked wealth, were to be shunned. No madmen, lunatics, simpletons, fools, blind men, and none of the maimed, the lame, the deaf or any minors were to enter the community. Those who were excommunicated were expelled, and might only be readmitted in order to die. If any member shared food or property with an excommunicate, he was to suffer the same fate.[64]

Conclusion

That was a sketch of some special aspects of the ethical environment within which Christianity was born. Christ and his disciples grew up as part of the jewish society which had developed the most spiritual and elaborate ethic of wealth in the ancient mediterranean world. The first gentile converts belonged to a society in which very different views and practices had currency, but in which stoic teaching in particular included a clear doctrine on wealth and liberality. It was a doctrine that was to help patristic writers of later generations in their attempt to interpret the difficulties and apparent contradictions in Christ's teaching on wealth and poverty.

While making no detailed claims on influences, I believe it would be wrong to look to the content of his ethical teaching to understand the revolution and transformation effected by Christ. It would not disturb me if his teaching contained nothing 'impressive or new' (see p.15). Dr. Vermes, in *Jesus the Jew,* writes: 'In one respect more than any other he differed from his contemporaries and even his prophetic predecessors. The prophets spoke on behalf of the honest poor, and defended the widows and the fatherless, those oppressed by the wicked, rich and powerful. Jesus went further. In addition to proclaiming these blessed, he actually took his stand among the pariahs of his world, those despised by the respectable. Sinners were his table companions and the ostracised tax-collectors and prostitutes his friends.'[65] I am certainly not denying that Christ should disturb a complacent assessment of ourselves or of the poor who call on us. That is not my point.

The gospel of Luke summarizes John the Baptist's teaching in a way which explicitly anticipates Christ's teaching on wealth and justice: 'He that hath two coats, let him impart to him that hath none; and he that hath food, let him do likewise.' To the publicans he said: 'Extort no more than that which is appointed you'; to the soldiers: 'Do violence to no man, neither exact anything wrongfully; and be content with your wages' (Luke 3, 10:14). One could suppose that attention is being diverted from Christ's ethical doctrine to some other point. If *The Testaments of the Twelve Patriarchs* ante-date Christ's preaching, even the beatitudes and the declaration 'the poor man ... is blessed beyond all men' were anticipated.[66] The point, I shall argue, is not an ethical doctrine; it does not matter that a teacher before Christ could have anticipated his entire ethical doctrine, point by point.

3

New Testament

In this and the following chapter, I shall examine the New Testament's teaching on wealth and the ways this was developed in the early centuries of the church's growth.

The Gospels

Jesus and his disciples were not poor. They were tradesmen, craftsmen, small businessmen who chose for a time an itinerant life as preachers, sharing a common purse, but who could return to their nets, their workbenches or their tax offices if they needed to do so. Like most of their jewish contemporaries, they were literate. While they themselves were not wealthy or aristocratic, from the beginning rich men like Joseph of Arimathea and Zacchaeus were among Jesus's followers. They preached to the poor; this was selected by Jesus as a characterizing feature of his ministry. The epistle attributed to James describes both well and poorly dressed people mixing in the church congregation.

Jesus, especially in the parables, describes a world of production, traffic, investment, commerce, where there are employers and employees, buyers, sellers and borrowers, where some men are better than others at business, where risky decisions have to be taken, wages paid, contracts observed, the harvest gathered. In tune with such contemporaries as Seneca and Philo, Jesus taught: 'Take heed and beware of covetousness: for a man's life consisteth not in the abundance of his possessions' (Lk. 12:15); and: 'Do not be anxious about your life, what you shall eat, or what you shall drink; nor yet for your body, what you shall put on ... Do not be anxious for tomorrow: for tomorrow will be anxious for itself' (Mt.

6:25, 34). In the story of the wealthy farmer, who said, 'I will pull down my barns and build larger ones ... and I will say to my soul, Soul, you have ample goods laid up for many years; take your ease, eat, drink and be merry', God replies: 'Fool!, this night your soul is required of you' (Lk. 12:16-21). There is a coincidental parallel here with Seneca's: 'What difference does it make how much there is laid away in a man's safes or in his barns ...?' (see p.16). Those thistles of 'wealthy cares and the false glamour of wealth' which choked the seed in the parable (Mt. 13:22) and the theme of corruption through the love of money, which destroyed Jesus' friend Judas (Jn. 12:5-8) and discredited the Pharisees (Lk. 16:14), were consonant with stoic teaching. Jesus declared: 'You cannot serve God and money' (Lk. 16:13); Plato had taught that love of money and self-discipline could not exist together (see p.18).

Jesus, however, went further. He said 'But woe unto you that are rich! ... that are full now! ... that laugh now! ... when all men shall speak well of you!' (Lk. 6:24-26). He said: 'How hard it is for those who have riches to enter into the kingdom of God' (Lk. 18:24). He instructed the very rich young man: 'Sell all that you have, and distribute unto the poor, and you will have treasure in heaven: and come follow me' (Lk. 18:22). He said: 'Blessed are you poor ... you that hunger now ... you that weep now ... when men hate you, and when they exclude you and revile you, and cast out your name as evil, on account of the Son of Man.' (Lk. 6:20-23). There is no qualification given, as in *The Testaments of the Twelve Patriarchs*, which says: 'For the poor man, if free from envy he pleaseth the Lord in all things, is blessed beyond all men, because he hath not the travail of vain men'.[1] Jesus's warning against wealth and to the wealthy man are more than an argument for detachment; and his blessing is for the poor, not in the qualified roman sense, but as hungry, miserable and outcast. This is the poverty of destitution.

It does not seem that Jesus and his disciples were themselves destitute, or even notably ascetic. I set aside the most dazzling aspect of his poverty, as God made man: 'For you know how generous our Lord Jesus Christ has been: he was rich, yet for your sake he became poor, so that through his poverty you might become rich' (II Cor. 8-9). He and the disciples observed the fasts required of good Jews, though without obsessive scrupulosity; he went into the desert for forty days, and occasionally retired into the hills to pray; he allowed himself to be stripped of friends, honour, clothes and life itself at the crucifixion. But his daily routine included parties, dinners, conversation with friends, laughter, at least one expensive luxury, in addition to the labour of missionary work, preaching, healing, public and private debate with antagonists and the frequent pressure of crowds — from which he deliberately escaped from time to time.

This was not a Jesus who would change wine to water. He made the point: 'For John came neither eating nor drinking, and they say, he has a devil. The Son of man came eating and drinking, and they say, Behold, a glutton and a drunkard, a friend of publicans and sinners' (Mt. 11:18, 19). The ointment poured over his head was no waste, he declared (Mk. 14:3-9). He defended his disciples when it was said: 'The disciples of John fast often, and offer prayers and so do the disciples of the Pharisees; but yours eat and drink'; but went on to say that when he 'shall be taken away from them, then they will fast on those days' (Lk. 5:33-35). This is the balancing view. To the scribe who said: 'I will follow you where you go', Jesus replied: 'The foxes have holes, and the birds of the air have nests; but the Son of man has no where to lay his head' (Mt. 8:19, 20). When the twelve were sent on their preaching mission, Jesus instructed: 'Take nothing for your journey, no staff, nor bag, nor bread, nor money; and do not have two coats' (Lk. 9:3). Jesus's followers would have to take up their cross; should see no profit in gaining the whole world if this meant they must forfeit their true life (Mt. 16:24-26). He argued against dissipation and drunkenness (Lk. 21:34); but when, after the resurrection, Jesus surprised the disciples on the dawn sea, he had bread there, and fish cooking for them (Jn. 21:9).

Jesus did not discourage work or fiscal responsibility, although he lived in a subject nation. The labourer is worthy of his food and hire (Mt. 10:9, 10; Lk. 10:7). Caesar should receive his due tribute and a miraculous half-shekel found in a fish's mouth supplied a tax-demand (Mt. 17:24-27). When he expelled the money-changers from the Temple, it was because the house of prayer had been turned into a den of robbers (Mt.

21:12, 13) (the *Mishnah* permitted the tables to be set up there at certain times).[2] When he rebuked the Pharisees, it was not because they paid 'tithes of mint and rue and every garden herb', but because they neglected justice (Lk. 11:42).

He also rebuked them for scorning so many fellow beings, neglecting charity. In discussing that critical priority in jewish and christian teaching, love of the neighbour (*cf.* p.30) Jesus describes Priest and Levite as aloof and negligent, preserving themselves uninvolved, presumably allowing themselves only a partial awareness of the man glimpsed naked, battered and inconveniently lying in the sun beside the hot road as they hurried by on the other side. There was too much risk, too much of the unknown, for them to break the onward rush of their probably unurgent journeys. For them, the odds made it likely the victim was a fellow Jew; for the Samaritan, the odds were that this man was an alien Jew, hostile to his people. As Calvin and Hans Küng have said, the parable defines neighbour as stranger.[3] The Samaritan gives emergency care to the victim, transports him, pays for his accommodation, secures him and promises to return with further aid. He still does not know the victim, but has allowed himself to be thoroughly inconvenienced, has given freely expecting no return, has involved himself and committed himself for the future (Lk. 10:30-37).

There is no escaping Jesus's teaching on care and love for our fellow men. There is no essene exclusivity: the hungry, thirsty, naked, sick, prisoners, children, poor, crippled, lame, blind, widows, even enemies are his followers' responsibility and are to be welcomed into the christian community (Mt. 25:35-44). Jesus in one description explains his own life as a ransom for captive man (Mt. 20:28). There would be no escape; the theme, 'The poor are always with you' (Mk. 14:7), had its origin in the *Torah,* and its reality abides today. Benevolence should look for no reward in this life: 'When you give a dinner or banquet, do not invite your friends, or your brothers, or your kinsmen, nor rich neighbours; lest they also invite you in return and you be repaid. But when you give a feast, invite the poor, the maimed, the lame, the blind; and you will be blessed; because they cannot repay you. You will be repaid at the resurrection of the just' (Lk. 14:12-14). It should be secret, not seeking public honour: 'When you give alms, sound no trumpet before you, as the hypocrites do in the synagogues and in the streets, that they may be praised by men. Truly I say to you, They have their reward. But when you give alms, do not let your left hand know what your right hand is doing, so that your alms may be in secret: and your Father who sees in secret shall reward you' (Mt. 6:2-4). Charity should be ready and open: 'Give to everyone who asks you' (Lk. 6:30). It is not to be measured by size alone: as with the poor woman's handful of meal (p.34), the widow's mite is valued because 'she out of her poverty put in all the living that she had' (Lk. 21:4). No one should be proud to have acted thus: 'When you have done all that is commanded you, say, We are unworthy servants; we have only done that what was our duty' (Lk. 17:10).

The motives given by Jesus are various, and mostly familiar by now. There are rewards in heaven: treasures which thief cannot steal nor moth destroy (Lk. 12:32-4). There is the argument that our lives and possessions are in trust from the Father, so that we must husband them loyally, energetically and justly: the steward is blessed 'whom his master when he comes shall find so doing' (Lk. 12:43). There is the argument for our imitation of God: 'be compassionate as your Father is compassionate' (Lk. 6:36). In any case, the good man does good works simply because he is good; the tree is known by its fruit. These are important arguments, but they certainly are not new.

What is new can be seen by comparing two stories. A rabbinic gloss on Psalm 118 runs: 'In the future world, man will be asked, 'What was your occupation?' If he reply, 'I fed the hungry', then they reply, 'This is the gate of the Lord; he who feeds the hungry, let him enter' (Ps. 118:20). So with giving drink to the thirsty, clothing the naked, with those who look after orphans, and with those, generally, who do deeds of lovingkindness. All these are gates of the Lord, and those who do such deeds shall enter within them'.[4] The parallel text in Matthew shows the Christ saying to the merciful: 'for I was hungry, and you gave me food; I was thirsty, and you gave me drink; I was a stranger, and you welcomed me; I was naked and you clothed me; I was sick, and you visited me ... . Inasmuch as you did (this) to one of the least of these my brethren, you did it to me' (Mt. 25:35-40). Elsewhere, he says: 'Whoever receives one of these children in my name ... receives me; and whoever receives me, receives not me but the One who sent me' (Mk. 9:37). These are not figures of speech. They introduce the new dimension which transcends any ethical teaching; the claim that a follower of Jesus lives the life of Jesus, that every individual life is a further realization of the Incarnation, and that in all experience and contacts there is an encounter with Christ living, active and reaching out in the Christian and in the people or events he encounters: 'He who abides in me, and I in him, he it is that bears much fruit: for apart from me you can do nothing' (Jn. 15:5).

Acts and Epistles

The pauline epistles strengthen this theme. Jesus Christ is the foundation, the root, the body whose limbs we are (1 Cor. 3:11; Col. 2:6, 8; Romans 12:3-5, I Cor. 12:12ff.). The effects of incorporation with Christ should be that 'your minds be remade and your whole nature thus transformed' (Romans 12:2), so that a christian life is lived in union with Him (Col. 2:6). The social consequences are not merely incidental; they are essential: 'Spare no effort to make fast with bonds of peace the unity which the Spirit gives' (Eph. 4:3, etc.); 'Let your bearing towards one another arise out of your life in Christ Jesus' (Phil. 2:5). This is not Paul's voice only: 'God is love; he who dwells in love is dwelling in God, and God in him' (1 Jn. 4:16) but: 'If he does not love the brother whom he has seen, it cannot be that he loves God whom he has not seen' (I Jn. 4:20). In Paul's paean for charity, it is the social virtues of people associating with each other affectionately and unselfishly that are praised, not the spectacular gifts or conspicuous philanthropy: 'And if I bestow all my goods to feed the poor ... but have not love, it profits me nothing. Love is patient, love is kind; love is not jealous or boastful, it is not arrogant or rude. Love does not insist on its own way, it is not irritable or resentful; it does not rejoice at wrong, but rejoices in the right. Love bears all things, believes all things, endures all things. Love never ends ...' (I Cor. 13:4-8). Considering the famous eloquence of this passage, these characteristics seem very ordinary; but Christianity was to transform ordinary lives and people, not adepts only.

The earliest christian community, described in *Acts,* led a form of common life, unlike those we looked at earlier (p.38) in that it was open to all and involved no physical withdrawal of its members from society, but like them in the sharing of property and the provision for the needy. In detail, Luke says that they held all property in common, claiming nothing as a private possession. Those who had land or houses or other goods sold them and put the proceeds at the apostles' disposal. From this common fund, provision was made for what each member needed, so that nobody was lacking or indigent. Barnabas, a cypriot Levite, is the one contributor identified; he sold a field for the fund. When inequities allegedly arose in the daily distributions, the apostles followed the traditional jewish pattern by selecting 'seven men of good report ... whom we may appoint over this business' to become official distributors of the common fund; these were the first deacons (Acts 6:1-6). Meanwhile, the Christians continued to worship at the temple as well as holding their own services (Acts 2:44, 45; 4:32).

It does not seem possible that this is a complete picture or that it was the only model. Peter's statement to Ananias and Sapphira implies that they had the option to keep their property; they were punished for their premeditated lie about the price they had been paid (Acts 5:1-11). Although Tertullian was to say that the Alexandrian Christians of about 212 shared property in common (see p.62), it is clear that from the earliest times there were Christians who owned and held onto their possessions, some of them being relatively well-off (*cf.* the *Epistle of James*). It does seem, though, that everyone was expected to contribute according to their means to the needs of the community, as was the case with their jewish neighbours. The love of the brotherhood and the common life Paul alludes to (Rom. 12:10; 14:19) assume at least this degree of expected, common sharing.

As I have implied, what is original, revolutionary here is the leap beyond merely ethical teaching into the explicit reality of the Incarnation. The general motives cited are familiar and conventional: that 'the rich man will disappear like the flower in the field' (James 1:10); that men should not 'live for money' (Hebrews 13:1-5), although even in the last days, 'Men shall be lovers of self, lovers of money' (II Tim. 3:2), while a Christian should be here 'like an alien in a foreign land' (I Pet. 2:11); that we should be good stewards of all we are and hold since 'all good and every perfect gift comes from above, from the Father of the light of heaven' (James 1:16); that we should use whatever we have received 'in the service of one another, as good stewards, dispensing the grace of God in its varied forms' (I Peter 4:10); that we should imitate God in Christ and share the folly of his cross (II Cor. 8; I. Cor. 1:18-31); that in any case we should observe the law which requires that we relieve the needy and practise hospitality (Rom. 12:13).

There is an additional theme, which had been common in the jewish apocalypses for some generations: the approaching end of this world. Christ had said: 'Do not let your minds be dulled by dissipation and drunkenness and worldly cares so that the great Day closes upon you suddenly like a trap' (Lk. 21:34), the Day which comes like a thief in the night (I Thess. 5:2) and requires immediate attention since 'The end of all things is upon us' (I Pet. 4:7) and 'This is the last hour' (I Jn. 2:18). This was an outlook which affected thought and behaviour during the apostolic period, and doubtless helped condition the minds of the early Christians in their practice of communism and self-dispossession, but it was one that was shared with non-christians. Even when Paul insisted that he had not taken advantage of a preacher's right to pay for his labour but had worked night and day (*cf.* Acts 20:34; I Cor. 9:18; II Thess. 3:8), he was doing no more than was normal for many contemporary rabbis (see p.3). One must look to the special consequences of one's private and social relationships with Christ for the factor which is unique in his teaching. This does not diminish the importance of ethical behaviour; it enhances and transfigures it. Faith must show itself in action; there is no use if a man says he has faith and does nothing to show it (I Thess. 1:3; James 2:14).

It would be wrong to suppose that, in such a notionally ideal society, economic altriusm came easily; that all St. Paul had to do was utter his exhortation: 'Instruct those who are rich in this world's goods not to be proud, and not to fix their hopes on so uncertain a thing as money, but upon God... to be ready to give away and to share, and so acquire a treasure which will form a good foundation for the future' (I Tim. 6:17-19). The reason why St. Paul became a fundraiser was that well-disposed people were as reluctant and prompt with excuses then as now when the moment to make their commitment arrived; and like many fundraisers since, he attracted hostility and criticism, and sometimes failed to persuade a potential donor to give. Yet he was a powerful fundraising practitioner. He needed support for missionary activity. He wrote to the Philippians: 'No church entered into partnership with me in giving and receiving, except you only; for even in Thessalonia you sent me help once and again' (Phil. 4:16) and he acknowledged the help of the Thessalonians 'towards all the brethren which are in all Macedonia', though he asks them to 'abound more and more' (I Thess. 4:9, 10). Paul organized relief for famine-afflicted Jerusalem between AD 45 and 47. His technique depended partly on fundraising letters, as in Corinthians I and II; partly on personal fundraising, for which Titus was appointed as a proto-type of the campaign director; and very much on organization (II Cor. 8:16-21; 12:18). He instructed the Corinthians: 'Now concerning the collection for the saints, as I directed the churches of Galatia, so you also are to do. On the first day of every week each of you is to put something aside and store it up, as he may prosper, so that contributions need not be made when I come. And when I arrive, I will send those whom you accredit by letter to carry your gift to Jerusalem. If it seems advisable that I should go also, they will accompany me' (I Cor. 16:1-4). He did indeed take gifts to Jerusalem, and he was forced on occasion to protest his integrity as a trustee: 'I coveted no one's silver, or gold, or apparel' (Acts 20:33). He used the example of one church to encourage another, declaring that those in Macedonia 'from the depths of their poverty ... have shown themselves lavishly open-handed' (II Cor 8:2). He used arguments from self-interest and justice: 'For I do not mean that others should be eased, and you burdened; but that as a matter of equality, your abundance at the present time should supply their want, so that their abundance also may supply your want; that there may be equality: as it is written, He who gathered much had nothing over; and he who gathered little had no lack' (II Cor. 8:13-15); 'He who sows sparingly will also reap sparingly; and he who sows bountifully will also reap bountifully. Each man must do as he has made up his mind; not reluctantly or under compulsion, for God loves a cheerful giver' (II Cor. 9:6-8).

Beyond this, the epistles give instruction on priorities for donors and recipients, setting family and household first, defining the qualities of qualifying widows and the terms on which they might be permitted to become a burden on the congregation (I Tim. 5:8, 10, 16). All this has a familiar appearance: the gift to Jerusalem, the organized collection, the appointment as fundraiser of a man of known piety and trustworthiness (II Cor. 12:18; Tit. 1:4) and the congregation's selection of equally worthy distributors of the funds raised, the appeal of self-interest, even the popular proverb on giving (II Cor. 9:8) are adaptations of jewish lore and practice (see p.34).

4

Wealth, Poverty and Relief in the Early Church

On a purely ethical plane, Jesus had none the less set radical new standards. He had questioned the possibility of a rich man's salvation; he had exalted, not the poverty of an ordinary working man of moderate means, but the poverty of deprivation and abandonment; he had definitively confirmed the extension of charity to alien, even hostile strangers. The earliest christian writers had to cope both with this alarming doctrine and with the attitudes, fashionable thinking and literature of the contemporary graeco-roman culture. While Christians did, at some times and in some places, separate themselves from society, this was not the general trend. Early christian teaching was worked out within and not apart from a vigorous roman culture, as it borrowed from a jewish culture whose ethical outlook and social structures it originally shared. Origen and Plotinus both had the neo-platonist Ammonius Saccas as their teacher; Tertullian graduated through the advanced, secular education of the time to become an advocate; John Chrysostom was taught by the pagan sophist Libanius; Augustine was a professor of traditional rhetoric.

It was difficult for some of these early teachers to accept either that wealth could be damned or that poverty could be admirable. Therefore, through analogical and other forms of interpretation, through the adaptation of stoic principles, the hardest teachings might be softened, or explained away. Other schools reinforced severe interpretations of the implied requirement for real, material poverty, perhaps influenced by cynic or pythagorean traditions. The discussions had to consider concepts of benevolence and patronage, rights and justice, as well as the questions of who should be included within a Christian's charity, what sums should be given, how this should be done, what were the motivations and who the donors should be. The product of these discussions was not a single, coherent statement, but a spectrum of teaching whose potency may be the tension between its poles; it does not form an unequivocal, dogmatic doctrinal structure. The exclusive assertion either of a doctrine of absolute poverty or of one which places purely spiritual values on 'wealth' and 'poverty', seems to detach Christianity from the real world it must transform, pushing it to extremes at which the only effective means of achievement entail injustice.

John Chrysostom (patriarch of Constantinople 398-404) argued: 'Tell me, then, whence art thou rich? From whom didst thou receive it, and from whom he who transmitted it to thee? From his father and his grandfather. But canst thou, ascending through many generations, show the acquisition just? It cannot be. The root and origin of it must have been injustice. Why? Because God in the beginning made not one man rich, and another poor ... . He left the earth free to all alike. Why then, if it is common, have you so many acres of land, whilst your neighbour has not a portion of it?' A pelagian tract stated: 'It is not so much the possession of riches but their origin which I am questioning' since 'There is no other principal source of wealth than injustice and robbery.' On the other hand, said Chrysostom, 'Jacob had wealth, but it was earned as the hire of his labour.'[1]

The Shepherd of Hermas (c100-140) describes a literary vision of the tower of the Church being built. Some of the stones 'fitted in their joining with the other stones; and they adhered so closely one with another that their joining could not possibly be detected; and the building of the tower appeared as if it were built of one stone': these, in their various orders, were the saints. Amongst the unusable or flawed stones some were 'white and round and did not fit into the building'. Interrogating his rather impatient woman instructor, he asked: 'But the white and round stones, which did not fit into the building, who are they, lady?' She answered and said to me, 'How long art thou foolish and stupid, and enquirest everything, and understandeth nothing? These are they that have faith, but have also riches of this world. When tribulation cometh, they deny their Lord by reason of their riches and their business affairs.' And I answered and said unto her, 'When then, lady, will they be useful for the building?' 'When,' she replied, 'their wealth, which leadeth their souls astray, shall be cut away, then they will be useful for God. For just as the round stone, unless it be cut away, and lose some portion of itself, cannot become square, so also they that are rich in this world, unless their riches be cut away, cannot become useful to the Lord.'[2]

Origen, in his commentary on Matthew's gospel, argues that a Christian should actually sell his possessions and give the proceeds to the poor; that the teaching has to be taken literally.[3] On the other hand, Clement of Alexandria (who died about 215), in the tract *Who is the rich man who is saved?*, seeks to rescue the wealthy from despair, comforting his prosperous alexandrian friends. His principle of interpretation is that Jesus teaches his people 'by a divine and mystical wisdom', so that 'we must not understand his words literally'. The words, 'Sell what belongs to thee' (Mt.19:21; Mk. 10:21), are not 'a command to fling away the substance that belongs to him and to part with his riches, but to banish from the soul its opinions about riches, its attachment to them, its excessive desire, its morbid excitement over them, its anxious cares, the thorns of our earthly existence which choke the seed of the true life'.[4] In a similar spirit, Tertullian (writing about 187) protested that Christians were not Brahmans, Indian ascetics, 'exiles from life'. They acknowledge and enjoy what God provides, though 'Obviously we maintain moderation, so that we make use of His gifts without excess or abuse.'[5]

These texts expose a tension. When the monk Theodore of Pherme asked the great Macarius (c300-390) whether he should keep three books which he and his brothers found useful and profitable or should sell them and give the money to the poor, the reply was: 'Your actions are good: but it is best of all to possess nothing.'[6] While poverty could be regarded as a requirement by some, as a counsel of perfection by others, it was not the only way. Thus bishop Ambrose (bishop of Milan 373-397): 'If a man is reluctant to be a burden to the church in the priesthood or some other ministry, he should not hand over all that he owns; to manage, without deception, on however much the job requires, does not seem imperfect to me.'[7] Better to understand the different views, we need to examine some of the ways wealth was perceived.

Perceptions regarding Wealth and Poverty

Cain, whose name was early construed etymologically as meaning 'possession' and 'envy', killed his brother, according to a talmudic account, because of a property dispute.[8] Money is the root of evil. In any case, as we have just seen, it is unlikely that wealth will have been acquired honestly. Wealth is an encumbrance and a distraction from a holy life. Hermas claims that the rich man is 'distracted about his riches'; that the wealthy are like rods 'half green and half withered': 'These are they that are mixed up in business and cleave not to the saints. Therefore the one half of them liveth, but the other half is dead.'[9] A pelagian tract questioned the consciences of the rich, whether they could claim they had not neglected prayer, reading good books and other good works because of their wealth.[10] Chrysostom said: 'First in proportion to thy wealth, doest thou subject thyself to this curse' of dependence on the need for others 'both for land, and for houses, and for imposts and for wages, and for rank, and for safety, and for honour, and for magistrates, and those subject to them, both those in the city, and those in the country, and for merchants, and for shopkeepers.'[11]

However, spiritual as well as material independence is necessary; without true purity of heart, writes John Cassian (c360-435), there is no freedom from earthly distraction for a monk: 'This is the reason why some people, who have given away wealth in gold or silver or lands, are afterwards agitated about (possession of) a knife, a pencil, a pin or a pen.'[12]

What is more, there is an actual injustice in ownership of excessive wealth. The pelagian treatise on riches I have cited, probably written about 410 by a young british gentleman living in Sicily, argues that in everything which God rather than man distributes — air, sun, rain — there is an equal distribution of good things, a point Seneca had also made. Following a threefold distinction between wealth, poverty and sufficiency, the Pelagian has defined wealth as a superfluity of unnecessary possessions. 'The question whether (such wealth) comes from God, who is the source of fairness and justice, I leave to your judgement. Evidently, God did create (the objects) along with everything else, not with the purpose that one should become prosperous through holding limitless riches, while another suffers excessive deprivation, but so that everyone should in equal proportion and equitably own what the author of fairness has provided.' Poverty is seen as the direct result of an unfair distribution of goods: 'Some people are indigent for the very reason that others hold a superfluity. Take away the rich man and you will find no pauper. No one should own more than is necessary but everyone should have what they need. A few rich people are the reason why there are so many poor.'[13]

The heretic Pelagius stands near the beginning of a line of radicals who combined unorthodoxy with a plea for the just distribution of wealth: the line will be seen to include Langland, the Lollards, Winstanley and the Diggers, the Levellers, the Liberation Theologians and perhaps even Wedgwood Benn. However, this view of justice was not the unique property of any faction. 'A brother said to Abba Serapion, "Give me a word". The old man said to him, "What shall I say to you? You have taken the living of widows and orphans and put it on your shelves." For he saw them full of books.' Similarly Cassian taught that the needy are there, 'thanks to the wickedness of greedy men who have seized and kept for their use (though they do not use them) the goods which God created for all in common'; Chrysostom and Basil (bishop of Caesarea 370-379) used the same argument.[14] This was a viewpoint which necessarily affected understanding of christian almsgiving and community sharing, since it added equity in the redistribution of wealth to the motives of obedience to law, benevolence and the imitation of Christ.

The argument from justice anticipates that Christians will retain some possessions, and does not require that anybody should elect a life of indigent self-deprivation. The dominant views on poverty seem to have been the following. Voluntary poverty, as practised by the thousands of monks whose example would spread the self-denying monastic life well beyond the egyptian desert, was a most perfect way: 'For those who are capable of it, it is a perfect good', according to the abbess Syncletica.[15] Rich men like the Abbot Antony of Caesarea and Paulinus abandoned all their possessions to follow Christ. For others, it was right that they should keep their possessions, provided they avoided lavish display and expenditure, obtained and managed their possessions justly, but above all that they used them for the welfare of the christian community and for the needy outside it.[16] It is possessiveness not possessions that corrupt, Clement taught; St. Augustine (bishop of Hippo 395-430) reinforced this: 'Greed ... is not something wrong with gold; the fault is in a man who perversely loves gold and for its sake abandons justice, which ought to be put beyond comparison above gold.' These two writers present wealth as a necessity: 'How could we feed the hungry and give drink to the thirsty, cover the naked and entertain the homeless, ... if each of us were himself already in want of these things?'; what Paul (I Tim. 6:9) condemns in riches is the desire for them, not the opportunities they offer.[17]

With a different emphasis, Lactantius (c250-325) explicitly evokes the stoic philosophers when he writes: 'Why do you so pusillanimously fear poverty ...? That which you fear is a haven against anxieties ... He who is rich towards God can never be poor ... It is the part of a great and lofty mind to despise and trample upon mortal affairs.' If you cannot give everything away, 'Cultivate justice with all your power ... that you may excel others in work as you excel them in riches.'[18]

In the potent metaphor of the Two Cities, Augustine expressed the theme that Christians must work out their salvation in and through the world, through temporal action; but they must align themselves with the standard of God, of truth, of spirit, with Abel joining an eternal, heavenly city, and stand against the standard of man, of falsehood, of flesh, under which Cain founds his earthly city, the city of the Devil.[19]

In any case, the Christian was required to regard the holding of property, not in terms of absolute possession, but as a trust he was to administer as a member of the community on behalf of the needy. This was a much-repeated principle. 'This wealth', wrote Chrysostom, 'is not a possession, it is not property, it is a loan for use.' The early *Epistle of Barnabas* (written about 130) instructed: 'Give your neighbour a share of all you have, and do not call anything your own.' Clement of Alexandria taught that a Christian held possessions 'for his brothers' sake rather than his own', that 'all possessions are by nature unrighteous, when a man possesses them for a personal advantage as being entirely his own, and does not bring them into the common stock for those in need'.[20] Basil the Great said goods were not evil, if they were consecrated to God, and that they should not be managed negligently.[21] There is an extra-canonical saying of Jesus: 'Be ye approved bankers.'[22] For those who held wealth, this concept of stewardship or trustee-ship was an essential discipline for its management, and it expressed the principle by which all of a Christian's posses-sions, as resources available for the poor brethren, were common to all.

Early Christian Charity

Motives for Giving

Before considering the ways in which money was re-distri-buted and who benefited from this, I want fairly briefly to reconsider the motives for christian charity, apart from the fact that charity was prescribed by Christ. It is impossible to be comprehensive; the motives varied from a kind of bribery, in Constantine's gifts to converts, to penitence ('You have money, so make good your sin' wrote Ambrose), to the acquisi-tion of poor bedesmen, as when the rich Pammachius gave an *Agape* or feast for the poor, in return for their prayers.

The sayings of the Desert Fathers, with rabbinic pragmatism (see p.33), argued that it was better to do the right thing for wrong motives than to leave it undone: even if alms-giving' ... is only done to please men, through it one can begin to seek to please God.'[23] This required that the motivation should pro-gress from a lower to a higher level. Ambrose argued: 'It is not enough to be disposed to do good, you must also do good; nor is it enough to do good, unless this is done from a good cause, in other words from a good disposition', and: 'It is not a good act if there is no good will.' Certainly, the motive should not be personal glory. Continuing with Ambrose: 'Generosity is perfect when one screens the good action with silence, and secretly takes care of each person's need; when the mouths not the lips of the poor give praise.'[24]

Augustine writes that charity is a function of justice and righteousness, whose origin (as Seneca would agree) is 'a kind of fellowship based on a common nature'.[25] *The Epistle to Diognetus* (written c124) says: 'If a man will shoulder his neighbour's burdens; if he be ready to supply another's need from his own abundance; by sharing the blessings he has received from God ... such a man is indeed an imitator of God ', and an imitator of Christ.[26] Most potently, though, in a radical transformation of Seneca's teaching that we are responsible for each other because 'we are members of one great body', Ignatius of Antioch (where he was bishop from 69 to c107) argues: 'Whatever we do ... let it be done as though He Himself were dwelling within us, we being as it were His temples and He within us as their God. For, in fact, this is literally the case ...'[27] Once again it is the reality of the Incarnation more significantly than the ethical theory derived from the New Testament which gives energy to the christian life and teaching. As Minucius Felix (a Roman writing about 210) declared: 'Everywhere, God is not just close, but intermingled with us.'[28]

Principles for Charity

This is the ideal context of early christian community, welfare or charity activity. In principle, everyone was to be cared for out of the common stock, and everyone should give. The *Epistle to Barnabas* says: 'Never hesitate to give'; the *Didache* (written before 150): 'Give to everyone who asks,' guided in almsgiving, prayer and all else 'by what you read in the Gospel of our Lord'.[29] Tertullian boasts that the Christians give more to the needy in small alms than the pagans, who complain their temple revenues are declining: '... Our compassion spends more street by street than your religion temple by temple.'[30] Clement of Alexandria even teaches: 'Do not yourself decide who is worthy and who unworthy, for you may happen to be quite mistaken in your opinion, ... it is better to do good even to the unworthy for the sake of the worthy than by being on your guard against the less good not to light upon the virtuous at all. For by being niggardly and pretending to test who will deserve the benefit and who will not, you may possibly neglect some who are beloved of God, the penalty for which is eternal punishment by fire.'[31] This too is very close to rabbinic teaching (see p.31).

The result was that the Christians' charity was seen as a distinguishing characteristic by some pagan writers, even if it was not especially admired. In a satire written about 165, the playwright Lucian shows the Christians tending the mountebank philosopher Peregrinus. The Christians, he wrote, moved with incredible speed, as was their manner, in providing him with relief in prison: 'In no time they lavish their all. So it was with Peregrinus; much money came to him from them by reason of his imprisonment ... they despise all things indiscriminately and consider them common property ... So if any charlatan or trickster ... comes upon them, he quickly acquires sudden wealth by imposing upon simple folk.'[32] The apostate Emperor Julian (ruled 361-363) saw the Christians' charity to everyone, whether believers or not, as a propaganda-threat to his pagan revival; he had to encourage his priests to be even more benevolent. He complained: 'No Jew is ever seen begging, and the impious Galileans support not merely their own poor but ours as well.'[33] These early centuries were remarkable for the confirmation of christian systems of almsgiving and, by the fourth century, for the development of sophisticated welfare institutions. Origen, defending the Christians against their critic Celsus about AD 246-248 asked: 'How could people with a wicked motive practise chastity and self-control, or generosity and social service?'[34] What substance can be put to all of this?

While all categories of the needy were to receive aid, grades or rankings were frequently observed. Polycarp (c69-153; allegedly a disciple of John the Evangelist) wrote in a pastoral letter: 'Treat no-one as inferior'; the poor were described variously as 'the Church's treasures' and 'our souls' benefactors'.[35] However, as Origen made clear, not all Christians were indiscriminate in their approach to the poor: if Celsus had been honest, 'he would not have left unexamined Jesus' pronouncements about the blessedness of the poor and the miserable lot of the rich'; did he have in mind 'a poverty which is blessed without qualification and a wealth which is without qualification blameworthy? For not even a stupid person would praise the poor indiscriminately; the majority of them have very bad characters'. Origen recommended a thorough vetting of all candidates for relief.[36] Ambrose argued that there were many who sought relief fraudulently, so that it was best to provide it where the cause of the hardship and the people concerned were known, or where there was real urgency.[37] The concept of deserving and undeserving poor, and wariness of importunate vagabonds, were not eliminated by Christianity nor invented by Tudor or Victorian legislators: 'Those genuinely needy will come to you, as well as those whose only reason for needing help is that they are vagabonds.' Therefore a right balance must be maintained between inhumanity and a random liberality which would deprive those in genuine need of adequate relief.[38] The *Didache* quoted an old saying: 'Let your alms grow damp with sweat in your hand, until you know who it is you are giving them to'; yet, while no blame attached to the man who gave to a fraud, 'Woe to the taker!'[39]

Distribution of Charity

Lactantius (whose language has been described as 'only half-christian')[40] described the following as the principal works of mercy: '... Hospitality is a principal virtue, as the philosophers also say; but they turn it aside from true justice, and forcibly apply it to advantage ... . The ransoming of captives is a great and noble exercise of justice, of which the same Tullius (Cicero) also approved ... Nor is it less a great work of justice to protect and defend orphans and widows who are destitute and stand in need of assistance ... there have not been wanting those who esteemed burial as superfluous, and said it was no evil to lie unburied and neglected; ... do not think that you are advised to lessen or exhaust your property; but that which you would have expended on superfluities, turn to better uses. Devote to the ransoming of captives that from which you purchase beasts; maintain the poor with that from which you feed wild beasts; bury the innocent dead with that from which you provide (gladiators to fight in the amphitheatre).'[41] Ambrose taught that, considering the age and vulnerability and feelings of the recipient, children, the old, the feeble, those impoverished (especially if not through their own fault), prisoners (especially women and children) should be helped; that the dead should be buried and churches built, and that, even in times of famine, travellers or pilgrims should not be expelled from the city and abandoned.[42] Elsewhere, lunatics and the shipwrecked were added to the list of those deserving relief.[43] Ambrose, like Lactantius, was indebted to Cicero in his categorization. He also gave priority to one's fellow Christians and, like Augustine, to family and household.[44]

The pagan Porphyry (233-c305), a pupil of Plotinus and a critic of Christianity, would further extend the scope of man's concern: 'He who does not confine harmless conduct to men alone, but extends it to other animals, is more similar to divinity; and if it was possible to extend it even to plants, he would preserve this image in a still greater degree.'[45]

Within each community, the bishop and deacons were primarily responsible for the distribution of relief. The bishops had special responsibility for hospitality, widows and orphans, and Augustine pronounced: 'He is no bishop who seeks eminence rather than service.'[46] As we have seen (p. 46), one of the original reasons for creating deacons was to solve problems in allocating alms. The deacons were to be selfless, honest, uncovetous: 'They must be men utterly self-disciplined, humane and hard working.'[47] Inevitably, they were more than 'mere dispensers of meat and drink'; they had also to assist at services, and provide comfort and counsel.[48] They or their equivalents (the words 'almoners', 'deacons', 'distributors' were all used[49]) had a critical role as operators of the christian welfare or community chest system, although in all that they did they were subject to the bishop.

The late second century writer Justin described this operation clearly: 'And those who are well to do, and willing, give what each thinks fit, and what is collected is deposited with the president, who succours the orphans and widows, and those who through sickness or any other cause are in want, and those who are in bonds, and the strangers among us, and in a word takes care of all who are in need.'[50] The deacons, as trustees and dispensers of relief, were inevitably suspect and criticized at times. They were the wild, spotted beasts of

Hermas' vision, who 'exercised their office ill and plundered the livelihood of widows and orphans, and made gain for themselves from the ministrations which they had received to perform'.[51] The system survived, none the less, although some preferred to bypass it. Chrysostom argued in one place: 'Give not thy alms to those who preside in the Church to distribute ... Be thou the dispenser of thine own gifts.'[52]

Relief was not confined to the residents and visitors within a community. The fourth century *Ecclesiastical History* by Eusebius (c260-340) quotes a letter from the Corinthian bishop Dionysius to bishop Soter in Rome: 'This has been your custom from the beginning, to do good in manifold ways to all Christians, and to send contributions to the many churches in every city, in some places relieving the poverty of the needy, and ministering to the Christians in the mines, by the contribution which you have sent from the beginning, preserving the ancestral custom of the Romans, true Romans as you are.'[53] In 253, Cyprian sent 100,000 sesterces from Carthage to the Christians in devasted Numidia. About the same date, the roman church was caring for some 1,500 needy people, many of them refugees and strangers, and Rome was a major source of funds for other Italian communities and fugitives from persecution.[54]

Relief did not merely take the form of grants and doles. Apart from the community chest itself, other institutions for self-help or relief evolved. There were burial societies and associations of widows, virgins and deaconesses, as in contemporary, pagan society.[55] From 372, perhaps partly inspired by Eustathius' hostel at Sebaste, Basil developed a complex outside Caesarea which included monastery, hostel and hospital. Basil wrote in a letter to the provincial prefect: 'We build hospices for strangers, for those who visit us while on a journey, for those who require some care because of sickness, and ... we extend to the latter the necessary comforts, such as nurses, beasts for travelling and attendants.' This venture became a model for others, and after Basil's death, it is recorded that Praindes presided over this 'hospital of great celebrity'.[56]

Fundraising

The means of raising the necessary money varied considerably.

In the case of Basil's hospital foundation at Caesarea and Fabiola's at Rome, there were personal fortunes, given away in Christ's name, to launch the projects.[57] Such formal measures as first-fruits and tithes were promoted by the *Didache* before AD 150. It said that the missionary or prophet, and the poor as well, should be provided for by giving up 'the first products of your winepress, your threshing-floor, your oxen and your sheep .... And when you bake a batch of loaves, take the first of them and give it away ... Similarly when you broach a jar of wine or oil ... So too with your money, and your clothing, and all your possessions; take a tithe of them in whatever way you think best, and make a gift of it, as the commandment bids you.'[58] It is assumed that, in many places, the clergy were supported through a variable share of the regular offerings.[59] However, perhaps partly for propaganda reasons against the pagans, the christian writers emphasized that the offerings were voluntary (although we also know non-givers were sometimes penalised).[60]

Tertullian's description complements Justin's (p.60 above): he says that there is a chest, but that the sums paid in are not a fixed fee or subscription. Monthly, each member freely and spontaneously gives what he can afford. The funds are not for banquets and luxuries, but for the poor, those needing burial, boys and girls, elderly slaves, the shipwrecked, those imprisoned for their faith in mines, islands or gaols. As a result, he says, some people say: 'Just see how they love each other.'[61] Justin adds that alms for the poor are collected weekly, on Sundays.[62] References to collection boxes, often in public view, occur frequently; Cyprian urges the faithful to put in their gifts to the poor before the Eucharist.[63] We even find criticism of the appointment of full-time fundraisers. Eusebius quotes from Apollonius's refutation of the 'so-called Montanist heresy' (which Tertullian joined). Montanus is blamed because he 'appointed collectors of money, who organized the receiving of gifts under the name of offerings, who provided salaries for those who preached his doctrine ...'.[64]

Virtually everybody gave. The scale varied between the entire properties or large gifts handed over by the wealthy and the small, regular gifts of an ordinary villager; it was always 'the attitude which makes a gift rich or poor'.[65] Even the desert monks worked in order to support themselves and to give alms: one is reported saying 'Every day I get two pence from my manual work, and I keep a little for food and give the rest in alms ...'[66] If a Christian fasted, the object could be specifically to provide for the needy, as Aristides claimed about 147. Or almsgiving could be secondary: Hermas instructed that, even when obliged to fast, 'from thy meats, which thou wouldst have eaten, thou shalt reckon up the amount of that day's expenditure, which thou wouldest have incurred, and shalt give it to a widow, or an orphan, or to one in want ...'[67]

It is clear there were distinctions, as there had been with the pagan writers, between small, casual gifts (see p.22), regular, generous, medium-sized contributions and gifts on a grand scale. Jerome criticized the traditional, ostentatious gifts made by wealthy Romans seeking civic honour.[68] In cities such as Tours and Bourges in the fourth century, and probably in Britain at the same time, this was not a problem, since there were no magnificent benefactors. In Tours, part of a senator's house had to be used for a church, until in 397 the money came to hand to put up a small basilica.[69] In the East, however, by the year 372, inscriptions commemorating founding donors had appeared in christian buildings;[70] pagan tradition had been transferred to the new church. Capital gifts by bequest were encouraged by Basil, who recommended that the person leaving or receiving money by legacy should give a fixed proportion, desirably 50%, to the poor.[71] At least from the beginning of the fourth century, a flow of bequests to the church had begun, and after such bequests had been legalized in 321 by Constantine, the flow greatly increased.[72]

Church and State

By the fourth century, the church's relations with the state had indeed changed radically. It was a mark of the change when Constantine entrusted distribution of the corn or bread dole, the major form of statutory relief, to the christian clergy.[73] The emperor allocated a proportion of state revenues to christian charities, and exempted the churches and clergy from tax.[74] In this, he was giving them privileges previously enjoyed by

pagan religious institutions. There was a critical contest with
the temples, reminiscent of reformation Europe, over revenue
and endowments. The temples had received their incomes
partly through offerings and fundraising (hence Tertullian's
jibe at the impoverished pagan temples: 'Let Jupiter hold out
his hand for alms!'), partly through substantial patronage from
the rich, but also through endowment and the gift of revenue-
earning property, such as shops and breweries, for which tax
exemption was sought then as it is today. Under Constantine,
some of the temples' revenue-earning assets were transferred
to the church, a process Julian sought to reverse, with more
success than Queen Mary achieved in sixteenth-century England.[75] In the end, of course, it was the Christians who enjoyed
these valuable concessions.

It was not only the christian churches and clergy who sought
support and exemptions; their charitable institutions did so as
well. Basil, writing to one of the prefect's accountants in 373,
says: 'In particular, you will have the kindness to inspect the
home for the poor in the district under his care, and to exempt
it entirely from taxation (for it has already pleased your colleague also) to make the small property of the poor immune
from assessment.' Writing to the other accountant in the same
year, he says: '... When you are kind enough to look at the
home for the poor that is administered (by my brother in
Christ) ... you will furnish him with whatever he requests. For
already your colleague has also promised me some beneficence for the homes for the poor. But I am saying this, not to
induce you to imitate another (for there is every reason why
you should be the leader of the rest in noble deeds), but in
order that you may know that others also regarding these
matters have shown us a reverent respect.'[76]

Conclusion

Throughout this chapter, I have suggested that Christianity
had introduced some new teaching and practice, or at least a
different emphasis even on a purely ethical plane, despite
Celsus's sneers, but that the theological fact of the Incarnation
was essentially more important, effectively transforming the

realities as observed or experienced. Early Christianity was indebted to jewish tradition for its attitudes to wealth and welfare, for fundraising techniques and the community chest, and much else. It also built on established graeco-roman attitudes and systems of thought, which affected some Christians' structured approach to benevolence and welfare relief through the stoic tradition, while for others cynic and pythagorean traditions confirmed a disposition to despise wealth and elect a life of voluntary austerity. This may be a simplification of the facts, but the literature demonstrates it is not a caricature. What emerged was a group of attitudes and practices, already defined by the early fifth century, never in harmony and sometimes incompatible, but usually capable of generating dynamic and constructive evolutions of christian behaviour.

It seems to me that a false value is placed both on the gospel text and on Clement of Alexandria when it is stated as a complaint that he made an unsuccessful attempt to blend christian and stoic doctrine. His work was part of the process through which Christianity has transformed, not necessarily for the better, the attitudes, systems of thought, behaviour and organization of the societies it has encountered, leaving nothing quite the same. Jesus argued there was a sacredness in poverty and the poor; this endowed the church with conflict. Was actual poverty required of Christians, or was the requirement for spiritual poverty which might be achieved with difficulty by the wealthy man? There was a challenge concerning a Christian's selection of the poor who should be helped, who had been defined in the great parable as the unsightly, inconvenient, disliked, hostile and alien stranger; did this definition embrace the slothful, the blameworthy, the heretical, the insubordinate, the disruptive? Jesus said that it was hard for a rich man to be saved, and also that each man was called on to exploit his talents to the full. Did this damn the man who worked hard and successfully? Was the teaching coherent, unless it was reduced to platitude? Did the concept of stewardship require the gifted christian businessman to pursue increasing prosperity ruthlessly and insensitively? Was a Christian required to give everything away or to make increasing sums so that he could give more away? How should he give his wealth away?

Nor did Christianity leave the teaching or the language of Cicero and Seneca unchanged. By Tertullian's time, the *agapē* had become a meal for the poor and a charge on the common chest, as a demonstration of mutual love within the community.[77] Concluding her study of the early christian vocabulary of charity, Helene Pétré argued that the preachers we have been studying were trying to restore the strong meaning to the universal terms 'brother' and 'neighbour', because they were specific and fundamental to christian morality; and that 'charity' and its synonyms recurred so frequently because the christian religion was 'above all, the religion of love'.[78] It is significant and unsurprising in this context that, between the late third and early fourth centuries, the principal ethical loan-words from Latin to British were 'charity' (*caritas*) and 'alms' (*eleemosyna*).[79]

We have seen, complainingly from the emperor Julian and boastfully from Tertullian, that the christian community (like the jewish) was characterized by its charity. The growth and importance of christian charitable practices and institutions is reflected, it has been suggested, in civic demoralisation in fourth century Athens, as the increasing number of Christians admitted to curial rank diverted funds from pagan, civic to christian, ecclesiastical purposes.[80] As the standing of Christians was raised, formal or statutory tasks were added to the Christians' informal, voluntary roles. The historian Jean Danielou reflects: 'The historian of civilization is bound to stress that (the institutions such as public assistance and social security which are now secularised and an essential feature of every civilized State) owe their origin to Christianity, that they were born, grew up and for many centuries yet were to live under the Church's protection. They give the fourth century its real value.'[81] As roman civilization declined, the church took on the care of education, health and welfare services, particularly through its monasteries. By 410 Pope Leo the Great, urged on by John Cassian, had set up registers and systems of relief for the poor, and in the Eastern Empire, by the sixth century, the Church had special privileges and financial support so that it could undertake full official responsibility for the relief of the poor.[82]

Here the dangers sat. As the church aligned itself with the

state, the landowner, the investors, the financially powerful it became better able to operate as an efficient, effective and increasingly powerful organization, and simultaneously became strange and a stranger to the poor.

I end this section with four christian voices from the period when the power of civil Rome was in final decline. The philosopher and wealthy public man Boethius wrote in AD 524 while waiting in prison to be executed by the gothic emperor Theodoric: 'You, therefore, who had lately abundant riches, shall first answer me. With all that great wealth, was your mind never perturbed by torturing care arising from some sense of injustice?'.[83]

The senator Cassiodorus, compiling about 550 an academic syllabus of classical and patristic learning for his monks at Vivarium, unaffectedly included the instruction: 'Above all else welcome the traveller, give alms, clothe the naked, break bread for the hungry, because he is truly comforted who comforts the wretched.' He added a prayer for charity.[84]

Benedict, drawing on earlier rules but creating the pattern for almost all monastic founders and reformers who would follow, included the works of mercy as an essential element in his Rule (written before 580); the monks were to 'relieve the poor, clothe the naked, visit the sick, bury the dead, help those that are in trouble, comfort the afflicted'. His rule provided means to effect this. The Cellarer was to be particularly considerate to the sick, to children, to strangers and the poor; the sick were to be cared for above all. Guests, especially the poor, were to be welcomed, and there should be a special kitchen to cater for them.[85] The impetus and framework for massive, monastic welfare relief during the Middle Ages were thus provided.

Meanwhile, in Britain, about AD 540, the monk Gildas, raging at the fading of the long-established roman civilization, partly blamed the wealth, greed and selfishness of the clergy, and described a church already corrupt: the priests 'certainly do not care for the wellbeing of the people, but make sure their own bellies are full'. 'They regard the honourable poor as snakes, and cultivate the wicked rich; they say with their lips that alms should be given, but give not a halfpenny themselves.'[86] These are the forces of destruction: wealth's corrupting power and the decline of charity.

Part Two: Developments

5

Christian Poverty

The acquisition and distribution of resources, the disaster of involuntary deprivation, and the ideal of voluntary poverty, the consequences of economic injustice: hunger, homelessness, disease, unpitied handicap, unemployment, the inequitable subjecting of man to man, revolution, war and spoliation; these are our familiar crises. Our failure to resolve them is partly inherited from the past, exacerbated by our inability to benefit from others' experience of former crises. The inheritance of concepts, prejudices and structures of thought concerning wealth which we have received is misunderstood sufficiently to justify a short archaeology of ideas. This section of my essay is not a history. It is an examination of a series of critical themes.

Most christian reforming movements and heresies, where any difference has been admitted, have been based on a return to the New Testament, the assumed behaviour of the primitive church and an imitation of Christ. The quaker founder of Pennsylvania described his reforming movement as 'Primitive Christianity Revived' in a 1696 tract. The return to origins has frequently demanded a transformation of economic behaviour; from this, contradictions have followed. An extreme of absolute, evangelical poverty may produce an access of wealth; advanced theories on christian stewardship or on worldly rewards and punishments for moral behaviour have justified the oppression of the poor and christian employers' brutality to workers. I shall argue that the absence of a credible, viable christian response to marxist or capitalist theses on wealth could result from our failure to note or understand what has happened, many times, before. To begin with, I shall look at christian traditions concerning poverty and wealth.

Babylon and Jerusalem

Returning to the image of the two cities (see p.55), Peter Lombard (c1100-1160) declares: 'Covetousness is the characteristic of Babylon's citizens; charity constitutes a man citizen of Jerusalem.'[1] Ignatius of Loyola (1491-1556,) in one of the exercises in prayer and contemplation with which he armed his special troops in the counter-reformation, sets out the exercise as follows:

'First, the story: Christ asks and wants everyone to come together under his standard; Satan wants them under his.

'Second, see where this happens: Visualize on one side a plain surrounding the whole territory about Jerusalem, where Christ Our Lord is commander in chief of all the good; and on the other, a plain around Babylon, where Satan is leader of the damned.

'Third, ask for what you want, which will be to recognize the deceptions of the evil leader, and for help to avoid them; and for recognition of the true life, which the highest and true commander shows us, and for grace to imitate him.

'The first point (in the contemplation) is to imagine the leader of all the enemy sitting on that great plain of Babylon, as though on a huge throne of fire and smoke, dreadful and frightening to look at.

'Secondly, reflect on how he calls together a meeting of countless devils, and how he sends them out, some to one state and some to another, throughout the whole world, leaving out no place or class or individual.

'Thirdly, pay attention to the speech he makes them, instructing them to capture men in nets and chains: first tempting them to desire riches, which is his usual method; so that they will come more easily to empty, worldly reputation, and so to massive pride.

'So, the first step is wealth; the second high reputation; the third pride; and by these three steps, Satan leads them to all other sins.

'On the other hand, think of the highest and true commander, Christ our Lord.

'First, think how Christ our Lord sits in the great plain around Jerusalem, in a place that is unpretentious, lovely and attractive.

'Secondly, reflect how the Lord of all the world selects so many apostles, disciples and others and sends them throughout the world to spread his holy teaching through every state and to people of every kind.

'Thirdly, attend to the address Christ our Lord makes to all the servants and friends he sends on this great mission: He urges them to train themselves to help and lead everyone first to the highest spiritual poverty; but if his Divine Majesty wishes, and he chooses to select them for it, to actual poverty as well; secondly, to persuade them to want criticism and contempt, because from these two (poverty and contempt) humility follows.

'Thus there are three steps: first, poverty opposed to riches; secondly, criticism or contempt opposed to worldly honours; thirdly, humility opposed to pride; and from these three steps, they would lead people to all the other virtues.'

The contemplation ends in a conversation with Mary, asking to be received under Christ's standard, for spiritual and (if possible) actual poverty and for the grace to imitate Christ.[2]

This potent but late model combines a number of key elements. These include the imitation of Christ, poverty as the route to other virtues and wealth as a principal cause of moral corruption. The example of Christ and the almost universal theme that money is the root of evil are combined through the image of two standards in a manner which had become popular at least since the time of Augustine of Hippo. The same theme is implicit where the augustinian Luther says: 'It is no wonder that Satan is an enemy to Christ, his people and kingdoms, and sets himself against him and his word, with all his power and cunning. 'Tis an old hate and grudge between them, which began in Paradise; for they are, by nature and kind, of contrary minds and dispositions.'[3]

Medieval Religious Orders

The implications affect wealthy and poor, but I begin with the concept and practice of voluntary poverty, in the first instance within the medieval religious orders. Contrast two historians, who are speaking of different stages in the process of institutionalising poverty. David Knowles: 'Throughout the history of the Church, the great monastic corporations and the religious orders have professed, at root, but one thing, the perfect following of the precepts and counsels of Christ in the gospel. They invite men, that is to say, to aim at, to tend towards, not the natural perfection of a life in a human society, but the supernatural perfection of a life of abnegation of self and imitation of Christ ...' He quotes Ailred, twelfth-century cistercian abbot of Rievaulx, speaking in his *Speculum Caritatis:* 'To put all in brief, no perfection expressed in the words of the gospel or of the apostles, or in the writings of the Fathers, or in the sayings of the monks of old, is wanting to our order and our way of life.'[4] R. W. Southern, dealing with developments not origins, finds the following principle 'most fully exemplified in the medieval religious Orders': 'a strong grasp on the things of this world, and an ardent desire for the rewards of eternity'.[5] The recurrent sequence appears almost inevitable: a life of dedicated poverty attracts importunate benefactors, their gifts stimulate greed in the monastic community, so that wealth and power and the corruption of ideals follows. The theory and process need closer examination, especially since the corruption of clergy, monks and church by wealth and worldly power are an enduring pretext for reforming movements.

It hardly needs to be said that monasticism and the rules of the non-monastic religious orders required a renunciation of wealth and possessions. Benedict's rule stated unequivocally: 'The vice of possessing property is particularly to be banished from the monastery.'[6] By the test of Christ's 'If thou wilt be perfect ...' and 'by such a standard and by these alone, must the monastic order in any age and in any country, be judged', wrote the benedictine David Knowles.[7] I intend to look more carefully at the consequences of observing this principle, by studying a few examples of theory and practice.

St. Francis was an inspirational example rather than an ordered legislator. The man, to the extent he can be known, is more coherent than his rules or *Testament.* It was the friars of his order who issued one of the most fundamental challenges on the renunciation of wealth; they were also, not coincidentally, amongst the butts as well as the prime movers of the reforming movements. It is not clear exactly how St. Francis wanted his followers to live their christian poverty, although poverty was an essental feature of any Franciscan's life. This lack of clarity was one cause of division and conflict within the order following Francis's death. His inspiration was the most perfect possible following of Christ, and the method was poverty. Asked by his brethren how they should make themselves acceptable to Christ, he replied: *'Knowe ye my brethren, that poverty is the special way of salvation,* as being the nutriment of humility and the root of perfection.'[8] The perfect poverty he taught implied that the individual should renounce all his possessions, doing simple work or begging for food and other necessary things but not handling money ('Flies' was his name for pieces of money), and that he was 'not only to renounce all worldly wisdom, but in some sort also the knowledge of secular learning'. The postulant was to carry his imitation of Christ to the letter in joining himself 'to the poor ones of Christ'. When one aspirant 'relinquished his wealth to his kinsfolks, reserving for the poor no whit at all', Francis said to him: 'Go thy ways, brother fly, for that thou has not as yet departed out of thy house and kindred: but hast given thy goods to thine own blood and allies, having defrauded the poor, wherefore thou art unworthy to be associate unto the holy poor servants of Christ.'[9] The poverty Francis expected of his followers, though joyful, seems to have come at times near to the poverty of destitution. His 1221 rule tells them to rejoice when they find themselves among the despised, poor, sick, lepers and beggars. His friars were to refuse ecclesiastical privileges. Further, the order itself was to be barred from corporate ownership.[10]

It may be thought that this doctrine of poverty is selective and unbalanced in its claim to New Testament authority, and it is not surprising that its extreme interpretation led to conflict. Bonaventura's *Apologia Pauperum* was to distinguish between the controlling ownership of property, which he said was forbidden to the order, and the use of property (eating food, wearing clothes, handling utensils, enjoying shelter), which was to be permitted though restrained.[11] There were clearly problems, in practice, in sustaining such a distinction, but it was upheld by the Spiritual faction amongst the Franciscans, who argued that Christ and his apostles exercised neither individual nor common ownership of property.[12] The inspiration was the perfect following of Christ, but the teaching and its implications were opposed by the franciscan Conventual faction, by the Dominicans and, eventually, by the papacy itself.

There were practical difficulties, and an element of self-deception, in the stratagems used to solve the problems caused by the needs of the rapidly growing order to clothe and feed its members and care for its sick. Various forms of trusteeship were developed: the benefactor would retain ownership while granting use of his gift to the friars, a 'spiritual friend' outside the order would own the property on the friars' behalf (Maitland saw in this the impetus behind the development of english trust law), the papacy would take the property under the control and ownership of St. Peter.[13]

The ideological problems were much greater, and Pope John XXII's Bull of November 1323, *Cum inter nonnullos*, condemned the views that 'Our redeemer and Lord Jesus Christ and his apostles did not have anything, either privately or in common' and 'that our redeemer aforesaid and his apostles in no way had a right of using those things which holy scripture testifies that they had, or that they had no right of selling, giving or exchanging them.' This did not settle the matter within the order; on 26th June 1328 the great english franciscan William of Ockham fled from Avignon to join Michael of Cesena and the other rebels against the papal and conventual Franciscan position.[14]

Neither the ideal of poverty nor the discussion about it were exclusive to the Franciscans. Bede's *Ecclesiastical History* (finished 731) praises the irish monks who had only those buildings essential to the communal life, and: 'Owned no property except cattle; and if they received any kind of contribution from the wealthy, they promptly gave it to the poor.' Bede describes the monk Owine 'who so completely abandoned worldly matters, that he left all he possessed, wearing only a simple garment and carrying an axe and an adze in his hand ...'; and the East Saxon king Sebbi who, with his wife, after thirty years of rule, brought the bishop 'no small sum to be given to the poor, keeping nothing for himself, preferring to stay poor in spirit for the sake of the kingdom of heaven.'[15] Norbert, archbishop of Magdeburg and founder of the premonstratensian order, about 1115 abandoned his wealth and became an itinerant preacher in northern France.[16] On 15th August 1173 the layman Valdes of Lyon, a rich merchant and money-lender, decided to abandon all and follow Christ, establishing a lay, poor movement which, like others of its kind, was eventually judged to have fallen into heresy.[17]

Two masters of the university of Paris, corresponding during the Spring or Autumn of 1256, about twenty-five years after Francis's death, argued for and against the practice of evangelical poverty. Master G reproved Master T for renouncing his possessions. He quotes Ambrose, saying that, having regard for the realities of life, a man should observe the mean, 'So that nobody should denude himself of everything, but should share what he owns with the poor.' G continues: 'Saint Martin did not give his whole cloak to the beggar', alluding to the story, related in the popular life written by Sulpicius Severus about 403, in which Martin, serving in the roman army, has only his cloak left to dispose of, encounters a beggar, divides the cloak with his sword, and is rewarded by a dream of Christ wearing the half-cloak he has given away.[18] The response given by T runs, in outline, as follows. Taking the text, 'Sell all that thou hast', he argues: 'The general rule is: if someone says "all", he allows no exceptions', so that logic insists that the counsel of perfection embraces everything that a man owns. If the clergy must have possessions, they should manage them 'not as owners, but as the Lord's stewards, allocating them to themselves and the poor as property held in common'. He cites Cyprian's complaint that, far from distributing all their possessions to the poor, the Christians of his day would not even give a tenth, preferring to increase their wealth. Master T then gives a long series of examples from scripture, the fathers and the lives of the saints. Ambrose urges the imitation of Christ. Jerome argues that those seeking perfection must sell *all* not *part* of their goods, and give to the poor not to their families. Augustine concedes that those who supported Christ and his disciples did well, but insists that they did better who abandoned everything to follow him. T concludes from Bede: 'To give everything away is not blameworthy, but is a measure of perfection.' He cites the example of Paulinus who gave away all he possessed after being made bishop of Nola, and then gave himself into slavery in Africa for the release of a widow's son: 'O marvellous lunacy!' T exclaims. He restates the themes that property is to be treated as a common resource, that we should manage it as stewards not owners, and quotes Ambroses's statement that everyone without exception has a duty of charity. 'Rich and poor alike, all alike are instructed to care for those who have nothing.' Finally, T thanks G for his advice, and admits he has kept a few unnecessary things for himself, including his books: 'Nor did my weakness enable me to follow St Martin's act in this, that he not only gave away what was extra and superfluous, but also clothed the poor in the clothes his body needed, so that he went half-naked.' This sober argument is set out by a secular priest apparently disapproving of the Friars (he disassociates himself from 'vagabonds').[19]

The Valdesians, the heretical Beghards with their houses of voluntary poverty, and the Templars, like the Franciscans themselves, started as basically lay movements. Not all were sane, holy or honest. The ferocious Tafurs of the People's Crusade claimed riches as a reward for poverty, and Gregory of Tours (c539-594), in his *History of the Franks,* tells the story of a mad, false Christ from Bourges who wandered through the land in animal skins, handing to the poor all the gold and silver given to him by his growing, adoring band of followers. Three thousand people, including priests, were said to be following him at the time he was killed by the Bishop's men while preparing to attack Le Puy.[20]

It is difficult to trace either the behaviour or the attitudes of the ordinary poor in the histories or literature. It seems that, for the shepherds of Montaillou at the turn of the fourteenth century, 'poverty was not only a frequent fact and a cheerfully accepted companion, but also an ideal and a system of values'. Their attitudes were affected by the unavoidable realities of their lives and by franciscan and cathar teaching. On the other hand, 'nobility without money conferred little prestige: *I am generally held in contempt because of my poverty,* declared the noble Arnaud de Bédeillac, of the village of that name ...'; and Pierre Maury could scorn the amassing of riches while regarding poverty as a disease. Emmanuel Le Roy Ladurie concludes: 'When poverty was factual it was a source of shame. But as an ideal, or when it was practised for itself, it was admired.'[21]

Mystical Teaching regarding Poverty

Before shifting attention from poverty to wealth, I want to broaden the focus a little, to illustrate the variety of teachings and practices relating to poverty. The english mystic Walter Hilton (d 1396) distinguishes between the active and contemplative lives: 'Active life lieth in love and charity showed outward by good bodily works ... . This life belongeth to all worldly men who have riches and plenty of worldly goods; and also to all other which either have state, office, or cure over other men ... and generally all worldly men.' The Contemplative life belongs 'specially to them which forsake for the love of God all worldly riches, worships and outward businesses ...'.[22] These are people like the young recluse Margaret whom Hilton's contemporary Richard Rolle (c1290-1349) addresses thus: 'At the beginning turn thee entirely to thy Lord Jesus Christ. That turning to Jesus is nought else but turning all thy covetousness and pleasure and the occupations and business of worldly things and fleshly lust and vain love, so that thy thought, which was always downward, grovelling on the earth, whilst thou wast in the world, now be always upwards, like fire, seeking the highest place in heaven, right to thy husband, where he sits in his bliss.'[23] This is paralleled by the sixteenth-century mystic Teresa of Avila (1515-1582), who writes: 'Now we come to the detachment that we must have because everything lies in this, if it be practised with perfection. I say here that it is everything, for if we cleave uniquely to the Creator, and attach ourselves in no wise to the created, His Majesty infuses virtues in such a manner, that working ourselves, little by little, according to our capacity, we shall not have much fighting to do, because the Lord takes upon Himself to defend us against the demons and against all the world.'[24]

The experience of the perfectly detached contemplative is described by another fourteenth-century, english mystic in the *Cloud of Unknowing*: 'And although your bodily wits can find there nothing to feed on, because they think it nought that thou dost, yea! keep doing this nought, and do it for God's love. And do not give up, but work busily at that nought with a waking desire to will to have God whom no man may know. For I tell you truly, that I had rather be so nowhere bodily, wrestling with that blind nought, than to be so great a lord that I might when I would be everywhere bodily, merrily playing with all this ought as a lord with his own.'[25] Teresa of Avila's friend and confessor, John of the Cross, describes an inner emptiness and destitution. In his exposition of the third verse of the Canticle of Love, he explains the verse: 'If riches abound, do not attach your heart to them' (Ps. 61:11), in this way: 'This precept applies not only to the renunciation of the desire for physical and temporal things, but also to the desire for spiritual things ...', such as consolation and tranquility of soul. It was his doctrine that: 'The tremendous gifts of God can be contained only in a heart that is empty and alone', and also: 'Never refuse, if it depends on you, to give from what you possess, even when you have need of it.'[26] This combines the charity which must be conjoined with renunciation to that terrible, inner destitution, described by T. S. Eliot in *Burnt Norton:*

> Descend lower, descend only
> Into the world of perpetual solitude,
> World not world, but that which is not world,
> Internal darkness, deprivation
> And destitution of all property,
> Desiccation of the world of sense,
> Evacuation of the world of fancy,
> Inoperancy of the world of spirit.[27]

Monks, nuns and hermits, physically separated from the world, did not monopolise even these most spiritual teachings on poverty. There was a range of movements which had direct and powerful influence on the laity in the Reformation and Counter-Reformation. I noted above occasional inter-action between the Spiritual Franciscans and such radical, sometimes anti-clerical, often heretical lay groups as the Beghards and the Brethren of the Free Spirit. Opposed to the latter were the Friends of God, a fourteenth-century movement teaching self-renunciation and union with God; it was a member of this group who wrote the *Theologia Germanica* about 1350. This popular work was edited in 1518 by Martin Luther and banned by the pope in 1612. The *Theologia* taught a rigorous inner detachment, with the same mystical intention we have already witnessed: 'Leave aside all creatures with all their works, first of all my own self'; 'The more of self and I, the more sin and wickedness; the less of self and I the less of sin. It has also been written: The more Mine and I, that is to say I-attachment and selfishness, recede, the more God's I, that is God himself, increases in me '; 'The greater the desire to possess and own, the more hell and wretchedness he will have.'[28] An even more influential work was the *Imitation of Christ* by Thomas à Kempis (1380-1471). It became the guide for the Brethren of the Common Life, a body given to piety and practical good works, who had Erasmus as a pupil in one of their pioneering secondary schools. It has been in vogue in catholic and protestant circles ever since. In his first chapter, Thomas à Kempis states: 'It is vanity to love the thing that passeth away with all manner of swiftness ... Study therefore to withdraw thy heart from love of things visible.' This is a pre-condition for any holy Christian's life, whose closeness to Christ will be in proportion to his withdrawal 'from the consolation of creatures': 'Nature laboureth for his own profit and taketh heed what lucre may come to himself alone, but grace considereth not what is profitable and advantageous to one but to many.'[29] The lovely fourteenth-century poem *Pearl* offered its ideal of poverty to everyone:

This pearl immaculate purchased dear
  The jeweller gave all his goods to gain
Is the realm of heaven's sphere
  There my Lord, the lamb that was bleeding slain,
In token of peace it placed in state.
  I bid you the wayward world disdain
And procure your pearl immaculate.[30]

The reformed churches were not going to abandon the ideal of inner, spiritual poverty; according to Owen Chadwick they 'no longer revered poor men. The holy beggar was no longer the object of unqualified admiration; partly because experience had shown too high a proportion of frauds, but partly because the moral ideal was to be modified in the presence of social and economic changes. Yet the devout men still assumed the ancient ideal of poverty and detachment.'[31]

6

Christian Wealth

Corruption through Wealth

The majority of Christians have always possessed wealth, or have wanted to possess it, whether in humble or extravagant measure, and have recognized at least notionally its power to corrupt. The *Theologia Germanica* argued: 'What else did (the devil's) apostasy and fall consist of but that he assumed for himself that he, too, was something, and that something was his and that something was his own property?'[1] Property was a principal cause of monastic as of angelic corruption. It has been estimated that in 1086, the monasteries earned one-sixth of the national income in England.[2] David Knowles gives an excellent description of the course of their disease.

The Cistercians, originally an austere, reforming, monastic movement, settled in remote and isolated places such as Fountains and Rielvaux, Tintern and Valle Crucis. Because of their high reputation, they attracted growing numbers of monks and lay brothers, so that they had to increase their lands. They also attracted an increasing flood of gifts; some, such as tithes, parish churches and populated and developed land, were forbidden to them. They often added to their unpopularity by evicting the people from the land, better to preserve their isolation.[3] The cistercian monk Caesarius of Heisterbach (writing 1220-1235) gives a horrifying illustration of the convenient reasoning which justified such action in the monks' minds. A german nobleman decided to found a cistercian house on his estates: 'Now the abbot, who was to send a convent to this place, was afraid that it might be displeasing to God that the poor should be driven out from their homes in such a way; wherefore he prayed earnestly that God would design to show him His will about this. Nor was that just man allowed to distress himself for long in this matter; for one day when he was engaged in prayer he heard a voice saying: *Thou hast given an heritage to those that fear thy name* (Ps. 61:5). Rising from his knees, he at once understood by the prophet's words thus sent from heaven, that it was the Divine will that worldly-minded men should be ejected from their houses, and that the God-fearing should be settled there to praise His name in that place.'[4]

A significant point, in the case of the english monks, was the fact they they needed greater quantities of wool for their cowls, at the same time that the demand for wool was increasing in the flemish market: 'And it so happened that (the cistercians') sheep were set to graze upon the rolling pastures of Lincolnshire and Yorkshire, which ever since that time have proved among the best in the world for the rearing of noble sheep and the production of the finest fleeces.'[5] These cistercians pioneered the English wool-producing industry, generating a vast income and suffering a consequent moral decline. It could thus be argued that the very features which characterized the great cistercian reform were the causes of corruption. It was their primitive, austere life of prayer which attracted postulants and benefactors, and it was because of the seclusion of their lands and the cheap labour available to them that their sheep farming prospered.

Envy as well as reformers' zeal were inevitably drawn by such wealth. Criticism of the Cistercians' greed and of their excessive tithe-charges against parishes is the subject of a letter from Pope Innocent III, possibly sent to the english cistercian abbots in 1214. He says there is an outcry because of their ruin of the parish churches, their extortionate behaviour in forcing neighbours to give up or sell their property, and their business conduct 'which would be condemned in laymen or people of the world'.[6] Early in 1308, a French clerk, lamenting the fall of the Templars, says that 'the irregular and wicked action' taken against them could be attributed to the greed of the Friars: 'For they hoped to make their monks and associates rich through the downfall of others, to grow fatter on the Templars' property ...'.[7] It was not only the Friars' enemies who saw avarice spreading amongst them. Writing in July 1227, less than a year after St. Francis's death, his follower Giovanni Parenti wrote the *Sacrum Commercium Beati Francisci cum Domina Pauper-tate*. In it, he criticized those who regarded profit-making as a holy work, and who brought in avarice under the names of prudence and common sense, and said the evil was not in possessions but in the mind. His criticism was of a re-entanglement in worldly cares and riches which would leave the friars in a worse condition than before they joined.[8] It was an attack on the corruption traditionally embodied in Friar Elias. In all such cases, the fact that wealth corrupts was starkly clear.

The corruption was not restricted to monks and friars. Walter Map (Chancellor of London, Archdeacon of Oxford in 1197, died 1210) wrote a latin poem describing the bribery which infected the legal processes. These are the first two stanzas:

> Fingers bearing gifts on them
>   Make a virtue out of sin;
>   Money ties the contract up,
>   Money brings the judgement in,
>   Money sugars bitter cups,
>   Money halts the skirmishing;
>   Money for a prelate is
>   Good as many witnesses;
>   To money give your places,
>   Magistrates and justices.
>
> Money when it has the say
>   Turns justice into Chaos,
>   Poor men are sent away
>   Although truth is their buttress,
>   While the rich are begged to stay
>   Because their fee is precious;
>   This the man a judge admires
>   Granting all that he requires
>   He for whom money's prayer is
>   Satisfaction of desires.[9]

William Langland, writing and revising his great poem on charity *Piers Plowman* between the 1360's and 1387, describes Lady Meed ('Lady Reward', 'Lady Bribery'), the personification of the evil power of wealth, who corrupts all kinds of men, showing 'how money dissolves all bonds of nature between man and man, and twists every relationship to its own remorseless ethic'.[10] Meed herself is an almost innocent figure, causing harm She does not really intend or understand because, as the stoics have taught us, money is in itself neutral. Yet, when she marries False Faithless 'of the devil's family', almost half the nation is invited:

> Some knights, some clerks, and other common people:
> Such as jurors, summoners, sherrifs and their clerks,
> Beadles and bailiffs and middle-men in business,
> Purveyors and publicans and pleaders in the courts,
> I cannot count the crowd which clung to Lady Meed.

Wealth was 'sly and unnatural' and threatened everyone with corruption.[11]

The Christian Pursuit of Wealth

At this point, one of the major tensions must be shown. On the one hand there are those who, with the Bohemians, have regarded private property as a sin, or, like Zwingli (1484-1531) or Gerrard Winstanley (c1609-c1660), as a direct consequence of sin;[12] on the other hand are those who have regarded it as a duty to create as much wealth as possible or who have even seen wealth as a sign of God's favour and indigence, if not decent poverty, as a punishment for sloth and immorality. There is an apparently unbridgeable gulf between the ideals of poverty considered in the last chapter and the views that 'to choose the less gainful way, when God showed a lawful way to make money, was refusing to be God's steward' (Richard Baxter, 1673) or that gold buys heaven (Columbus c 1446-1506), or that: 'Religion promotes industry, industry gains respect, respect gains recommendation, recommendation gains business, business gains wealth; and thus religion itself naturally leads to prosperity' (*Evangelical Magazine,* 1804).[13]

The latter view entails propositions of this type: that 'No man in England, of sound limbs and senses can be poor merely for want of work' (Daniel Defoe, 1704),[14] so that laziness is the cause of poverty; or that no man need be destitute, since it is possible for any man 'by the careful and thrifty use of all his endowments' to provide for himself and his family by his own efforts while 'Any class of men that lives from hand to mouth will ever be an inferior class', but little removed from slavery, 'fixed to his parish like a limpet to its rock.' (Samuel Smiles, 1859).[15] Christians of the industrialized West were to develop some strange and brutal attitudes to their neighbours in the names of stewardship and God's providence for his favoured children, disregarding starvation in the next street and destroying childhoods in factories, mines and rich men's chimneys. Of course convenient economic theory was another cause, and today Christians have an equally effective blindness to the injustice suffered by other neighbours. But it is also clear that there is a viable christian morality which admits within some measure the creation and enjoyment of wealth, and this is the next matter for inspection.

There are two major questions: how can wealth be rightly held by a Christian? and how can it be rightly earned? The Dominican Thomas Aquinas (1224/5-1274) taught that it was quite proper for a man to own private property. However, the use of material goods should be common, in the sense that the owner should share the use of his possessions with others and should not unreasonably prevent others from having access to them. He taught: 'When Ambrose said *Nobody should call that private property which is common to all,* he is speaking of property from the point of view of its use; this is why he added: *Whatever exceeds the consumer's requirements is held violently.*'[16] A distinction between 'private' and 'personal' property is implied here. The principle expressed permits someone in urgent need, in certain circumstances, to take another's property secretly or overtly without incurring the moral guilt of theft.

Tawney has shown that economic theory concerning the ownership and role of capital, pricing principles and trade had been developed by Aquinas, Gratian and especially Antonino well before the Reformation.[17] Economic realities forced these developments. But it was after the Reformation, and in response to the economic and social forces which made the Reformation a possibility and a necessity, that christian ethics of wealth and business conduct were maturely developed. Luther could say: 'The god of the world is riches, pleasure, and pride, wherewith it abuses the creatures and gifts of God.';

and: 'Wealth is the smallest thing on earth, the least gift that God has bestowed on mankind'; but he also said, in criticizing the monks: 'He who has chosen poverty ought not to be rich. If he wants to be rich, let him put his hand to the plow and seek his fortunes from the land .... It is not fitting that one man shall live in idleness on another's labour, or be rich and live comfortably at the cost of another's hardship ... '[18] An unjust and self-deluding poverty is as blameworthy as an obsession with wealth, and it is proper that a Christian should earn his keep.

What is required is a correct attitude to the possessions everybody without exception requires. Calvin writes in the *Institutes:* 'We have a frenzied desire, an infinite eagerness, to pursue wealth and honour, intrigue for power, accumulate riches, and collect all those frivolities which seem conducive to luxury and splendour. On the other hand, we have a remarkable dread, a remarkable hatred of poverty, mean birth, and a humble condition, and feel the strongest desire to guard against them. ... the course which Christian men must follow is this: first, they must not long for, or hope for, or think of any kind of prosperity apart from the blessing of God; on it they must cast themselves, and there safely and confidently recline. ... since those on whom the curse of God lies do not enjoy the least particle of true happiness, whatever we obtain without his blessing must turn out ill. But surely men ought not to desire what adds to their misery.'[19]

A principal controlling concept was the doctrine of stewardship, which affected the exploitation of one's talents through industry, labour and profit-seeking endeavour and also the proper disposition towards any wealth acquired and a just management of it. Calvin's teaching is very clear: 'We are not our own ... We are God's'; 'All the endowments which we possess are deposits intrusted to us for the very purpose of being distributed for the good of our neighbour'; 'We are (God's) stewards, and are bound to give account of our stewardship; moreover, ... the only right mode of administration is that which is regulated by love.'[20] Writing in 1715, Robert Nelson argues that riches are 'talents the Providence of GOD hath committed to your management'; and 'if you do not Good with your Riches ... You use them contrary to the Intention of God who is absolute Master of them.'[21] What this means as far as private affairs are concerned will be studied presently, but one conclusion is almost universal: that the rich are responsible for the poor. In his 1658 *Warning to all the Merchants in London,* George Fox demanded: 'For how can you go up and down in your superfluity, and abound in your riches, and see the poor, blind, and cripples go about your streets?'[22] The same attitude was evident in Aquinas, and neither this view of the rich man's responsibility to the poor nor the basic concept that we hold our goods in trust were original or exclusive to the protestant churches; we have seen the same viewpoint in classical and medieval times and it was shared by Jews and Muslims. The *Koran* taught: 'Bestow in alms of that which God hath made you heirs.'[23] However, as their members prospered in business and became the leaders in a revolution in manufacture, distribution and trade and in new patterns for mass employment, the protestant churches were to give the idea of christian stewardship a special emphasis, at different times enlightened and benighted.

Christian Commercial Practice and Theory

The process of accumulating wealth occupied protestant minds, but here again it is wrong to think that the Reformation was an impassible frontier, with trade and commercial expansion on one side and feudalism on the other. Aquinas the poor friar was readily able to discuss commercial exchanges, conceding that there may be added values over and above direct costs and prices: there should, he says, be equity between buyer and seller, so that it would be wrong 'if the price excelled the value of the goods, or if the value of the goods exceeded the price'; but 'If someone very much wants to possess something, whose loss will harm the other; in such a situation the just price will have regard not only for the object itself, but also for the loss the vendor will suffer from the sale.' Similarly, it is legitimate to sell an object above the purchase price if, for example, its value has been increased because it has been improved or because its value has been increased as a secondary effect of a change of time or place. Aquinas anticipates the protestant discussion.[24]

The puritan Bunyan in his turn discusses commercial practice, buying and selling, and fraud — Aquinas's topics — in *The Life and Death of Mr. Badman* (1680). He tells at length how Mr. Badman went against scripture in using false weights and measures, and gives several reasons 'why a man who hath (a commodity) should not always sell too dear nor buy as cheap as he can, but should use good conscience to God and charity to his neighbour in both'. More than worldly justice is expected of a Christian; wealth, for Bunyan, is not the goal: 'Let the tradesman or others consider that there is not that in great getting and abundance which the most of men do suppose; for all that a man has over and above what serves for his present necessity and supply, serves only to feed the lusts of the eye.' Marketing his wares, the tradesman must observe secular honesty and christian charity, and should avoid misleading advertising: 'If thou sellest, do not commend any otherwise but to give the thing that thou hast its just value and worth; for thou canst not do otherwise, knowingly, but of a covetous and wicked mind.'[25]

Jeremy Taylor is apparently more permissive where he writes of *Civil Contracts* (1650): 'In prices of bargaining concerning uncertain merchandises, you may buy as cheap ordinarily as you can, and sell as dear as you can', but he restricts this commercial behaviour by the requirements of truth and justice and by an insistence that such bargaining should be between equals: 'merchants with merchants, wise men with wise men, rich with rich'. Justice and charity are required of the Christian: 'Let no prices be heightened by the necessity or unskilfulness of the contractor: for the first is direct uncharitableness to the person, and injustice in the thing; (because the man's necessity could not naturally enter into the consideration of the value of the commodity;) and the other is deceit and oppression: much less must any man make necessities; as by engrossing a commodity, by monopoly, by detaining corn, or the like in direct arts; for such persons are unjust to all single persons with whom in such cases they contract, and oppressors of the public.' In every transaction, 'the rules of friendship and neighbourhood, and the obligations of charity' are to be observed; no man's poverty, for example, could excuse his becoming 'more oppressing and cruel in his bargain'.[26] Considering the christian teaching rather than the implied economic theories, the simple point to be made here is that it concentrates, not on market forces, national or international trends, but on the just, loving, individual treatment of man by man. Only in this way can Luther's *dictum* be upheld: 'Buying and selling are necessary. They cannot be dispensed with and can be practised in a christian manner.'[27]

We know that the growth of trade and the monstrous development of economic theory, feeding each off the other, were to overwhelm such simple teachings, leaving christian moralists dazed and staggering behind. It is possible to watch this happening in the case of usury. There is no need to repeat the condemnation of usury from the Fathers from the medieval papacy (by the Second Lateran Council in 1139, the Third Lateran Council in 1179, Urban III in 1150, the Second Council of Lyon 1270, the Council of Venice 1311); from the medieval moralists and lawyers (Gratian in 1140, Thomas of Chobham in 1215, Caesarius about 1223, Jacques de Vitry 1230); from canon and civil law (by canon law in 785; by civil law under Edward in 1064)[28]; from the Muslims (the *Koran* states: 'They who swallow down usury, shall arise in the resurrection only as he ariseth whom Satan hath infected by his touch ... God hath allowed selling, and forbidden usury ... God will bring usury to nought.');[29] from the reformed churches (George Fox and other Puritans as well as Martin Luther).[30]

In literature, usurers have always been attacked and abused — one lay under the pelting fire in Dante's Hell amongst the miserable spirits of his fellows.[31] Langland said a whore could tithe her arse-winnings before a usurer could tithe his gains,[32] and variants of an eighteenth-century Alphabet have the usurer as one who, disgracefully, 'took Ten per cent':

> U was a usurer, a miserable elf,
> V was a vintner, who drank all himself.[33]

Hilaire Belloc, in an essay published in 1931, wrote: 'A sum of money lent has, according to our present scheme, a natural right to interest. That principle is false in economics as in morals. It ruined Rome, and it is bringing us to our end.'[34] More eloquently, Ezra Pound:

With USURA

With usura no man has a house of good stone
each block cut smooth and well fitting
that design might cover their face
......
Usura rusteth the chisel
It rusteth the craft and the craftsman
It gnaweth the thread in the loom
None learneth to weave gold in her pattern
......
They have brought whores for Eleusis
Corpses are set to banquet
at behest of Usura.[35]

An early, fairly crude argument against usury, as stated by
Thomas of Chobham in 1215, was that the usurer had nothing
to sell which justified charging interest: 'What the money-
lender sells to the debtor is not something which is his own but
only time which is God's.'[36] Another, classic doctrine, which
was still being taught twenty years ago in the catholic church,
depended on defining money as a thing whose proper and
principal function is to be consumed by being used, like bread
or wine. With such, the use may not be distinguished from the
thing itself. Thomas Aquinas argued: 'I cannot say "I charge
this for the wine, plus this if you drink it." If it is lent, the
possession of the thing is handed over with its use; a loan
confers both use and possession. Therefore, if a man sells the
wine and the use of the wine, he is either selling the same thing
twice, or selling something which does not exist, and so
commits an injustice.' Since money is of the same kind, 'It is
not permitted to charge a price for the use of a loan of money,
which is called usury.'[37]

Even as these teachings were being elaborated, they were
being circumvented. In 1083, Paul the money changer had
made a loan to St. Peter's church in Rome at 20%. The Jews
were certainly used at some times and places to preserve christian consciences, but seldom exclusively. The great bankers of
Valencia in the thirteenth-century, the Ricciardis (c1240), the
Bardi and the Peruzzi (c1340), the Frescobaldi (who trained
Thomas Cromwell), the municipal Taula de Canvi in the early
fifteenth century, the Medici in the later fifteenth century, the

banks of Ludwig Menting, the Hochsteters and Anton Welser
in Antwerp during the same period, the Fuggers who became
after 1487 massive owners of mineral resources as well as
money-lenders to Maximilian, Charles V and the papacy —
they were all Christians. Pope Innocent IV (c1207-1254)
describes these christian bankers or money-lenders as 'the
favoured children of the Roman church'.[38] Eleven of the great
italian banks, in the late thirteenth century, were appointed to
receive funds raised by the papacy outside Italy.[39]

It is not that there was a universal flouting of law, since
distinctions and devices had been introduced to justify and
effect technical avoidance of usury. If the lender suffered a
loss or endured significant risk, for example, or if he was
investing in a profit-making enterprise, a charge for use of the
money could be justified. The bill of exchange, because it
produced a return which was not fixed but which fluctuated
with the international money market, had by the late thirteenth century become 'a simple, effective loan contract that
fully circumvented the ecclesiastical and civil bans on usury
without any taint of fraud'.[40] Luther raved against *zynkauf,*
another technical device for evading usury, because if it
continued 'Germany will not have a penny left, and the
chances are we shall have to eat one another '; it was the
devil's invention. He urged: 'We must put a bit in the mouth of
the Fuggers '; but it was the Fuggers who prevailed, paying
counsel for the defence of such interest charges against
Luther's attack.[41]

Calvin's condonation of usury was, according to Tawney,
'protected by such embarrassing entanglements' that it 'can
have offered but tepid consolation to the devout money-
lender.'[42] What he and other, more permissive teachers on
usury urged was that rates of interest should not be excessive
and that charity should be observed. But the moralists were
trailing and tidying up the real development of money
markets, very much as abstract theory may trail technological
development as an effect not a cause. Practical measures
which attempted to meet the demand for loans, without
resource to usury, such as the Franciscans' interest-free pawn-
shops, the *Montes Pietatis* (starting about 1462) were, like their
victorian successors, a business and charitable failure. Also, in

ciceronian style (see p.17) there was a tendency to condemn the small, back-street usurer or pawnbroker but to admire the merchant-prince or the massive, institutional moneylender; to salute the international banker's throne and kick at the bench from which it was descended.[43]

The Protestant Ethic

It would, of course, be naïve to imply that Puritans, Quakers, Methodists, Brethren throve in business, as they so evidently did, merely as a result of certain christian ethical teaching on earning and owning money; as the universal doctrine acknowledged, money and power and greed were a trinity to which man was instinctively but destructively drawn. It was some time after he preached the great sermon *The Use of Money* in 1744 that John Wesley commented: 'The Methodists grow more and more self-indulgent *because they grow rich.*', and the Methodist Conference minuted that: 'Many Methodists grow rich and thereby lovers of the present world.' In his sermon, Wesley had outlined a classic formula for the Christian involved in commercial business. Its main tenets were: 1. Gain all you can; 2. Save all you can; 3. Give all you can. In his attitude to money, he was influenced by Robert Nelson (see p.87 above). Money, says Wesley, is an 'excellent talent', not to be despised; he echoes Augustine (p.55 above): 'For let the world be as corrupt as it will, is gold or silver to blame? ... The fault does not lie in the money, but in them that use it. It may be used ill; and what may not?'; money 'is full as applicable to the best as to the worse uses'; it is 'food for the hungry, drink for the thirsty, raiment for the naked'. Therefore, he sets out 'three plain rules, by the exact observance whereof we may approve ourselves faithful stewards of "the mammon of unrighteousness" '.

It is right to *Gain all you can,* but without sin or damage to health of body or mind. This excludes some practices and occupations. Pawnbroking, gaming, medicine or the law, where they charge excessively, are excluded. So is the sale of 'that liquid fire commonly called drams, or spirituous liquors', except as medicines. Common retailers of spirits are poisoners, who break the precept: 'Neither may we gain by hurting our neighbour *in his body.'* Surgeons and apothecaries who cause pain to the body and many of those concerned with such places as 'taverns, victualling-houses, opera-houses, play-houses, or any other places of public, fashionable diversion', who may hurt their neighbour *in his soul,* should take heed. But the man who gives all his time and energy in his work will have no time for 'silly, improfitable diversions'. He should not put work off till tomorrow, should spare no pains, do nothing by halves, because 'It is the bounden duty of all who are engaged in worldly business to observe that first and great rule of Christian wisdom with respect to money: *Gain all you can.'* You will achieve this 'by common sense, by using in your business all the understanding which God has given you'.

Having observed the first precept, it is important not to throw the precious talent away or waste it. The second rule of Christian providence is: *Save all you can.* Money should not be spent on gluttony or drunkenness, or even on a 'regular, reput-able kind of sensuality, an elegant epicurism'. Wesley com-mands: 'Cut off all this expense! Despise delicacy and variety and be content with what plain nature requires.' Money should not be wasted on 'superfluous or expensive apparel or by needless ornaments', or on the house by buying expensive furniture, pictures or decorations. No expense should be com-mitted to vanity, buying men's honour and praise. 'And why should you throw away money upon your children any more than upon yourself ... ?'; if they would use the money extrava-gantly or vainly, it should not even be given to them by bequest. The bulk of a man's fortune should be left to that child 'who knew the value of money', while the rest of the children should be given only what would keep them above want.

'But let not any man imagine that he has done anything barely by going thus far.' You may as well throw your wealth away or 'bury it in the earth as in your chest or in the Bank of England'. Like Calvin, who held that 'the only limit to (a Chris-tian's) beneficence is the failure of his means', Wesley taught: 'Having first gained all you can and, secondly saved all you can, then *give all you can.'* The reason for this is that God placed man on earth 'not as a proprietor but a steward'. As a good steward, the Christian should provide first for himself;

secondly for wife, children, servants and other members of his household; then, from what is left, he should 'do good to them that are of the household of faith'; finally, if there is still a surplus, he should 'do good unto all men'. Wesley provides guidelines for reaching a decision on expenditure. He gives a prayer for a Christian's determination of his expenditure, to the end that he should 'act therein with a single eye as a steward of thy goods'. After a jibe against the Jews, based on a misunderstanding of their tithes, he urges: 'Render unto God not a tenth, not a third, not a half, but all that is God's (be it more or less) by employing all on yourself, your household, the household of faith and all mankind, in such a manner that you give a good account of your stewardship when ye can be no longer stewards.'[44]

Wesley's teaching is directed to people who *should* be immersed in business and the affairs of the world; there is no anxiety that this might be a less perfect way, and that it could be more excellent and Christ-like to renounce all possessions, and even to rely on alms rather than productive work for a living. It is a fine statement of the protestant ethic, which Christopher Hill has summarised as 'an emphasis on the religious duty of working hard in one's calling, of avoiding sins of idleness, waste of time, over-indulgence in the pleasures of the flesh'.[45] It would be wrong to suppose that its faults and strengths were absent from catholic lands, but it was one major factor in the development of the nineteenth-century industrial culture, with its formidable polarising momentum in the growth of private wealth and the deterioration of conditions for labour, fixing a great gulf of indifference, despair and rage between the two. Other factors in this development were the secular teachings of Adam Smith, Bentham, Ricardo, James and John Stuart Mill, which opposed interference from government in the operations of a free market on the basis that the welfare and liberty of the individual would best be preserved by unrestricted competition. The burgeoning industrial revolution had to be fed by an untrammelled deployment of private capital. It was natural that the prospering, bourgeois, christian capitalist, bewitched by the glamour of prospective wealth, should often have observed only the first of Wesley's precepts, while assenting to the entire doctrine of *laissez-faire*.

As medieval doctrines of poverty created a cycle of self-corruption, the protestant doctrine of stewardship created a comparable cycle of its own. The requirement was that a man should be a good steward of his innate talents and external endowments, so that he was to work tirelessly and industriously, measuring his stewardship by his profits. Samuel Smiles declared: 'The honest earning and the frugal use of money are of the greatest importance.'[46] A Christian's profits were a reward for virtue. He was required to be charitable to the poor, but outside certain categories there was a presumption that the poor were lazy, corrupt, even debauched; poverty could be imputed to many of them as just retribution. The effect of this doctrine on an emergent and ambitious bourgeoisie, who were at the same time indoctrinated by a non-interventionist economic doctrine of self-sufficiency, was to encourage the creation of a system which sanctified profits and transformed labour and the unemployed into the talents available for exploitation to God's and the State's chosen stewards. If some suffered, this was an intention of Providence accommodated by political economy.

The Use of Wealth: Sumptuary Regulations

Sumptuary regulations and customs have been concerned with controlling expenditure beyond the purchase of necessities, with restraining luxury and with maintaining the social mythology of wealth. They presuppose some degree of enjoyment of wealth. At their simplest level, they are intended to protect people. This was Luther's intention: 'There is a great need for a general law and decree in the German nation against extravagant and costly dress, because of which so many nobles and rich men are impoverished.'[47] In 1637, the Jewish Council of Lithuania demonstrated a similar intention: 'With respect to banquets: Inasmuch as people are spending too much money unnecessarily on festive meals, every Jewish community and settlement which has a rabbi is expected to assemble its officers and rabbi and to consider the number of guests which it is suitable for every individual, in view of his wealth and the occasions, to invite to a festive meal.' To avoid attracting the envy and hostility of the christian community in which they lived, the Jews of Forli, Italy in 1418 were ordered by the elders not to be so arrogant as to wear a fur-lined jacket ('unless of course, it is black') or sleeves lined with silk, unless the linings were hidden; if 'the sleeves and the garments themselves (were) closed at the sides and at the back', all was well.[48] In *Utopia,* Thomas More suggests that display is foolish: 'So whereas in other countries you won't find anyone satisfied with less than five or six suits and as many silk shirts, while dressy types want over ten of each, your Utopian is content with a single piece of clothing every two years. For why should he want more? They wouldn't make him any warmer — or any better looking.'[49] In any case, as Richard Rolle wrote in a letter to a nun near Pickering about 1343: 'As soon as you feel savour in Jesus, you will think all the world nothing but vanity and a nuisance to men's souls. You will not covet then to be rich, to have many mantles and fair, many gowns and ornaments; but you will set all at nought ... and take no more than you need.'[50] Therefore sumptuary self-control, which limits consumption to what is necessary, should be instinctive for a dedicated Christian. This need not preclude pleasures because, Luther insists, 'Our loving Lord God wills that we eat, drink and be merry, making use of his creatures, for therefore he created them.', but it does require restraint, an avoidance of superfluity.[51]

Conspicuous christian austerity can draw ridicule. Nicholas Ferrar's (1592-1637) biographer, Dr. Jebb, reports that as a boy Ferrar 'fancied being a clergyman, and he made his friends laugh heartily by a request he very solemnly made to his mother; that whatever his brothers wore, he might wear no lace, for he was resolved to be a clergyman; and he would take no denial, but all his clothes must be plain'.[52] Milton's quaker secretary, Thomas Ellwood, describes the mockery attracted by their sober clothes in his *Speculum Saeculi* of 1667:

> And he that in a modest garb is drest,
> Is made the laughing-stock of all the rest.
> Nor are they with their baubles satisfied,
> But sex-distinctions too are laid aside.
> The women wear the trousers and the vest,
> While men in muffs, fans, petticoats are drest.[53]

For many Quakers, formal austerity of dress (as well as their use of 'thee' and 'thou' and refusal of 'hat honours') still distinguished and separated them from the rest of english society as late as 1835. Owen Chadwick remarks: 'To adopt Quaker garb for the first time felt like ordination, experience of affection, committal of soul ': its role was like that of the religious habit.[54] This illustrates another aspect of sumptuary regulations: a recognition that a style of dress may identify the individual with his group.

This is only the beginning. Clothes in a way express or even create the man; they can increase the height, bulk and impressiveness of the wearer, as they do for a policeman, guardsman or (as we see in Holbein's portraits), for Henry VIII. If a man, without entitlement, puts on the clothes appropriate to a group with particular authority or to a higher social class, this may be an impersonation, an act of insolence or presumption or, worse still, it may be subversive, a threat to the established order. Chaucer's Poor Priest gives a detailed argument on sumptuary matters, criticizing superfluity in clothing. He complains against the waste of using too much material for gowns, so that they trail in the dung, and by wasting cloth create scarcity for the poor. On the other hand, he says the clothes are in other ways too scanty, 'to wicked intent' showing the man's 'horrible swollen members', which look like hernias in their tight trousers, 'and also their buttocks move along like the hindparts of a she-ape at the full moon'. In a critical passage, he says: 'Moreover, if it happened they would give such (decoratively) pierced and slashed clothing to the poor people, it is not fitting for them to wear because of their position in society, nor sufficient to meet their needs, to keep them from the affliction of bad weather.'[55] Here, in addition to the point about justice, there is a concept of an ordered society in which there are clothes proper to each grade. In the middle ages, it was defined as a deadly sin for a man to dress beyond his station.[56]

Clerical Extravagance

One group which attracted and at times deserved criticism for extravagance during the middle ages was the clergy. Monks with fur-trimmed sleeves, friars in double worsted, canons with silk girdles and jewellery and over-dressed priests were a great distance from the evangelical ideal.[57]

Here, it is perhaps more significant to consider, not the behaviour of individuals, but the relation of the church itself to property. It had been an object of the argument on Dominion and Grace to establish the church's unique title to property ownership. This generated its own contradiction: that the church, grown greedy and luxurious through property ownership, had fallen from grace, and should therefore be despoiled.[58] There were other arguments for the dispossession of the church. Marsilius of Padua, starting from an assertion of the supremacy of the civil state, concluded in his *Defensor Pacis* (1324) that it was for the lay rulers to provide ministers of religion with just sufficient resources to meet their needs. The church itself should not have property, and any gifts it received were for use only; ownership remained with the donor.[59] The reasoning was not always as disinterested as this. In 1410, the english parliament was asked to dispossess the monasteries, largely because they were conspicuously rich, while the government's domestic and overseas financial requirements were vast and unfulfilled. Adam Smith was to be equally pragmatic: 'It may be laid down as a certain maxim, that, all other things being supposed equal, the richer the church, the poorer must necessarily be, either the sovereign on the one hand, or the people on the other.'[60] Bentham's imagination was inflamed by the supposed wealth of the English church; the principal utilitarian view was that the church's property should be redistributed to contribute as much as possible to the welfare of the greatest possible numbers in society.[61]

The church's wealth was to stimulate argument of a different, though now familiar kind. Teresa of Avila, in her *Way of Perfection,* told her nuns: 'It looks very bad, my daughters, to build large houses with the gifts of the poor. May it please God not to permit it, but let them be poor in every way, and small.'[62] This was the true spirit for a religious, but it could also reflect the peoples' feelings. In 1839, a fundraiser for the movement to build more working-class churches in England's inner cities 'was told that they would give him a shilling to hang the bishop but not a sixpence to build a church. They said that they wanted food, not churches.' This was an attitude Pugin decried in the roman catholic community of the time; instead of his elaborate and richly furnished, neo-gothic buildings the poor 'actually propose deal and plaster', he wrote in 1848; 'Ere long they will advocate a *new service,* suited to these (Quaker-like) conventicles — as sort of *Catholic Methodism.*'[63]

The debate is an ancient one, and it re-establishes an essential theme in this essay. At the end of the twelfth century, the Parisian Pierre Le Chantre criticized the building of Notre Dame, then rising on a mass of endowments and donations, because this expenditure was oppressive, at the expense of the poor, and therefore an abuse of divine justice.[64] An english lollard polemicist brings the same criticism against lavish gifts for saints' shrines: 'Dear Lord! what alms is it to paint gaily dead stones and rotten lumps of wood with the very alms that are poor men's goods and livelihood'; the proud covetous clerks who spend money thus are 'wasting these poor men's property'.[65]

This argument is radically different from many we have been considering: the pursuit of poverty for the purpose of self-perfection, the pursuit of riches in the name of stewardship, the reward of virtue with wealth and of sloth and vice with destitution, the frugal management of one's own means to provide for home then household of faith then all other men, the equitable conduct of trade and employment — these in themselves grant only a secondary, still concessionary title to the poor for right of access to the resources concerned. For example, while Jeremy Taylor said that an employer should pay his employee 'exactly according to covenant, or according to his needs',[66] so that a christian concern for the individual is added to observation of contract, nothing is said or implied about the worker's entitlement to share in the wealth generated. This teaching, precisely because it places on the employer a responsibility to allow for the worker's finite needs, leaves the decision (and presumably an indefinitely large surplus) in the employer's or corporate owner's hands.

Christian Socialism

Christian socialism is a many-layered group of concepts. In its most familiar form, as we have seen, it argues that a man should provide for the poor from his surplus income or wealth; this is the gentlest sense in which the christian community can be said to share all things in common, when the less privileged are given access to whatever is left over.

There have been many communities of people sharing property in common and caring for the poor, extending the practice of creating small islands of common life in a selfish world which St. Gregory commended to Augustine and his monks at Canterbury in the sixth century. Langland declared: 'Christians should be in common rich', and the system described in *Utopia* was 'based on communal ownership instead of private property'.[67] The layman Nicholas Ferrar (later a deacon) created such a community in his household when he bought the manor at Little Gidding in 1625.[68] Robert Owen, having pioneered model working conditions for the labourers in his New Lanark mills early in the nineteenth century, in 1826 attempted to create a truly socialist community in the New Harmony village community in North America. Following this, 'A score of other Owenite communities were developed ... but soon ended, their idealistic theories inadequate to meet the stubborn realities of economics and human nature.'[69] Although Owen was a fierce anti-clerical, Bishop Stanley of Norwich in 1846 unsuccessfully attempted to transport the experiment to England.

This was the age of Christian Socialism, when F. D. Maurice espoused the co-operative cause, inspired by the principle 'The truth is that every man is in Christ', and that men had 'no existence save as sons, brothers, members of the community'. Conrad Noel was to write in 1910 that public ownership was 'a necessary deduction from the teachings of Christ'.[70] He also exposed a disastrous flaw in Owen's position: 'Mount your benevolent man on the high horse of law, and he will complacently trample on other men's wishes, "all for their own good". Mr. Robert Owen was one of the most benevolent of men; but a more unmitigated *tyranny* can scarcely be conceived than his "New Moral World" would have been if it could have been realized.'[71]

The Christian Socialists were apparently very clear about their position. In a letter to John Ludlow, another key figure in the movement, F. D. Maurice defended their title: ' "Tracts on Christian Socialism" is, it seems to me, the only title which will define our object, and will commit us at once to the conflict we must engage in sooner or later with the unsocial Christians and the unchristian Socialists. It is a great thing not to leave people to poke out our object and proclaim it with infinite triumph. "Why, you are Socialists in disguise." " In disguise; not a bit of it. There it is staring you in the face upon the title page!" "You want to thrust in ever so much priestcraft under a good revolutionary name." "Well, did not we warn you of it? Did we not profess that our intended something was quite different from what your Owenish lectures meant." This is the fair play which English people like, and which will save us from a number of long prefaces, paraphrases, apologetical statements which waste time when one wants to be getting to business.'[72] Christian Socialism would later be condemned as a contradiction in terms (see p.203).

The methods they used were perceived as honest and practical. In another letter to Ludlow, Maurice explained his intervention in the 1852 lockout as follows: 'I have not been urging the amalgamated iron trades to an unconditional surrender. I have not seen Newton, or any one who represents their interests. What I said to the council was that I believed an unconditional surrender might be the right way of showing the brute force there was in capital, and of bringing the case of the working-men fairly before the public, as a struggle of human beings against mere money power.'[73] Edward Vansittart Neale's promotion of the Co-operative cause was more pragmatic, and cost him a substantial fortune. He saw Co-operation as the most constructive way to achieve satisfactory conditions for the production, distribution, sale and purchase of goods, and thus as the most promising vehicle for the redistribution of wealth.[74]

Charles E. Raven, in his papers on *Christian Socialism 1848 to 1854,* describes the attitudes against which Maurice, Ludlow, Neale, Charles Kingsley and Tom Hughes were reacting. He says that, to Hannah and Martha More, conspicuous nineteenth-century philanthropists, 'God had made some men poor, just as He had made some men black: Scripture guaranteed that poverty and blackness were alike immutable ...'.

Raven saw it as 'a paradox which no cynic would dare to invent' that Evangelicalism could use prophets, Gospel, 'the little band who turned the world upside down ... to bolster up the doctrine of *laissez-faire* and the righteousness of unrestricted competition ...'.[75]

Yet, consistently with the pattern of corruption observed elsewhere in this essay, Neale's Co-operative movement quickly destroyed its original idealism: 'The great irony of Neale's life was that he ultimately became the leader of a powerful movement which benefited from the organizations he designed, while rejecting the purpose behind them.' Thus, the Co-operative Wholesale Society '... like private capitalist organizations, pursued a policy of monopoly at home and, whenever possible, economic imperialism abroad.'[76]

The ideal, expressed by Ludlow, was that 'Pure communism, the having all things in common, must always be the ideal of Socialism.' It has been said of the Christian Socialists that: 'In every field of social service the influence of their adventure was felt.'[77] However, although they with other churchmen such as Wilberforce, Shaftesbury, Ramsay McDonald and Keir Hardie, were to have a major impact on social legislation and the improvement of living conditions and resources, they achieved no radical, christian revolution of wealth. Secularist socialists complained precisely because their teaching was christian. Marx, who had some contact with the movement, commented: 'Christian Socialism is but the holy water with which the priest consecrates the heart-burnings of the aristocrat.'[78]

To see where christian radicalism bites, we must return to the heretic-radicals. There are many clear voices. For a time, under Cromwell, ordinary men could speak out. In 1646, some soldiers were demanding an upper limit on property holdings, and in 1647 on incomes. More fundamentally, the Leveller Gerrard Winstanley regarded the earth as a 'common storehouse', so that its Creator was insulted if private individuals bought and sold it or if it was 'kept in the hands of a few'. He continued: 'The poorest man hath as true a title and just right to the land as the richest man ... True freedom lies in the free enjoyment of the earth.' Oppression was maintained by the monarchy; with Charles I's execution: 'That top bough is lopped off the tree of tyranny ... But alas, oppression is a great tree still, and keeps off the sun of freedom from the poor commons still.'[79]

The conclusion, if the premise is accepted, must be that the issue is one of justice, not of 'charity', in the sense of 'philanthropy'. John Ball, in 1381, is shown by Froissart crying: 'It is from us and our labour that everything comes with which they (the lords) maintain their pomp.' The lollard *Lanterne of Light* (c1415) approved the saying of William de Saint Amour that those who build fine churches 'turn the bread of poor men into stones'; Langland longed for the day

> When the greed of the clergy is clothing for the poor
> And their fur and their fillies make a poor man's livelihood;

Dives and Pauper asserted that the monks held property which was the right or entitlement of the poor; Tolstoy believed that property claims were 'based on robbery and maintained by violence.'[80] It has been a christian tradition to dilute the rage. Latimer preached: 'The poor man hath title to the rich man's goods,' but he went on: 'so that the rich man ought to let the poor man have part of his riches to help and comfort him withal.' There has been a counter to compromise, though. In 1649, the Ranter Abiejer Coppe wrote: 'And I in thee, who am durable riches, commanded thy perishable silver to the poor.'[81] This restores the central christian issue of the Incarnation.

7
Christian Philanthropy

Christian teaching requires us to care for our neighbour. The responsibility has been acknowledged for poor as well as rich, in proportion to their means. This has not been an obligation exclusive to Christians, or to people who are religious. For all, it has created problems concerning the sums to be given, the ways they should be given and the recipients. The problem of choosing the right recipient contains, for a Christian, the question: 'Who is my neighbour?' The answers may not, perhaps should not, invoke 'charity' as 'philanthropy' rather than 'justice'. My intention in this chapter is to see who have been the almsgivers, who the beneficiaries and to examine the relationships and attitudes between them.

Almsgiving seems to have been practised by almost everybody, including the poor; it is implied that the practice is their right. Rowntree, in his study of poverty in York, lists the features of a family surviving at the official level of mere 'physical efficiency': they cannot afford to spend a penny on public transport, 'go into the country unless they walk', buy a newspaper or stamps for letters to absent children, go to a popular concert, save, join a sick club or Trade Union, give treats to their children, smoke, drink or buy any pretty clothes. Rowntree includes this in his schedule of deprivation: 'They must never contribute anything to their church or chapel, or give any help to a neighbour which costs them money.'[1]

It is difficult to glimpse the charity of the poor, which is often informal and can scarcely be either magnificent, in the aristotelian sense, or patronising. Yet, as Rowntree implies, charity is a normal function for christian as for jewish poor. The migrant shepherd Pierre Maury, early in the fourteenth century in the Pyrenees, declared: 'If we have but one farthing, we must share it with our poor brothers.'[2] In 1856, a con-

·gregation of slaves in Sharon, Tennessee raised $7 to buy
clothes for destitute children in West Africa.[3] During the late
1870s, William Carter, a working-class man by origin, raised at
least £100 annually from the poor at the New Cut Mission,
Lambeth.[4] Gifts from humble benefactors were received by
many nineteenth century charitable organizations. More
important, perhaps, are the spontaneous collections, meals,
hospitality and practical services for the unfortunate which
have been a feature of many working-class communities.[5]

I give prominence to this unspectacular charity because the
essence of christian doctrine may be clearer here than with the
conspicuous, better recorded, more elaborately organized
works which necessarily fill most of my study. When charity
grows remote from personal loving kindness it quickly contra-
dicts itself. The histories of philanthropy are necessarily
concerned with the institutions and organized movements,
and they show how their integrity and true effectiveness have
been vitiated when their inspiring motivation has decayed.

'Kindness' in its original meaning is a central concept. The
first chapter of the early fifteenth-century treatise *Dives and
Pauper* opens: *'Dives et pauper obviaverunt sibi; utriusque
operator est Deus*, Proverbs xxii (2). ... The rich man and the
poor met together; God is maker of them both, for he made
both rich and poor and bought them both with his blood full
dearly. They are both like in kind, like in beginning, like in
ending '; both came into the world naked and poor.[6] This adds
the theme of a common redemption to the stoic teaching of the
brotherhood of men. Later in the same century, Langland
wrote in *Piers Plowman:*

And for love to lend (give) and live well and believe
Is ycalled *Caritas*, Kind Love in English.[7]

Charity is a response between people who, because they are of
one 'kind' or 'nature', must treat each other with natural sympathy. Another central feature of christian teaching is the Incarnation; by suffusing man with divinity so intimately that
'you are to God as your hand is to you' and 'God and man are
one', it transforms the merely human action into an act of
Christ.[8]

Donors

When we turn to the historic records of giving, the problem is that the lists of founders, donors or benefactors appear endless. The monarchs, in establishing churches, monasteries, hospitals and schools, must head the list, though they have not always been the most generous philanthropists. Edward the Confessor committed a tenth of his income to the construction of a noble building in the fertile lands and green fields near the river outside London, at Westminster. Hospital founders include Stephen, John and Henry VIII.[9] William III, Queen Anne and Queen Victoria were all, on a less spectacular scale, prominent benefactors of the S.P.C.K. and the Society for the Propagation of the Gospel.[10] The nobles have been equally active. One historian (misrepresenting the degree to which an unjust social structure was acknowledged by the aristocracy during the middle ages) says: 'Men of property were expected to give to the church and to the poor, during life and at death, both to justify their inequitable status in the social hierarchy and to buy prayers for their own souls.'[11]

For the clergy, the role of philanthropy was a requirement. The pope was father of the poor, as Luther reminded him: 'How can a man rule and at the same time preach, pray, study, and care for the poor? Yet these are the duties which most properly and peculiarly belong to the pope ...'[12] For bishops, at least from the fifth century, a four-fold division of ecclesiastical funds was recommended. Pope Gelasius anticipated the formula used in a letter from Pope Gregory to Augustine of Canterbury: 'All receipts should be divided into four parts: namely, one for the bishop and his household for hospitality and other commitments, another for the clergy, the third for the poor, the fourth for mending churches.'[13] A canon issued in Orleans in 509, included in an English collection of canons by Ecbricht in 740, stated: 'Let the bishop give food and raiment, to the utmost of his power, to the poor and infirm, who cannot labour with their hands, by reason of weakness.' The general clergy had a similar responsibility, and even some monks, despite their elected poverty, were given an allowance so that they could hand out small alms.[14]

As the wealth and power of burghers and merchants grew

during the middle ages, they took on increasingly important roles in the funding of charitable institutions and churches and in the relief of poverty. The great cathedrals of Paris and Strasbourg depended on them. In York, the profusion of beautiful medieval churches may be attributed to the exclusivity of the Minster, which discouraged gifts from commoners.[15] Dick Whittington, that exemplary merchant, was a major benefactor of the London hospitals in the late fourteenth and early fifteenth centuries, and had also 'made a new chamber with eight beds for young women that had done amiss in the hope of a good amendment'.[16] Merchants supported the protestant reformers, sending funds to them in exile, and the puritan businessmen and gentry became active benefactors of very diverse charitable activities, ranging from the financing of Tyndale's work about 1524 to the founding of 'that Puritan seminary Emmanuel College' by Sir Walter Mildmay in 1584.[17]

As wealth increased for larger sections of the community, patterns of philanthropy changed. In her study of the charity school movement, M. G. Jones writes: 'The success of the voluntary societies was closely bound up with what contemporaries termed the joint-stock method of finance. In industry and commerce joint-stock companies, during the seventeenth century, had tapped new sources of capital, hidden hitherto in the stockings of maiden ladies and country clergy. When eighteenth-century reformers for the education of the poor required funds to finance their work the joint-stock method supplied them the means.' As a result, large numbers of small donations from the 'middling classes' were added to the gifts of the rich.[18] There had been the earlier guild movements for mutual aid and external charity (see p. 136 below), which drew on the funds of ordinary tradesmen, and there had been humble gifts at all times, but the late seventeenth century introduced powerful changes in the scale and practice of philanthropy. Throughout the eighteenth century, parallel developments were taking place in North America, where they were to produce a movement in philanthropy more massive, highly organized and popular than any that had existed before.[19] Subscription lists to churches, welfare and educational institutions and such pioneering fundraising bodies as the charity schools, S.P.C.K. and S.P.G. (founded in

1698 and 1701 respectively) and the other new Societies give the impression that by the middle of the eighteenth century most trades people and gentry were having their donations noted down in the annual reports of charitable societies and on boards in hospitals and churches. The more devotedly religious groups such as Nicholas Ferrar's Little Gidding community, or Wesley's Holy Club at Oxford or the evangelical Clapham Sect included charitable action as an integral aspect of their christian regimes.[20]

The point I am making here is that one can take the simple act of giving virtually for granted. It was required of saints, expected of citizens, observed with little amazement from bankers, villains and even from non-Christians. During the period 1868-92, the pagan king in Mandalay gave land and funds for the christian mission, and buddhist gifts accounted for 44% of the offertory there. The Fuggers founded churches and almshouses. In this they resembled Robin Hood who, seafaring in a late ballad, disowns his share of plunder:

> It shall be so, as I have said;
>> And with this gold, for the opprest
> An habitation I will build,
>> Where they shall live in peace and rest[21]

Finally, as the nineteenth century progressed, increasing numbers of religiously inspired industrialists committed corporate funds to charity, often channelling them through their eponymous trusts (see p.143).

Recipients

If the categories of donors are bewilderingly numerous, the categories of recipients and of recommended good works are more bewildering still. They have varied in details; during and immediately after a war, wounded soldiers and sailors appear, as in the preamble to Elizabeth's 1601 Act or in York in 1649 or after the Great War.[22] The Guild of St. Leonard at Lynn and the poor house in Penzance, both seaside places, provided for victims of shipwreck.[23] At times of high unemployment, special measures have been taken through both statutory and voluntary means. After 1257, Guglielmo Boccanegra created public works to help the unemployed, and from Tudor times onwards English poor laws stipulated: 'That in every city and town corporate within this realm a competent store and stock of wool, hemp, flax, iron and other stuff' should be held, which was to be supplied to the able-bodied poor for manufacturing goods, 'for which (the authorities) shall make payment to them which work the same according to the desert of the work' (from the *Poor Relief Act* of 1576).[24] On the side of voluntary initiative, the Society for Encouraging Industry and Employing the Poor, set up in eighteenth-century Boston, is a fairly typical example. Special measures were taken to relieve suffering when there was famine, plague and natural disaster; witness the conscientious, often frustrated fundraising of Cristofano in plague-stricken Prato during 1630 and 1631.[25] The categories of relief have, to some extent at least, been responsive to needs.

There is one apparently strange example of this. In wills, in Guild ordinances, in documents relating to fundraising and in legislation, there are frequent references to gifts for maintaining roads, bridges, causeways, fosse ways, sea walls, ports and havens. Bishop Grandisson, during the first quarter of the fourteenth century, was raising money both for his cathedral in Exeter and for the Exe bridge.[26] The people of that period would not have made the distinction between secular and religious acts to which we may be inclined. Some citizens of Lyon preferred their great Rhone bridge to the cathedral there, and found it perfectly natural to attach to a gift for the bridge the formula they would have used with a gift for the poor or for the cathedral: that it was made 'for the remedy of my soul, and those of my ancestors, and for my own salvation'.[27] It was a very practical work of mercy 'to help perilous ways and paths where man and beast is perished,' as a fourteenth century tract explains it.[28] Lives, beasts and property were often in danger. At an earlier date, probably about 1100, Eadmer's *Life of Anselm* described London Bridge as so full of holes that a baggage horse fell through into the Thames below.[29]

Responsibility for roads and bridges was often unclearly divided between landowners, monasteries, guilds and civic corporations, and there is much evidence of confusion and evasion. While the fifteenth century Ordinances of Worcester stipulated 'that the Bridge may be overseen at all times for the safety of the city. And that the repair of the said Bridge be over-looked by the chamberlains every quarter'; and while, with their concern for commerce, the Tudors in 1531, in 1555 and again in 1563 passed acts for the mending of bridges and highways, it is clear that confusion remained.[30] W. M. Hanyngfeld, esq, in his will of 1426, included this: 'And also I will that on the bridge between Easterford (Kelveden) and Chelmsford, if need be, be spended 500 marks, if it so be that no man be bound by his land to mend it.'[31]

The problems were intricate. The medieval system insisted on local responsibility for roads and bridges. The sheriff and his staff, working through jurors, had to assess maintenance needs and attribute responsibility for them.[32] Yet, as late as 1700, these were matters to arouse parish passions. Richard Gough, in his *Antiquities and Memories of the Parish of Myddle*, traced the course of Peine's brook as it passed down, from Dunstall Pitt through Newton, Alderton and 'Hardwicke grounds', to a common where it divided Myddle from Shawbury parish. 'In this common there is a bridge over this brooke. The west end or half of the bridge is maintained by the owners or tenants of Hardwicke; and the east end or half, by Shawbury parish, by which it appears that the brooke is in both parishes.' The purpose of this account was to explain a disagreement over maintenance of the bridge. Through a search of the books of Baschurch parish, 'It was found that Baschurch parish had formerly repaired the said bridge wholly.' In the end, the men of Marton had to repair the causeway, the parish of Baschurch the bridge.[33] The complexity of the situation, involving several parishes and estates, was typical.

Even where responsibility was clear, there might not be the means to fulfil it. The Report of the Commissioners of Henry VIII found that the town of Birmingham had been unable to maintain 'two great stone bridges, and diverse foul and dangerous highways', so that a Guild had undertaken this work.[34] The remedy was a long time coming. G. M. Trevelyan has commented: 'The unfairness of laying the burden of repair not on the users of the great roads, but on the parishes through which they happened to pass, was equalled by the folly of expecting farmers, who had no interest in the matter, to act gratuitously as skilled workers of highways.' The turnpikes, and the House of Hanover, went some way to remedying this.[35] Before there was any effective statutory remedy, road and bridge maintenance could be seen as a pious and charitable act, however odd this seems today. It was only in 1975 that the English Charity Commissioners made their final arrangements for diverting to the poor, elderly and sick of the contiguous boroughs the funds Edward Harvist gave in 1610 for 'repairing and amending the highway between Tyborne (Marble Arch) and Edgware.'[36]

The example of roads and bridges illustrates the original relationship between charity and social needs. The Diggers in the seventeenth century regarded the collective manuring of common lands as a religious act, wholly consistently with their beliefs and their perception of needs.[37] These were the more extraordinary expressions of 'charity'. The usual medieval categories embraced orphans and widows (one commentator believes that preoccupation with these two categories caused others to be neglected);[38] children and the elderly; the bedridden, lame, blind, deaf, dumb, maimed, bent and insane; lepers and the sick generally; the deserving poor and those who had fallen into sudden poverty; the hungry and the naked; pilgrims and travellers; prisoners and poor tenants; young women needing dowries and boys requiring education or apprenticeships; the churches and clergy. Christians were urged to bury the dead, to provide clothes and sheets for the sick and needy and for prisoners, to pay the debts of the poor, to ransom captives, to give hospitality to strangers, to help build churches.[39] Behind the benefactions named in the wills are fairly standard lists of charitable objects, with some personal variations: 'And if the vault of Okeham steeple be not made in my life, the which I have made covenant of with Thomas Nauton, Mason, ... I will the same covenant be fulfilled after my decease' (Roger Flore, 1424); 'Item I bequeath to the high altar of (Saint Augustine's church, Hackney) 20d. Item I bequeath to the reparation of the bells of the same church 20d. Item I bequeath to the amending of the highway in the same parish 20d. Item I bequeath Agnes my daughter, my dun bullock, and one pot of brass of a gallon' (Roger Barton, 1434).[40]

The celebrated lists of charitable objects in Langland and the

1601 *Charitable Uses Act* were by no means original, and the latter has been misunderstood. Picarda states that the *Charitable Uses Act* 1601 'was not passed for the purpose of giving a definition of "charity" but was directed to providing for the reformation of abuses in the application of property devoted to charitable uses.'[41] The main headings for the list, embodied in the 'seven works of mercy', had long been a regular subject of religious preaching as in this example by John Gaytryng in 1357: 'Of which the first is to feed them that are hungry. The second is to give them drink that are thirsty. The third is for to clothe them that are clotheless or naked. The fourth is to harbour those who are houseless. The fifth is to visit those who lie in sickness. The sixth is for to help those that lie in prison. The seventh is to bury dead men who need this. These are the seven bodily deeds of mercy that every man ought to do who has the might to do them.'[42] A lollard text, of the late fourteenth or early fifteenth centuries, makes it clear that there was back-sliding: 'And thus instead of works of bodily mercy and charity is come in hypocrisy of worldly name and covetousness and nourishing of sin and subtle excusing thereof; and evil is called good and good evil. ... but however we excuse ourselves, we waste needless many goods both in food and drink and clothes with which poor men should be helped ...'.[43]

I have lingered over this discussion of categories because of their influence on case law and on practice in the UK and USA. They were not in themselves specifically christian, as we have seen. The pagan Icelandic poem *Hávámal* taught:

> He needs a fire who comes in
> with cold in his calves;
> a man needs clothes and meat
> who has fared down from the fells;
> the stranger come to supper
> wants water, towel and a welcome;
> if he can get it, he should have comradeship
> and enjoy a ready answer.[44]

However, christian tradition has given these works special sanction, so that they have become part of our law, attitudes and accustomed patterns of behaviour. They are accepted so instinctively within our culture that we are scarcely conscious of them. There is a view today which regards this as harmful, on the grounds that, in a well organized state, the works of mercy are as obsolete as the charitable funding of roads and bridges. It is therefore useful to understand the origins of the prejudice which favours the traditional works and their some-times eccentric offspring.

There have been age-long attempts to find criteria for estab-lishing priorities amongst needs. The *Poor Relief Act* of 1598, predecessor of the 1601 Act, placed first responsibility for the indigent on their own families: 'And be it further enacted, that the parents or children of every poor, old, blind, lame and impotent person, or other poor person not able to work, being of sufficient ability, shall at their own charges relieve and maintain every such poor person in that manner and accord-ing to that rate as by the Justices of Peace of that county ... shall be assessed.'[45] The custom by which better-off families cared for their own poor relations, whether as servants or as less pri-vileged members of the household, was at least occasionally continued into this century. After the family, the parish tended to be the next unit on whom responsibility was placed, although allowance was made for parishes whose resources were over-extended to call on others which had resources to spare.[46] In any case, the normal christian interpretation of 'love thy neighbour' tended to be fairly literal; the poor within the village or town, and especially those of one's own religious sect, were to be preferred to others, equally or more indigent, who were geographically more remote. The guilds, by their ordinances, necessarily preferred their own members above outsiders; the Guild Merchant of Coventry in 1340 approved the hiring of chaplains, but only after 'the brothers and sisters of the guild who are fallen into poverty' had been provided for, 'according as need may be'.[47] In 1667, George Fox wrote to Peter Hendrix, a cheesemonger: 'And be diligent in all your meetings, and see to the setting forth of apprentices, all father-less and poor Friends' children.'; and William Croucher's 1712 account of the first London Quakers describes how the 'ancient women-friends' used to meet to provide for those imprisoned because of their quaker beliefs: 'These women did also inquire into, and inspect the wants and necessities of the poor, who were convinced of the truth.'[48]

Calvin had warned against a narrow charity: 'Our Saviour

having shown, in the parable of the Samaritan (Lk. x, 36), that the term *neighbour* comprehends the most remote stranger, there is no reason for limiting the precept of love to our own connections. I deny not that the closer the relation the more frequent our offices of kindness should be. ... But I say that the whole human race, without exception, are to be embraced with one feeling of charity: that here there is no distinction of Greek or Barbarian, worthy or unworthy, friend or foe, since all are to be viewed not in themselves, but in God.'[49] In the same spirit, the Diggers 'spoke on behalf of "all the poor oppressed people of England and the whole world" and hoped that the law of freedom would go from their country to all the nations of the world'.[50]

It is difficult, however, during these earlier periods, to find much evidence of the kind of disinterested, distant relief which has been promoted in the West since the late 1950s. The requirement that rich parishes should help those parishes unable 'to levy among themselves sufficient sums of money' to meet the requirements of the 1598 *Poor Relief Act* was scarcely voluntary. Peter's Pence was a tax not a donation; anyway, in Wolsey's time, it 'amounted to less than £200 for the whole of England'.[51] The Protestants did indeed support their co-religionists overseas when they were persecuted or in need. George Fox's *Journal* for 1658 records: 'About this time came forth a declaration from Oliver Cromwell, the Protector, for a collection towards the relief of divers Protestant Churches, driven out of Poland; and of twenty Protestant families, driven out of the confines of Bohemia.' and it invited the nation 'to a day of solemn fasting and humiliation, in order to a contribution being made for the suffering Protestants for the valleys of Lucerne, Angrona, etc., who were persecuted by the Duke of Savoy'. In his own, special fashion, George Fox then rebuked Cromwell for persecuting Protestants at home. William Penn, the founder of Pennsylvania, in his preface to the original 1694 edition of the *Journal*, records that George Fox used letters of distress 'from the many Meetings of God's people over all the world ... endeavouring speedy relief'[52] (see p.164). Governments joined with voluntary donors in contributing towards hospitals and schools in the missions, because these were major weapons in the extension of their empires. The pattern was the same in the catholic missions to portuguese Asia in the sixteenth century and in the english protestant missions to South Africa and India in the nineteenth; with both, the gifts had an explicit, proselytising and political purpose.[53]

The exceptions seem to be isolated. The work of churchmen for the abolition of slavery is a massive example, too complex to be considered here. The Sharon slaves who raised funds for west african natives would have been moved by sympathy only. About 1877, a drive in England to raise funds for indian famine victims was explicitly 'for the relief of 96,000 sufferers (without respect to race, caste or creed)'. The money sent by the christian churches to famine-afflicted Russia in response to Patriarch Basil Tikhon's appeal in 1921-2 was surely genuinely disinterested, but the funds were confiscated by the soviet government, to deny the church such advantageous propaganda.[54]

One example of genuinely disinterested, distant relief before our own period is a jewish meeting in New York called for March 8th, 1847. The Irish potato crop had failed the previous year, and this is how the Rabbi J. J. Lyons presented the case for the remote catholic Irish to the meeting: 'No devasting pestilence has invaded our shores; all with us is teeming with life and health. No dreadful blight has consumed our fields: all nature is smiling in beauty and abundance. ... Yet sadness and gloom pervade the land. A nation is in distress, a nation is starving. Numbers of our fellow-creatures have perished, dreadfully, miserably perished from hunger and starvation. Millions are threatened with the same horrid fate, the same dire calamity. ... We are told that we have a large number of our own poor and destitute to take care of, that the charity which we dispense should be bestowed in this quarter, that the peculiar position of ourselves and our co-religionists demands it at our hand, that justice is a higher virtue than generosity, that self-preservation is a law and principle of our nature. Examine these objections for yourselves. Reflect upon them seriously and conscientiously; then ask for yourselves whether they be forcible and true, or whether they are not in fact excuses which the lips utter, while they are rejected by the heart. Ask yourselves if the contribution which this day you are requested to make will diminish in the smallest degree the other calls which you admit are imperative and binding; and if the responses be those which I anticipate, our meeting for this purpose will not have been in vain. ... I have attempted only to express the one simple truth, that the sufferings of our fellow-men, wheresoever and howsoever situated, demand from us alleviation, assistance and relief. Grant it in this case, for it is a pressing one. Grant it mothers, for mothers once happy and blessed as ye are ask it of you for their own sakes and for the sakes of their suffering babes; they ask it of you by that bond of sympathy which nature has created between ye; they ask it of you with streaming eyes and outstretched hands, to save them from disease and starvation. Grant it wives: to save a famishing husband, a wife asks it of you, and what stronger claim can she present to you? Grant it sisters: in a brother's name, in the name of pure and holy love, it is asked of you, and you will not refuse. Grant it brothers; grant it men: in the name of God it is asked of you, and it is, I know it is granted.'[55]

Motives

The reasons why people have given to charity are often hidden, and are generally confused. Pride, vanity, advantage have always been potent motives. We saw earlier (p.20) how, in classical times, public good works were explicitly intended to secure attention for the philanthropist's name, in life and after death. The pagan, nordic view was expressed this way:

> Flocks die, family dies
> you will die the same way also;
> but the great name will never die
> of the man who has made it.[56]

Raymond de l'Aire of Tignac, near Toulouse, in the early fourteenth century, admitted: 'I am a great alms-giver. But not for the love of God. It is rather to win a good reputation among my neighbours. To have the reputation of being a good man ...'.[57] The self-glorifying motive was seldom admitted quite so openly, although there was certainly a spirit of emulation between medieval benefactors, seeking at the same time the temporal survival of their names and the eternal salvation of their souls: 'People asked for tombs like those of other peers who had predeceased them and who had attracted post-humous fame through the splendour of their monuments, benefactions, and funerals. The peers all knew each other and it is only to be expected that they kept abreast of each others' gift giving activities.'[58] If this is reminiscent of the philanthropy of many present-day companies, so is the conservatism which has been a feature of both noble and corporate giving.

Such vanity is, of course, a marvellous pretext for satire. Alexander Pope, in 1733, contrasted the self-effacing style of a perfect philanthropist with the display of a vain man's monument:

> The MAN of ROSS divides the weekly bread:
> Beyond yon Alms-house, neat, but void of state,
> Where Age and Want sit smiling at the gate:
> Him portion'd maids, apprentic'd orphans blest,
> the young who labour, and the old who rest.
> Is any sick? The MAN of ROSS relieves,
> Prescribes, attends, the med'cine makes and gives.
> .....
> 'And what? no monument, inscription, stone?
> His race, his form, his name almost unknown?'
> Who builds a Church to God, and not to Fame,
> Will never mark the marble with his Name.
> .....
> When Hopkins dies, a thousand lights attend
> The wretch, who living sav'd a candle's end:
> Should'ring God's altar a vile image stands,
> Belies his features, nay extends his hands;
> That live-long wig which Gorgon's self might own,
> Eternal buckle takes in Parian stone;
> Behold what blessings Wealth to life can lend!
> And see, what comfort it affords our end.[59]

At a meaner level, William Cowper (1731-1800) describes a charity collection in church after

> A conflagration or, a wintry flood
> Has left some hundreds without home or food.
> Extravagance and avarice shall subscribe
> While fame and self-complacence are the bribe.
> The collector approaches the squire first:
> With slow deliberation he unties

His glittering purse, that envy of all eyes!
And, while the clerk just puzzles out the psalm,
Slides guinea behind guinea in his palm;
Till finding, what he might have found before,
A smaller piece amidst the precious store,
Pinch'd close between his finger and his thumb
He half exhibits, and then drops the sum.
Gold, to be sure! — Throughout the town 'tis told,
How the good squire gives never less than gold.
From motives such as his, though not the best,
Springs in due time supply for the distress'd;
Not less effected than what love bestows
Except that office clips it as it goes.[60]

The combination of secular with spiritual motivation was encouraged by fundraising churchmen. Trade groups and individuals could be commemorated in stained-glass windows with their names and pictures, and the images of suppliant donors are a commonplace in medieval windows, altar-pieces and religious paintings.[61] Langland described Lady Meed with her friar-confessor:

And he absolved her soon and since that said:
'We have a window being worked will highly become us;
If you would glaze that gable and engrave your name there
At mass and at matins we shall sing for Mede
Solemnly and softly as for a sister of our order'.[62]

A combination of motives was quite readily accommodated by medieval writers. Caesarius of Heisterbach's Monk can say: 'To him that has the grace of hospitality, and receives his guests with kindness, goodwill and a cheerful countenance, and who freely welcomes God's poor; to him it is the Lord's will that there shall be given as much, and sometimes as is shown above, a hundredfold in this present life, and he shall have abundance, and in the world to come life everlasting.'[63]

Luther condenses a story from Caesarius to illustrate the text 'Give and it shall be given unto you' (193-4). 'There is in Austria a monastery, which, in former times, was very rich and remained rich so long as it was charitable to the poor; but when it ceased to give, then it became indigent, and is so to this day. Not long since, a poor man went there and solicited alms, which was denied him; he demanded the cause why they refused to give for God's sake? The porter of the monastery answered: "We are become poor;" whereupon the mendicant said: "The cause of your poverty is this: ye had formerly in this monastery two brethren, the one named *Date* (give), and the other *Dabitur* (it shall be given you). The former ye thrust out; the other went away of himself." [64] The same theme had occurred in the early Icelandic poem *Hávámal:* 'Give-away and Give-back-again are the oldest friends.'[65] At this level, the donor's more selfish motivations could be sensible, or at worst laughable. It was the practice of good works to purchase paradise and save the soul which drew rage rather than laughter from the reformers.

Yet the purchase of salvation is one of the motives most frequently expressed by medieval donors. It had been clearly taught, for example in Canons issued by Cuthbert, Archbishop of Canterbury, at Cloveshoe in 647, that alms are 'certainly ... not to be given to the intent that a man may commit any the least sins with greater liberty, on account of the alms given by him, or by any others in his behalf', nor in place of fasting and other mortifications, although they should be done daily 'that so past sins may the sooner and more fully be forgiven by God'. Therefore, in a decree of 925, we read: 'I Athelstan, king, declare to all my reeves, with advice of archbishop, bishops, and servants of God, that it is my will that for forgiveness of my sins ye always feed one poor Englishman, and give him, from two of my farms, every month an amber of meal and a gammon of bacon, or one ram worth four pence; and one shroud every year for the twelve months (wear); and that ye set at liberty some one that has for his crimes been condemned to slavery, for the mercies of Christ and for my love, with the testimony of the bishop in whose district it is ...' [66] The same aspiration is a regular formula in gifts and wills. Caesarius takes this conversation for granted: ' "I should like to leave something for the benefit of my soul, if I knew where it could best be placed," His friend replied: "Near Cologne there is a very holy monastery ... Nowhere could you place your alms better nor more profitably to your soul than there." '[67] The will of John Toker, Vintner, in 1428 is wholly typical: 'First, I bequeath my soul to almighty God my creator and maker, and to his blessed mother our lady saint Mary, and to all the holy company of heaven, and my body to be buried in the church of Saint Mildred in Bread Street in London. Also I bequeath to the high altar of the same church for my tithes and offerings forgotten and withdrawn, 40 shillings. ... Also I bequeath to be distributed among poor folk dwelling in the foresaid parish of St. Mildred, forto pray for my soul, 40 shillings. Also I bequeath to be distributed among prisoners in the prisons of Ludgate, Marchelsea, Kingsbench And the Counters in London, that is to say, in every of the said prisons, the prisoners to pray for my soul, 20 shillings.'[68]

A gift was made because it carried merit in itself, because it made up for sins and omissions and because it purchased prayers. There was rivalry to obtain burial in certain churches, those of the friars being especially desirable to some fourteenth-century benefactors. In 1327, Jean Ogier, a burgher of Lyon, left 2,300 livres to the Franciscan church to secure remembrance there. Roger Elmesley's will in 1434 stipulated: 'And my body (is) to be buried under the stone without the door of the porch, and my name written thereon when I am dead. Also I bequeath to the works of the same church of St. Margaret Pattens ¾d to have my burying there, and the stone free.'; a torch was to burn every Sunday in his memory at the elevation of the host.[69] The object with these benefactions, as with the endowment of chantry chapels and chantry priests, was to try to guarantee endless prayers for the soul of the donor, his family and friends. Dick Whittington clothed, fed and housed twelve poor bedesmen, who were to pray for him. In 1423, a pen-and-ink sketch of his deathbed was made, showing the good men in attendance, their leader with rosary poised. The Countess of Warwick, in 1439, instructed the masons: 'And all about my tomb, to be made poor men and women in their poor Array, with their beads in their hands'.[70] When the people of Wittenburg flocked across the border to buy indulgences from the Pope's fundraiser, Tetzel, they had the same intention (see p.160). An elaborate, and from the viewpoint of fundraising, effective system had been created on the basis that the performance or funding of good works and pious liturgies could help effect a man's salvation. Alms were a peculiarly potent remedy for avarice and other sins relating to the creation and deployment of wealth, 'on the principle that ''contraries are to be cured with contraries'' '.[71] Such aids to salvation were officially approved and available for sale.

Countering this, the reformers invoked a more spiritual tradition. Calvin quotes St. Bernard approvingly: 'The testimony of conscience, which Paul calls "the rejoicing" of believers, I believe to consist in three things. It is necessary, first of all, to believe that you cannot have remission of sins except by the indulgence of God; secondly, that you cannot have any good work at all unless he also give it; lastly, that you cannot by any works merit eternal life unless it also be freely given.'[72] Without faith, the raising of the dead or martyrdom or any other work is not good. Faith has primacy over love but, says Luther, 'All works are accursed which are not carried out in love.' He writes in *The Freedom of a Christian:* 'We conclude that a Christian lives not in himself, but in Christ and in his neighbour. Otherwise he is not a Christian. He lives in Christ through faith, in his neighbour through love. By faith he is caught up beyond himself into God. By love he descends beneath himself into his neighbour. Yet he always remains in God and in his love ...' Luther exposes a belief in good works for their own sake as superstition, and a trust in material immortality as folly: 'As all people feel they must die, each seeks immortality here on earth, that he may be had in everlasting remembrance. Some great princes and kings seek it by raising great columns of stone, and high pyramids, great churches, costly and glorious palaces, castles, etc. ... But as to the true, everlasting, and incorruptible honour and eternity of God, no man thinks or looks after it. Ah! we are poor, silly miserable people!' Good works are required as an expression of faith and love.[73] This is a teaching which, George Whitefield preached, 'excludes works ... from being any cause of our justification in the sight of God; but it requires good works as a proof of our having righteousness imputed to us, and as a declarative evidence of our justification in the sight of men.'[74] Here there is an echo from the articles of the Church of England: 'That albeit good works do not justify us, yet they will follow after justification, as fruits of it.' Dabbling in judgement, an old woman at Wreyland reflected to Cecil Torr: 'As for my grandfather, his works were undeniable; but she had her doubts about his Faith.'[75]

I am not going to dwell on the implied theological issues. They made little difference to christian, charitable practice. Reformation and counter-reformation were both character- ised by revivals of humanitarian concern for the unfortunate. They both also depended for their philanthropy on various meldings of self-interest with altruism and natural sympathy. George Whitefield, in the passage I have just quoted, mentions the esteem of others as an effect of charity. There was little fault in this, but it implies a fairly typical mixture of motives.

The contemporaries Barnardo and John Groom shared a similar, evangelical inspiration and were equally, humanly moved by the deprivation of the poor London children they originally helped. Jim Jarvis, according to the story, inspired the spurious doctor to respond to the condition of hordes of London waifs: ' 'Eaps of em! More'n I could count!', as Jim exclaims in the published account. Similarly, John Groom wrote in an autobiographical pamphlet (1919): 'My whole nature was stirred with deepest feelings of pity towards these street slum children, especially the girl child.'[76] John Groom was an industrious, devoted and very practical philanthropist, but a minor self-publicist. Barnardo was a practical philan- thropist, was ambitious for his personal reputation, and was prepared to lie for its enhancement; he was also a brilliant promotional and public-relations operator, skilled in exploit- ing print and photography to achieve the public impact he was seeking for his charity. Both Groom and Barnardo were typi- cal, concerned Christians of their day, and their organizations have energetically if unequally survived. In their motivations there is a mixture of humanitarianism and theology, with a substantial dash of vanity at least in Barnardo's case.

The outlook of a humane, thinking Christian is perhaps typically expressed by Sir Thomas Browne (1605-1682) in his *Religio Medici*: 'Now for that other Virtue of Charity, without which Faith is a mere notion, and of no existence, I have ever endeavoured to nourish the merciful disposition and humane inclination I borrowed from my Parents, and regulate it to the written and prescribed Laws of Charity. And if I hold the true Anatomy of my self, I am delineated and naturally framed to such a piece of virtue; for I am of a constitution so general, that it consorts and sympathises with all things ... All places, all airs, make unto me one Country; I am in England every where, and under any Meridian. .... In brief, I am averse from nothing: my Conscience would give me the Lye if I should say I absolutely detest or hate any essence but the Devil; or so at least abhor any thing, but that we might come to composition.'[77] A man's natural disposition, and his human virtues, are the raw materials from which faith and love construct a Christian's charity.

There could be self-interest of a wholly different kind in charitable gifts. Where there has been a close alignment between state and church, each has promoted the other's interests. On the one hand, gifts, benefits, grants or charity might be offered as an inducement to convert influential individuals to the alliance between church and state. This was Constantine's motive in offering gifts to converts, and it was the motive of the sixteenth-century Turks who were prepared to bribe the anatolian Christians to join Islam. The convert was publicly honoured and: 'If he is poor, they make a large collection and give it to him, and the great lords show particular honour to him, and make him rich; this they do, that Christians may be more willing to be converted to their faith.'[78]

On the other hand, charity and the established church could be used by the government or the colonial authorities to establish and maintain civil order. Partly charitable doles to the poor in London during 1649 were intended to help prevent an uprising. The same fear of riots inspired the doles and collections associated with the Mansion House fund in London in the late 1860s.[79] More ominously, there is this record of the anglican mission to the Eastern Division of Cape Colony during the last century: 'While the foundations of this mission were being laid, the Governor of the Colony, Sir George Grey, who had done so much by moral and religious means for elevating the conditions of the native tribes of New Zealand, determined to follow a similar method for reducing to peaceful and industrious ways the more barbarous and savage races of South Africa; and in December 1854 he called upon the Church to aid him in the enterprise.' An expenditure of £45,000 p.a. was required, to be drawn from the Government, the Imperial Treasury and such voluntary sources as the S.P.G. Governor Grey wrote to Bishop Gray: 'The Church has now an opportunity of retrieving her character, of recovering lost ground. She will greatly embarrass my Government, if she does not rise to her duty.' His anxiety was to ward off further rebellion from the hostile natives. 'The Clergy of Grahamstown Diocese "felt the crisis to be so momentous to the whole interests of the Church and that the Church of England was altogether so completely put upon her trial before the whole colony" that they unanimously assented to their Bishop's plans for expanding the mission.' In a fundraising letter, Bishop Gray wrote: 'Now, then, it is our time, or never. S.P.G. ought for the next few years to back up the bishop of Grahamstown more largely than any other bishop. The work will be done in ten years by us or by others, and Government will pay at least three parts of the expense.'[80]

It is not my intention to project a perception of charitable motives which is jaundiced or cynical, but it would be misleading to ignore the vanity, self-interest and imperial or political ambitions which have often been present. Of course the love of God and an attempted imitation of Christ have usually been present also. That inner man who, in Luther's words, has it as 'his one occupation to serve God joyfully and without thought of gain in love that is not constrained'[81] will sometimes be influenced by the baser motivations of his outer self; that is the character of the christian Redemption.

In March, 1846 *The Female's Friend* followed a tradition, well established by that date, of encouraging victorian women to good works (here, the care of prostitutes) by invoking the imitation of Christ: 'None other but He can know what unutterable agony goes up by day and by night from the loathsome chambers, the pestilential dens, in which these homeless, hopeless, and decaying mortals hide themselves in misery to die.'[82] George Fox saw it as his vocation 'to bring people off from all the world's religions, which are vain, that they might know the pure religion, and might visit the fatherless, the widows and the strangers, and keep themselves from the spots of the world'.[83]

With the Jews, while the charity of 'pure religion' was most praised, other grades were acknowledged as well. Perhaps the greatest master on the subject of charity is the twelfth-century jewish philosopher Moses Maimonides. In his *Guide for the*

Perplexed, he discusses the triple distinction implied by the hebrew terms *hesed* ('loving-kindness'), *zedakah* ('righteousness') and *mishpat* ('judgement'). The expression *hesed,* he says, is used of extraordinary kindness, especially when directed to those who have no claim to it whatever; it denotes pure charity. *Zedakah* 'denotes the act of giving every one his due, and of showing kindness to every being according as it deserves' and 'We do perform an act of *zedakah* when we fulfil these duties towards our fellowmen which our moral conscience imposes upon us; e.g., when we heal the wound of the sufferer.'; it is 'a means of attaining perfection for (the) soul'. Finally, 'The noun *mishpat,* "judgement", denotes the act of deciding upon a certain action in accordance with justice which may demand either mercy or punishment.'[84]

Elsewhere, in his *Mishneh Torah,* Maimonides distinguishes 'eight degrees of charity, one higher than the other': 'There are eight degrees of charity, one higher than the other. The highest degree, exceeded by none, is that of the person who assists a poor Jew by providing him with a gift or a loan or by accepting him into a business partnership or by helping him find employment — in a word, by putting him where he can dispense with other people's aid. ... A step below this stands the one who gives alms to the needy in such a manner that the giver knows not to whom he gives and the recipient knows not from whom it is that he takes. Such exemplifies performing the meritorious act for its own sake. An illustration would be the Hall of Secrecy in the ancient sanctuary where the righteous would place their gift clandestinely and where poor people of high lineage would come and secretly help themselves to succour (see pp.32 & 34).

'The rank next to this is of him who drops money in the charity box. One should not drop money in the charity box unless one is sure that the person in charge is trustworthy, wise, and competent to handle the funds properly, as was Rabbi Hananya ben Teradyon.

'One step lower is that in which the giver knows to whom he gives but the poor person knows not from whom he receives. Examples of this were the great sages who would go forth and throw coins covertly into poor people's doorways. This method becomes fitting and exalted, should it happen that those in charge of the charity fund do not conduct its affairs properly.

'A step lower is that in which the poor person knows from whom he is taking but the giver knows not to whom he is giving. Examples of this were the great sages who would tie their coins in their scarves which they would fling over their shoulders so that the poor might help themselves without suffering shame.

'The next degree is that of him who, with his own hand, bestows a gift before the poor person asks.

'The next degree lower is that of him who gives only after the poor person asks.

'The next degree lower is that of him who gives less than is fitting but gives with a gracious mien.

'The next degree lower is that of him who gives morosely.'[85]

It is a point of interest that these eight grades concentrate, not on degrees of theological purity, but on relations between donor and recipient; on the tact, good manners, sensitivity or constructive kindness of the benefactor. It is such relations and attitudes between donors and recipients which largely determine the forms taken by relief services, and their acceptability. It is only the beginning to acknowledge that we have a responsibility to assist the poor and needy, and that this must be catered for in our stewardship of wealth. The basic categorisations of the poor (orphans, widows, etc.) are a reminder of the places we should look to discover those in need, and even of the priorities we should set between them, but they do not solve the problem.

The Undeserving

One traditional argument may be articulated like this: Charity must be managed with judgement, and judgement tells us there is a limit to our means and that some of those who present themselves are less deserving than others; that some are deceivers or, as they now say, scroungers. Since the fraudulent or culpable poor man 'defraudeth the needy',[86] is an unjust drain on wealth and is reprehensible, he must be discouraged. He must also be goaded to improve himself through profitable work. Some more ingredients must be added: that poverty may be a moral failing; that it is economically misguided to interfere with natural, commercial patterns of profit-taking and earning; that the poor are pre-ordained to their position in society; that the soul must be considered above the body, so that true religion (preferably through conversion, but at least through observance) is a condition for receiving aid. Such a mixture necessarily distances the owner and dispenser of wealth from the dependent employee and from the man who suffers a poverty which may qualify him to receive help but which must not be encouraged and may even deserve punishment.

The conclusions to such arguments are seen in the punitive, unloving and positively proselytising institutions which have often been the vehicles for christian poor relief. I am not suggesting that the problem is trivial; indiscriminate alms may be harmful. Yet the Gospels teach, 'Give to everyone who asks you' (Lk. 6:30), so that Calvin could say: 'Therefore, whoever be the man that is presented to you as needing your assistance, you have no ground for declining to give it to him.'[87] The crisis is encapsulated by George Fox in his *Journal*. One morning, in 1652, he was with some people from Underbarrow: 'And as I was walking upon the top of the bank there came several poor people, travellers, that I saw were in necessity; and they gave them nothing but said they were cheats. But when they were gone to their breakfast it grieved me to see such hard-heartedness amongst professors that I ran after the poor people a matter of a quarter of a mile and gave them some money.'[88] Here again there is a tension, in this case between wise stewardship and open charity, which is intrinsic to the christian teaching. It requires some further examination.

The classic image of the undeserving petitioner for alms is the Sturdy Beggar. Langland's version of the traditional list of deserving charitable objects is associated with traditional descriptions and categorisations of the undeserving. The 'Bold beggars and big' who could work for their bread were to be given the bare minimum of food;[89] but they were well able to thrive, and were often poor only in appearance. Here is the ballad description of a beggar sturdy enough to better Robin Hood:

A clouted cloak about him was,
  That held him from the cold;
The thinnest bit of it, I guess,
  Was more than twenty fold.

His meal-pock hung about his neck,
  Into a leather fang,
Well fastened with a broad buckle,
  That was both stark and strong.

He had three hats upon his head,
  Together sticked fast;
He cared neither for wind not weet,
  In lands wherever he past.[90]

Such beggars, according to Thomas More, formed the 'most quarrelsome section of the community', and were a continual threat to its peace.[91] Some were political radicals and agitators. The potent image of the sturdy beggar was used by Simon Fish in *A Supplication of Beggars* (1528), addressed to Henry VIII, to express his attack on the clergy: 'And this most pestilent mischief is come upon your said bedemen by the reason for that there is, in the times of your noble predecessors passed, craftily crept into this your realm another sort, not of impotent, but of strong, puissant, and counterfeit holy and idle beggars and vagabonds, which, since the time of their first entry by all the craft and wiliness of Satan, are now increased under your sight, not only into a great number but also into a kingdom. These are not the shepherds but the ravenous wolves going in shepherds clothing devouring the flock — the bishops, abbots, priors, deacons, archdeacons, suffragans, priests, monks, canons, friars, pardoners and summoners. And who is able to number this idle, ravenous sort, which (setting all labour aside) have begged so importunately that they have gotten into their hands more than the third part of all your realm.'[92]

Extensive legislation attempted to eliminate the sturdy beggar, unpopular and omnipresent at least since Plato's time. Edward VI's 1547 Act provided for their branding; Thomas More, jokingly, would compel them to enrol as nuns and lay-brothers in monasteries; Bishop Berkeley, like Edward VI, would have them enslaved.[93] There was even a scriptural argument against supporting them. Luther interpreted Christ's saying 'He that desireth of thee, give to him' in this way: 'that is, to him that needs and is in want; not to idle, lazy, wasteful fellows, who are commonly the greatest beggars, and who, though we give them much and often, are nothing helped thereby'.[94]

The distinction between the deserving and the undeserving was not easy to apply, however, especially when judgement was made that nobody need be poor, if only they would be virtuous and industrious. This was a fairly characteristic nineteenth-century view. Its corollary was that indiscriminate alms were a cause of poverty. William Lecky, in his *History of European Morals* (1894), expressed a typical outlook: 'It has been shown that, where idleness is supported, idleness will grow; that, where systematic public provision is made for old age, the parsimony of foresight will be neglected; and that therefore these forms of charity, by encouraging habits of idleness and improvidence, ultimately increase the wretchedness they were intended to alleviate.'[95] The Reverend Thomas Malthus's argument to the same end had the different base of nineteenth-century economic theory. He states in the *Essay on the Principle of Population:* 'I cannot by means of money raise a poor man and enable him to live much better than he did before, without proportionately depressing others in the same class. If I retrench the quantity of food consumed in my house, and give him what I have cut off, I then benefit him, without depressing any but myself and family, who, perhaps, may be well able to bear it. If I turn up a piece of uncultivated land, and give him the produce, I then benefit both him and all the members of the society, because what he before consumed is thrown into the common stock, and probably some of the new produce with it.' He held that the real effect of the english poor laws was to increase prices and reduce wages: 'They have therefore contributed to impoverish that class of people whose only possession is their labour.' In his *Summary View*, he argues that, by increasing expectancy of relief, we lower resistance to dependence: 'The ground objection to the language used respecting the "right of the poor to support" is, that, as a matter of fact, we do not perform what we promise, and the poor may justly accuse us of deceiving them.'[96]

These were not new issues; we have seen the requirement that relief be constructively articulated especially clearly by the Jews, and both legislation and moral persuasion attempted to separate those suffering undeserved and unavoidable misfortune from those exploiting methods for its relief, and to develop remedies which would restore both groups to a productive role in society. These were the principles behind the registers, based on enquiry, of poor people qualifying for relief found in fourth century Egyptian monasteries, in fifth century Rome, in sixth and seventh century Gaul, and in sixteenth century Europe, including Tudor England. It was as part of this effort to eliminate mendicancy that, after 1349 in England, it was forbidden to give alms to vagabonds.[97] Parishes were to enquire carefully into applicants for alms, who were to be returned to their places of origin for relief. An illustration of the possible effect of this legislation is seen in an order from 1700 concerning George, Mary and Eve Smith, the eldest of whom was six, who under a pass dating December 1698, 'were sent and conveyed from constable to constable and from officer to officer from Southampton, by and thro the county of Kent, unto the city and county of Canterbury and after, by warrant and under the seals of two justices of the peace of Canterbury, were sent back again to Southampton and soe have been sent from Southampton to Canterbury through this county eight several times and are likely to bee soe sent forwards and backwards during their lives, to the great and apparent wrong of the said children and the charge of the counties thro' which they pass and repass ...'[98]

At the same time, the poor outside the workhouse were to be marked and distinguished by their pauper's badge. In Wenn parish in Shropshire, about 1700, the badge was of tin. At the same time, in Shoreham and Charing, Kent the 'parish badge or mark' was 'a large Roman P together with the first letter of the name of your said parish'; the wife of Edward Francis, miller, was rebuked because she 'does neglect to wear (it) in open and visible manner, on the shoulder of the right sleeve of her uppermost garment'. In 1770 Nicholas Toke, also of Kent, recommended '*Badging* the indolent and lazy poor *only* — and a punishment for those *who give* anything to Vagrants'.[99]

The attitudes which had corrupted relations between rich and poor by the nineteenth century mixed economic expediency, with pride and vanity, with motives which were genuinely benign. This was the case with a man as outspokenly hostile to the concept of inculpable poverty as Defoe, and with pious Miss Humphreys whose 1848 hymn in support of the established, social order has been a longstanding and popular success:

> The rich man in his castle
>   The poor man at his gate
> God made them, high or lowly,
>   And ordered their estate.[100]

As late as 1910, the voice of paternalism still boomed across the Empire: 'The time when men were most nearly equal was when they were all primitive barbarians a quarter of a million years ago. Ever since then they have been becoming more and more unequal, and the evidence is not only that there are grades but that those grades are increasing and steepening ... it is obvious that certain border races must inevitably come under the control, the protection, the administrative tutelage of certain higher races ... Protection, guidance, and tutelage of the weak by the strong, of the lower by the higher are, to my mind, an essential part of human development ... there are peoples who flourish best and who can most effectively develop their especial individuality when they are under the protection of a stronger, more practical race, who will do the, as it were, 'dirty' work of governing them ... The Tibetans *prefer* being under some strong temporal power ... And the Jews, though they did not come under Roman protection as a matter of choice, nevertheless, did, when under that protection, make their greatest contribution to the welfare of mankind, for it was then that Christianity arose' (Sir F. Younghusband).[101]

Ordered Charity

These good people, mostly christian, were determined to enforce the betterment of their fellows. Bentham's 'apostle to the new age', Edwin Chadwick, secretary to the Poor Law Commission in the early 1830s, was 'the greatest, in the character of his mind, in the machine-like simplicity of his ideas and the inexhaustible fertility of his applications, the most typical of the Benthamites'; and the mainspring of his career, says G. M. Young, 'seems to have been a desire to wash the people of England all over, every day, by administrative order'.[102] A like fervour and identical doctrine, combined with evangelical socialism, inspired the formidable, self-righteous and idealistic *Charity Organisation Society,* founded in 1869 as the greatest sorter of deserving sheep from undeserving goats yet seen in the philanthropic world. Its original name was the *London Society for Organising Charitable Relief and Repressing Mendicity,* and it aimed to provide 'machinery for systematizing, without unduly controlling, the benevolence of the public'.[103] The christian socialism of Octavia Hill, and such bodies as Mrs. Pennefeather's evangelical *Association of Female Workers* and William Rathbone's *Central Relief Society* in Liverpool (1863), were forerunners of C.O.S.'s idealism and practice.[104] It was launched by churchmen and by clergy in the presence of their bishops and was vigilant against all forms of indiscriminate charity or any measures which might encourage pauperism. C.O.S. favoured stricter vetting and categorizations of the poor, because it held that random doles, charity and applications of poor relief were a cause of mendicity. They opposed random relief, free medical missions, Dr. Barnardo's non-scientific charity and General Booth's open-handed charity and proposals for noncontributory pensions because, with Malthus, they held that such measures would entail 'legislation of a pauperising nature'. They established a charity blacklist. Fundamental to their beliefs was the familiar christian thesis 'that pauperism (and to a considerable extent, poverty) was the result of moral weakness on the part of the individual'.[105] For this reason they encouraged moves to render statutory relief as difficult as possible and to create the narrowest routes of access to voluntary relief. They represent an apotheosis of the two trends, christian and utilitarian, we have been observing. It was an effect of these trends, instituted in the name of political economy, on which Dostoevsky comments in *Crime and Punishment:* 'Compassion has been outlawed by science.'; but to Charles Stewart Loch, Secretary of C.O.S. from 1875 onwards, it was a proud ambition to 'discipline the life of the people by a nobler, more devoted, more scientific religious charity'.[106]

In the following chapters, I shall study charitable institutions, and the ways money has been raised for them. It seems proper, though, to end by remembering the unscientific kindness without which charity would be worthless. All was not bleak. That greatest english poem on christian charity, *Piers Plowman*, urges that there should be human warmth and kindness:

> Now lords, send them summer sometime to solace and to joy
> That lead all their life in lowness and poverty.

It also gives a perfect illustration of the way the unfortunate should be regarded, with an intelligent human sympathy and christian love:

> And yet are there other beggars, in health, as it seems,
> But they want their wits, men and women both;
> They are the lazy lunatics who leap all about,
> And grow mad with the moon, more or less.
> They don't care about cold nor consider the heat
> And are moved by the moon; moneyless they walk,
> With a good will, witless, many wide counties,
>   .....
> And to our sight, as it seems, since God has the might
> To give each man a right mind, money and health,
> And suffers such to go so, it seems, to my insight
> They are his apostles, such people, and his private disciples.
> And although they may meet with the mayor along the street
> He receives not their reverence, rather than others.
>   .....
> For they are merry-mouthed men, minstrels of heaven,
> And God's boys, his bawds, as the book tells us.[107]

8

Christian Charitable Organization

This chapter looks at the situations in which personal christian kindness passes over to organized or institutionalised charity, and even to statutory measures, to remedy needs. I have published studies elsewhere on funding and on institutionalised charities. Only one observation from those studies needs to be repeated here: that it is a 'demonstrable fact that political regimes and other human institutions seem to gather into themselves the causes of their own corruption and the contradiction of their inspiring idealism almost from the moment they are formed'.[1] Religious institutions are fully subject to this law of decay.

Not that organized charity is always formally institutionalised. The return for the medieval Guild of Smiths in Chesterfield stipulated: 'If any of them fall into poverty, they shall go, singly, on given days, to the houses of the brethren, where each shall be courteously received, and there shall be given to him, as if he were the master of the house, whatever he wants of meat, drink and clothing, and he shall have a halfpenny like those who are sick; and then he shall go home in the name of the Lord.' In a like spirit, it was required that the Mayor of Bristol should visit the brewers' houses on certain days, to guarantee the quality and measures for free beer assigned to the poor.[2] Similarly the polish Jews about 1648 would lodge wayfarers for 'as many days as they wished', sending them on with food and transport for their journey.[3]

It has been suggested that the hagiographical accounts of the twelfth century Elizabeth of Hungary represent a trend towards the personalisation of charity. It was in pursuit of a more personal charity that she set up her hospital at Marburg, where she sought out the vilest tasks. Amongst the children, she 'more specially loved the pocked, sick, weak and those most repulsive and deformed, taking their heads in her hands and drawing them to her breast'. On occasions, 'She gathered a crowd of lepers, washing their feet and hands, and she kissed their most septic and appalling sores.' Her motive was expressed thus: 'How good it is that we can this way bathe and touch our Lord.'[4]

The problem is that, after the death of a St. Elizabeth, the institution and practice must be left to others, probably less inspired; yet, once the inspired founder has withdrawn, or the work has grown beyond a certain size, institutionalisation may be essential if the work is to be continued. It is a further problem that any large-scale relief of need necessarily becomes ineffective if it is randomly dispensed. Also, individuals and communities have wanted to set limits to the sums they could be called on to provide, and to ensure that what they gave was honestly and efficiently managed, to the maximum advantage of the recipients and of the community itself. The intervention of institutions is inevitable, and it is perilous. It sets a distance between donors and receivers, and entails a categorization of recipients. It almost certainly requires professionals to provide the necessary services and organized fundraising to sustain them. In doing this, it puts great potential power in the hands of both benefactors and staff, and leaves the recipients vulnerable.

Guilds and the Community Chest

Returning to the methods which have attempted to keep the organization of relief human and personal by putting responsibility for the necessary works expressly on the individual families within a community, I quote Maimonides' assertion: 'Never have we either seen or heard of a community in Israel that should be without its Public Charity Fund.'[5] The community chest has particularly flourished amongst the Jews. In Nathan Hannover's account of late seventeenth century Poland, we see a system within which meal and lodging tickets were issued to wayfarers and others, because 'The system of ticket-relief did away with the humiliation of begging.' By the terms of the Constitution of the jewish community in Sugenheim, Franconia in 1756, the funds for such meal tickets were levied according to each man's means: 'eight for every family head and two for every hundred florins capital. ... the cantor is to apportion them properly and impartially so that the poorer (citizens of the town) do not have too heavy a burden and the richer do not have too few (meals to supply).' The community would take care of young boys and girls, providing for their education and apprenticeship and setting them up, even to the extent of providing a wife and her dowry.[6]

This is reminiscent on the one hand of the systems represented by the medieval guilds, and on the other by the organized, civic collections and doles embodied, for example, in the sixteenth century *Aumone-Générale* in France. The english guilds, of which the City of London Livery Companies are the transformed progeny, originated in anglo-saxon times. A guild was 'an institution of local self-help'. They were 'associations of those living in the same neighbourhood, and remembering that they have, as neighbours, common obligations'.[7] The instrument for the collection and distribution of funds by these community chest organizations was usually a real, physical box, of which some massive and elaborate examples survive.[8] A typical regulation stipulated: 'The money and goods of the Gild shall be kept in a chest having two locks and two keys; of which keys one shall be kept by each of two Aldermen of the Gild.' All members of the guild, while they had the means, were required to make regular contributions. The rule of the Tailors of Exeter carried the financial obligation further: 'Item ye shall give, in your testament (will), to the alms of (the guild of) Saint John Baptist, more or less according to your means and devotion ...'. There was an explicit intention to provide charity and mutual help: 'Vain is the gathering of the faithful unless some work of kindliness is done', said the rules of the guild formed to act a play in York setting forth the goodness of the Lord's Prayer. The primary beneficiaries of a guild's distributions were the members themselves: 'Item, ye shall be helping and counselling with all your power, if ye know any brother of this fraternity, that hath done his duties well and truly to the fraternity, come or fall to poverty by the visitation of god, or by casual chance, and hath not where-of (he may live), that he may have, every week, of the alms of the said fraternity, 10 pence; and, if he has been Master, to have 13 pence a week.'[9] Non-members also benefited, though, and the relief provided by the guilds ranged over all the traditional categories, from the poor, sick and handicapped and travellers through schools and schoolmasters, to roads, bridges and causeways. There were specialized bodies such as the 'fraternity throughout the province of Canterbury to last for seven years from this year of grace 1186', which Archbishop Baldwin set up to build a church in honour of St. Thomas.[10]

The guilds appointed official collectors of dues and guardians of the chest. St. Katherine's, Aldersgate had four officers accountable for handling the funds, one to keep the box, one to hold the key, and two to receive the dues. This was fairly typical. With the guild of St. Christopher, Norwich a weekly payment was to be made to the keeper of the chest. However, the system was not always rigid. The Guild of Furriers at Norwich did not exact fixed sums, but raised however much was needed from the 'brothers and sisters' as occasions required. As with the Jews, loans might be offered, to provide more constructive assistance than outright gifts. Sometimes, discretion was left to the donors in allocating their funds, as with the Tailors of Lincoln: 'Each brother and sister of the gild shall every year give one penny for charity, when the Dean of the gild demands it; and it shall be given in the place where the giver thinks it is most needed, together with a bottle of ale from the ale store of the gild.'[11]

The medieval guilds and fraternities suffered variously in the Reformation. In Munster they were crucial promoters of Protestantism; in England, the religious fraternities were suppressed on account of their superstition and commitment to the purchase of salvation, while many of the more powerful secular gilds survived.[12]

By the sixteenth century, though, revolutionary measures to deal systematically with urban poverty were being introduced in both protestant and catholic Europe. While those involved were, inevitably, active Christians, the forms of relief selected were often more secular than religious. The English *Beggars Act* of 1536 laid down: 'And for the avoiding of all such inconveniences and infections as oftentime have and daily do chance amongst people by common and open doles, and that most commonly unto such doles many persons do resort which have no need of the same. It is therefore enacted ... that no manner of person or persons shall make or cause to be made any such common or open dole, or shall give any ready money in alms, otherwise than to the common boxes and common gatherings ... upon pain to lose and forfeit ten times the value of all such ready money as shall be given in alms contrary to the tenor and purport of the same (Act).' All alms were to be distributed to 'common boxes, to the intent the same may be employed towards the relieving of the said poor, needy, sick, sore, and indigent persons, and also toward the setting in work of the said sturdy and idle vagabonds and valiant beggars ...'.[13]

Meanwhile, in 1534 in Lyon, the *Aumone-Générale* had been established, with identical purposes. It was a civic, lay-directed movement, dominated by lawyers and businessmen. Random distributions of alms were forbidden; all alms were to be put into the common box or sent to an official collector. Officers of the Common Fund made visits to the houses of the poor, and a list of the needy was created. The sick were sent to the *Hotel-Dieu* (where Francis Rabelais was a doctor at the time), while the other deserving poor were issued with tokens which entitled them to relief. The Common Fund kept detailed accounts. Like the C.O.S., the Fund carried out investigations to establish how much bread a man needed daily (one and a half pounds); whether the numbers of the needy were increasing or decreasing; what was the prognosis for those entering the *Hotel-Dieu*.[14]

Scope and Adequacy of Relief Measures

With all these movements, as with Luther in Wittenberg and Zwingli in Zurich, the intention was to make relief more effective and to meet the growing urban crises of the time. They all combined systems for the central collection and distribution of funds and support for the deserving poor with an attempt to discourage indiscriminate charity. They also marked an early stage towards the national extension of official or statutory methods to encounter all of society's welfare needs.

This does not imply any unqualified criticism of pre-reformation provisions. Although medieval measures were, in some times and places, random and disorganized, this was not always so. The system which created rosters of the poor qualifying for aid in the cities of merovingian France had aimed to limit the community's liability, to specify its responsibilities and to control and hopefully remedy mendicity. This anticipated the sixteenth century developments we have been studying. Monastic measures were inconsistent in the services they offered and in their geographical distribution; but where, as at Cluny, elaborate facilities for the needy and the staff to deploy them were available, funded by the monastery's massive endowment and its continuing flow of gifts, it would be unreasonable to belittle the achievement.[15] The monasteries had set standards, goals, challenges to stimulate more adequate measures in later providers who had different attitudes to wealth and to poverty. The monks' ideal of poverty had also challenged, in anticipation, the christian mercantile ideals with whose consequences many Christians are now in conflict. The normal channels of benevolence which concentrated on bishop, priest and deacon, and which may merit some critical hindsight, also established mechanisms which survived to co-exist with more secular provisions. Similarly, such groups as the Austin Friars who, from the twelfth century, effectively provided community-chest facilities and welfare services in many of Europe's burgeoning towns, anticipated the creation of specialised orders dealing with poverty and sickness by Vincent de Paul and Camillus de Lellis in the seventeenth century, and even the work of Florence Nightingale in the nineteenth. With the Order of St. John, the institutionalised regime for hospital care and the provision of relief for the poor was tempered by the recommended christian attitude of reverence towards the sick and poor, who were to be called 'Our lords the sick', 'Our lords the poor.'[16]

Indeed, one is in danger of applying a kind of systematic misjudgement to these medieval measures, which were available to all but which could not provide the even, universal, demographic coverage which is the aspiration of our modern welfare states. The ideal expressed by the monk William of Dijon (961-1031) was that his monastic schools should be open 'as much to serfs as to freemen, to rich and poor together'. This does not discredit the later judgement: 'Outside the universities monks played an almost negligible role in early Tudor education.'[17] The ideal might remain, but the scale and nature of the demands and people's expectations grew beyond the scope of the older religious institutions to meet them.

Some aspects of medieval practice are undeniably baffling. With measures to relieve the sick or injured, there is a combination of science with superstitution which is only partly intelligible today. However, attendance at miraculous shrines, the recital of healing formulae which resemble spells more closely than prayers, the application of relics and other holy objects, even revivals of asclepian incubation in temple or church, were one aspect only of what happened. The anglo-celtic monastic hospital at St. Gall, Switzerland had ordinary wards, an intensive care unit, a dispensary and reception room, as a plan dating from 830 shows. In the twelfth-century leper colony at Amiens, the hygienic methods imposed were exemplary. In most hospitals in the middle ages, formal medicine and various forms of religious healing were both employed.[18] Even if many such english medieval foundations 'had vanished long before the Reformation owing to neglect, declining revenues or perversion of the founders' intentions', others survived under municipal patronage, and many that vanished were acutely missed. From 1538 until 1544, the Mayor and citizens of London petitioned Henry VIII to re-found the hospitals of St. Mary's, St. Thomas's and St. Bartholomew's: 'for the aid and comfort of the poor sick, blind, aged and impotent persons, being not able to help themselves, nor having any place certain wherein they may be lodged, cherished and refreshed till they be cured and (eased) of their diseases and sickness'.[19]

The reasons for the decline of these hospitals were, according to Henry VIII's letters patent, 'the abuses, in long lapse of time lamentably occuring'.[20] In this they were subject to the laws of decay generally affecting human institutions. During the period of the Reformation, there were major improvements in methods for delivering relief, and there was the opportunity to dismantle systems and institutions which had irrecoverably decayed or had lost their relevance; but the causes of change were often economic, social or political rather than religious. The apparent increase in the value of philanthropic bequests following the Reformation in England had as much to do with inflation as with increased, protestant benevolence, according to A. G. Dickens. Gerrard Winstanley and Samuel Herring were inspired by a new christian awareness when, in the 1650s, they pressed for social reforms in England, including the introduction of a free national health service; but in Italy, free health services had been provided in some places by *medici condotti* or *medici del pubblico* since the thirteenth century.[21]

One significant point that emerges is the combined importance of a revived christian outlook and of responsiveness to emergent social pressures and to the new learning as a cause of constructive, charitable initiatives in both Reformation and Counter-Reformation. Another is the tendency for social demands and expectations to outstrip the charitable resources to meet them; this was as much the case with Peabody, Guinness and other nineteenth-century philanthropists in housing or education, health care and poor relief. This implies that charity, particularly when institutionalised, cannot rest unreformed for long, if it is to stay close to justice.

This is not to deny the importance of religiously motivated individuals as founders and operators of charitable institutions. In nineteenth-century England, virtually all the major charitable foundations were established by committed Christians. Lord Shaftsbury was apparently ubiquitous in the charitable world of the day. In 1884, he pronounced that 'Most of the great philanthropic movements of the century have sprung from the Evangelicals.'[22] Philanthropy had been led by such figures as Wesley, Wilberforce and Hannah More. In G. M. Young's words: 'By the beginning of the nineteenth century virtue was advancing on a broad invincible front ', its charity supported through the good stewardship of the new generation of 'money-making witness-bearers'.[23] Committed Christians, whether of the established or other churches, were responsible for virtually every institutional welfare measure taken in the last century. Dr. Barnardo's, John Grooms, NSPCC, the Salvation Army, the Society of St. Vincent de Paul, founded on the basis of strong, personal religious belief, were all active by 1890 with a style and a momentum which have carried them most of the way through the twentieth century. They have therefore been forced to adapt to the more secular trends which have only recently become dominant amongst emergent, charitable institutions.

Religious belief powerfully motivated initiatives of other kinds. The famous names amongst the grant-making foundations belonged to disciplined religious men. The Quakers George Cadbury and Joseph Rowntree saw their wealth as a trust from God, to be handled for the welfare of others. John Davidson Rockefeller, while still a teenager, gave a tenth of his income to his Sunday school and its missions, and never in later life broke this habit of regular giving. Even if Carnegie in his 1889 *Gospel of Wealth* emphasized that philanthropy was a social rather than a religious obligation, his philosophy is a product of radical christian thought. In our own century, Israel Sieff excellently expresses the basic, religious outlook of such philanthropists: 'To live justly before God is to behave charitably to one's fellow man. This is whether he is a Jew or not. Justice is the condition in which men help each other. This idea is the essence of being a Jew.' The same outlook inspired those who established philanthropy as a feature of their business activities, a pattern which became more common in the second half of the nineteenth century. Henry Wellcome, whose company passes its undistributed profits to a medical grant-making trust which currently distributes £13M annually, declared at the age of twenty-one that he intended to be rich so that he could fund medical research for the glory of God and the good of mankind. On the other side of the Atlantic, the remarkable philanthropy of such groups as Levi Strauss, Cummins Engine and Dayton Hudson can be attributed to their founders' personal convictions.[24] Finally, such committed Christians as Lord Shaftsbury, Dr. Barnardo and Charles Booth, as well as the nonconformists Ramsay MacDonald and Keir Hardie, were major advocates of statutory measures to relieve poverty. In promoting the concept of state Old Age Pensions, for example, Charles Booth was opposed by the C.O.S., which saw pensions as a threat to constructive, ordered relief. The familiar insistence on the separation of deserving from undeserving poor would be abandoned only with difficulty: 'If poverty was often the outward and visible sign of an inward and spiritual disgrace, then the poor needed to be punished or rewarded. The Old Age Pensions Act of 1908 sought to apply this principle by separating the worthy poor from the unworthy and witholding pensions from those deemed lazy or improvident.'[25]

Before looking at the effects on their institutions of such religious commitment amongst founders, organizers and funders, I set down two incidental notes. One concerns the contribution of the clergy in an apparently lay-dominated sphere. The clergy were, of course, prominent in the Christian Socialist Movement, and were in attendance at all charitable institutions and on all philanthropic occasions, even the initiation of the R.S.P.C.A.; but E. R. Norman has commented on a paradoxical feature of anglican church leadership. He remarks on 'the adoption, in almost every generation, of diluted versions of the most progressive ideas available, by that section of the leadership most in touch with academic idealism'. This has meant that the clerical leadership has been ineffective, 'because it has been too much in advance, too academic, too removed from the practical assumptions of ordinary men'. Thus: 'In adopting criticisms of *laissez-faire* practice and competitive principles at the same time (in the second half of the nineteenth century), church leaders managed, once again, to cut themselves off from the main current of working-class thought.'[26]

My second note concerns a long-established strand of thinking, which has become accepted doctrine today amongst the socialist left and in the communist block generally. Rousseau had asserted that there should be no independent associations within the State, and his teaching was echoed in the decree of the French Revolutionary government of 18th August 1792, which outlawed all independent associations or corporations, even those which had served the nation well.[27] This has been one reason why organized philanthropy has had a stunted and slow development in modern France. The consequences of such attitudes today I leave to the final chapter, merely commenting that the state's tolerance or encouragement of charitable institutions has never been a thing to be taken for granted.

Christian Charitable Institutions

Religiously-inspired charitable institutions have operated as centres for sectarian indoctrination as well as for relief. Many had an explicit, evangelizing intention, both at home and in the colonies. Free food could be used to entice the poor into the chapels or the mission churches. In the refuge for prostitutes opened in 1843 by the York Penitentiary Society, a bleak but well-intentioned establishment, generously supported by the local Quakers, there seems to have been positive persuasion against Roman Catholicism, a sect proportionately under-represented amongst the poor prostitutes of the town. In October 1851, Mary Robinson was commended because, though a papist, she was willing to attend a protestant place of worship. Amongst the bad 'circumstances which occurred in the home of poor Mary Robinson' was her return to roman catholic ways. After her mother had been reasoned with by the Gentlemen's Committee, 'Robinson expressed her willingness to remain (in the refuge), if her house is considered completely an unfit one, till she could be placed in the house of some dress-maker in the country. She will be happy to make any declaration necessary that she is advised to, as to renouncing the errors of Rome.' Grim and punitive though the refuge was, there was no alternative; many inmates readily regarded it as home.[28]

There was the same tendency elsewhere, for example in Dr. Barnardo's homes. Barnardo was hostile to Roman Catholicism; this caused him to resign from the N.S.P.C.C. and involved him in litigation over the custody of roman catholic children. The issue was resolved through a pact between Barnardo and Cardinal Vaughan, by which they agreed that information would be exchanged on protestant and catholic children being considered for admission to the home of either sect.[29] This reflects the unedifying, negative aspect of committed belief. The charitable institutions were there because of their founders' strong faith, and the salvation of souls and formation of character were frequently given a higher priority than bodily comfort or even human justice. There were, however, some spectacular exceptions to sectarianism, as when in 1887 Dean H. Martyn Hart (Episcopalian), Monsignor William J. O'Ryan (Roman Catholic), the Reverend Myron Reed (Congregationalist) and Rabbi William S. Friedman launched the Charity Organization in Denver — the first United Way.[30]

Moral and economic principles combined to convince legislators and governors that workhouses should be made as uncomfortable and unattractive as possible, so that they would be perceived by the labouring poor as the worst option available to them. The nineteenth-century commissioners, against pressure from some of the dissenting churches, insisted that workhouse inmates should not be let out even for Sunday services: 'Life in the workhouse must be made more unattractive than life outside. Since well-meaning endeavours found it impossible to lower diet and rooms to standards below those of surrounding labourers without starving the inhabitants of the workhouse, this comfort of living must be compensated by imprisonment. So long as a man was receiving relief he must be confined to the workhouse.'[31] There was a mixture of motives: to discourage mendicity and idleness, to encourage godly observance and habits of industry and to preserve the interests of the parish and nation.

There was tolerance. At Goudhurst, in 1744, the Workhouse Rules insisted on scripture reading, prayer and attendance at services, but allowed 'That any dissenter shall have liberty to resort to any meeting house on Sundays, returning home as soon as the meeting is done.' Even where the regime was harsh, there might be kindness. To the severe 1756 Dietary for the Farnborough workhouse, someone added: 'Sometimes biscuits for the children', and there was provision for beef and plum pudding on holidays. Nicholas Toke, writing on measures to care for the poor in Kent in 1770, would see penalties imposed on those who missed religious services, and would 'prevent vice, profaneness and immorality' in the poor 'by putting an effectual stop to tipling in public houses, and dram drinking in private gin shops'; but he was also anxious to prevent the 'injury to the poor' which could be inflicted on them by any 'Egyptian Taskmaster' who might take on the poor 'by the lump', and his recommended regime was intended to ensure that the workhouse inmates should be warm, well-nourished, clean and healthy. Not far away, Charles Chambers, vicar of Dartford from 1718 till 1746, had paid careful, daily attention to the wellbeing of the 'family' in the Dartford workhouse: 'June 1 1732 Some cheese being wanting I order some to be sent ... '; 'June 5 All Latter's children being well recovered of the itch I think the 2 eldest boys should be sent out this summer to work ... I sent for Mr. Dalton ... and desired him to find some easy imploy proper to the biggest boys ...'; 'May 9 1733 I think it most reasonable that the poor people should have some change in their diet on the great festival days of our church ...'[32]

It would be too much to expect even such individuals to be free from the prejudices of their day. Thus Nicholas Toke argues of Charity Schools: 'There certainly should be a limitation of knowledge. And an ability to read the Gospel, and to receive with humility the great truths it contains, is perhaps as much as prudence, policy, or charity, would advise in the education of poor children.'[33] A century later, Dr. Barnardo preferred to provide industrial training rather than academic learning for his children, continuing the same prejudice.[34] There are good grounds for the charge that, in the nineteenth century, the poor schools provided a training for subservience while the privileged schools trained their pupils for government and leadership. Good Christians, through their charitable institutions, perceived it as a godly duty that they should reinforce the social order and hierarchy of the christian state.

Church, Charity and State

If there is confusion in such cases between civic duty, christian charity and instinctive kindliness, the confusion is worse when one looks at the institutions such as schools, hospitals and dispensaries which were founded throughout the christian missions, often with a combination of church and state finance. Good Nicholas Toke and Dr. Barnardo instinctively favoured christian institutions which reinforced the established social order; where church and state were one, godliness entailed conformity.

Early in our century, Bishop Dudley of Kentucky could say, in praising the work of the Society for the Propagation of the Gospel, that the extension of the British Empire 'had been hardly a possibility save for the development of the Missionary spirit in the Church of England, largely through the operations of this Society'. When the history of the S.P.G. declared: 'The Church of England was the first Christian body to occupy

Swaziland', it found it natural to use the language of state imperialism. Where the empire reached, the mission schools followed, for the 'taming and refining (of the native races) into a nobler, purer manhood'. Hospitals followed as well, which might be praised, like the one in Madras, because it 'led to the conversion of many an afflicted woman'. In Hawaii, the success of the Anglican Ladies Visiting Society caused the Catholics to send out Sisters of Charity, like sectarian marines, to ward off the charitable threat to their works of indoctrination.

In almost every case, the schools and hospitals were supported by gifts from home, often substantially supplemented by government grants in the case of the established churches. Thus the Negro Education Fund for the West Indies and Latin America between 1835 and 1845 received £24,463.3.11 in Donations against £62,385.1.0 in Parliamentary Grants.[35] Such missionary imperialism was not exclusive to the Old World. It has been argued that U.S. missionary activity prepared the way for the annexation of Hawaii in 1898, and that, in the war with Spain, there was a strong, pan-sectarian religious motivation in early U.S. imperialist ventures.[36]

The privileges of institutions of the established church, as we shall see in another context presently, have been the stimulus for revealing confrontations between different sects and religions. All have had their own, often irrationally competitive institutions. These have aimed to meet a religious and humanitarian responsibility towards the young, the old, the feeble, the poor and other needy groups, as well as to evangelize or to preserve the purity of sectional doctrines. Conspicuously and as a frequent occasion of harmful social division, this has been the case with schools. The Jesuits were not alone in identifying the education of young people as the most promising method for securing both minds and souls; 'To form the child instead of reforming the man was a sound commonsense proposition which appealed to the puritan mind' as well.[37] Under Henry VIII, new schools were founded, and many were re-founded under Edward VI, with large endowments derived from the dissolution of older foundations.[38] In the optimistic 1640s, puritan reformers were aspiring to free, universal education.[39] The Charity School movement has been presented as a characteristic product of eighteenth-century puritans.[40]

When, by the nineteenth century, the demands for national education were being pressed with increasing force, there was a potential conflict. The Dissenters were as effective in education as in all other areas of welfare initiative, and were not willing to see the established church hold any monopoly of religious teaching. Statutory grants were therefore given to the *British and Foreign Schools Society* (1814), which included the dissenting churches, as well as the Church of England's *National Society for promoting the education of the poor in the principles of the established church* (1811) in proportion to the funds each group raised. While this meant that 70% of the grants went to the established church, it admitted the principle that dissenting schools were eligible for statutory support; indeed, after 1839, even roman catholic schools might receive it.[41]

9

Finance and Fundraising

Tithes

The last chapter leads directly into the theme of finance, and I stay initially with some of its controversial aspects. Tithing was a cause of conflict from medieval times, when it was the principal source of income for beneficed clergy, right up to the 1930s. The Ecclesiastical Laws attributed to Edward the Confessor, but probably drawn up under William Rufus, stipulate that the tenth sheaf, colt, calf, cheese, lamb, pig should be paid: 'Likewise the tenth is to be given to God, who gives the nine parts, as well as the tenth of wood, meadow, waters, mills, parks, warrens, fisheries, osiers, gardens, and negotiations; let him that detains it be constrained to pay it by the bishop's court and by the King's, if that be necessary.'[1] Tithes were a motive for the english peasants' revolt of 1325, and the Lollards were blamed for asserting 'that no man is bound to tithe in the manner now used by the church, but such tithes and offerings by the law of God should be given to the poor needy men.'[2] Tithes were a major cause of resentment in England and elsewhere at the time of the Reformation[3] but, despite minority pressures for their abolition, they were retained. A statute of 1534 annexed papal firstfruits and tithes to the crown, and this held until 1703, when the establishment of Queen Anne's Bounty applied these funds to augment poor clerical livings, an initiative which Gerald Cragg has described as 'one of the few disinterested acts in an age in which advantage was the determining consideration in official dealings with the church'.[4] Meanwhile, the practice of tithing remained as the normal source of ecclesiastical revenue. George Fox saw Oliver Cromwell's dishonourable disinterment and reburial at Tyburn by Charles II as a just punishment. At the battle of

Dunbar, he wrote, Cromwell 'had promised to the Lord that if he gave him victory over his enemies he would take away tithes or else let him be rolled into his grave with infamy' yet when 'he came to be chief, he confirmed the former laws that if people did not set forth their tithes they should pay treble, and this to be executed by two justices of peace in the country upon the oath of two witnesses.'[5] The Quakers, like many other dissenters, suffered for their resistance against tithe-paying. The Epistle of the Yearly Meeting in London, 1688 says: 'And it is the desire of Friends generally, that you all be careful in your Monthly and Quarterly Meetings, in collecting the sufferings of Friends by priests and impropriators for their testimony against tithes and what goods are taken away from them upon that account, with the value thereof as also about repairs of steeple-houses ...'[6]

It is easy to see why tithe-payments were unpopular, but it is also clear why they were regarded as a desirable and necessary source of income by the established church. It was in fact difficult to replace them. About 1654, the Puritan David Davies, who had been given the cure of Gelligaer in Wales, 'preached down tithes for three years, but finding that this gift did not come up to the value of the living at the 4th Harvest, began to be mutinous and to preach up the divine right of 'Tyth', which greatly offended the parishioners'.[7]

Tithes were an embarrassment to some clergy, who felt at a disadvantage seeking them. At 'The Yearly Distress, or Tithing Time', at Stock in Essex, the priest was heavy-hearted according to Cowper, who wrote in 1779:

This priest he merry is and blithe,
   Three quarters of the year,
But oh! it cuts him like a scythe,
   When tithing time draws hear.

Now all unwelcome, at his gates
   The clumsy swains alight
With rueful faces and bald pates,
   He trembles at the sight.

And well he may, for well he knows
   Each bumkin of the clan
Instead of paying what he owes
   Will cheat him if he can.[8]

The other side could perceive tithe-dependent clergy as grasping. Writing in 1528, Simon Fish protested: 'Yea, and they look so narrowly upon their profits that the poor wives must be countable to them of every tenth egg, or else she getteth not her rights at Easter, shall be taken as a heretic.'[9] The fact that tithes might be owned by monasteries or by lay landowners and others made them more contentious. So did the growing difficulties of levying tithes on industrial production and from those liable to pay 'personal tithes' who, after 1549, made up a financially weighty proportion of the population. Tithe wars lasted into the twentieth century: neither catholic Irish nor non-conformist Welsh were willing readily to pay tithes to the english ecclesiastical establishment, and the final revolts by english tithe-payers occurred in the 1920s and 30s. The 1936 Tithe Act virtually eliminated the tithe as a required contribution to the english church.[10]

The disappearance of the tithe as a legally required contribution to church finances has added to the established church's financial problems, particularly as its endowment income has reduced in value. This has necessitated a greater recourse to Voluntaryism, the principle that church and state should be separate and that the church should depend on the direct support of its members, despite resistance from elements in the anglican church during and since the nineteenth century.[11]

That is not the issue here, however. The point I would make is that the removal of legal sanctions on tithing does not affect the biblical concept that a tenth at least of what man produces belongs to God. On the one hand, this is how in 1816 Lord John Russell expressed the legal principle: 'The tythe is part of the gross produce which never belonged to the landowners, but was always the property of another person.' On the other hand, Quaker Richard Baxter retorted to Quaker James Mayler's criticism of tithes thus in 1655: 'And where you ask whether the apostles took the tenths, I tell you again they took more, that is men sold all and laid down the money at their feet. It's true that then the poor also were maintained out of it, and if you will show a commission to examine us, we will give you an account how far we maintain the poor out of our mere tenth.'[12] This is in sympathy with Maimonides' *dictum*, quoted earlier, that tithing trains a man to be liberal; that it is a preparation for charity (see p.27).

Christian Endowments

The church's productive and income-earning assets have been another cause of controversy. To endow an institution is an obvious and often constructive way to secure its operations and safeguard its future. As with tithes, my account will be summary. The western church had been endowed from expropriated pagan property, from the spoils of conquest, from property left by or seized from Jews, from lands received in commutation of tithes, and above all from many, massive gifts. The capital has most usually been in the form of land, but tithe-earning churches as well as shops, mineral holdings, markets, fisheries, mills and other commercial property and money-bearing assets have frequently formed a significant part of the endowment. Taking some fairly random, medieval examples, in 1145 and 1151 the cathedral chapter at Amiens was created co-owner with the commune of the city's main commercial port, the Great Quay. In 1098, Pedro I of Aragon gave the monastery of Leire a half-interest in the Jews of Ruesta, so that the monks would receive half the custom dues levied on them; in February 1210, Pedro II made a gift to the monastery of Sigena of the Jew Vitalis, his family and property.[13] Still in Aragon, in 1379 the christian bankers Pere and Franesc de Gualbes lent the hospital of Pere dez Vilar in Barcelona 52,000 sous for the purchase of mills. Revenue from the mills was intended to establish a secure source of income for the hospital by eliminating a large number of small donations by private citizens, and to repay the loan.[14]

The detail is unimportant; what matters is that the medieval church and its institutions accumulated extensive property throughout Europe, suffering the corruption we considered earlier and drawing the enmity of reformers and of covetous men. When the property was seized in the Reformation, the main benefit went to the crown and certain favoured individuals, with a proportion passing to such institutions as the Oxford and Cambridge Colleges. Thus the proceeds from Bayham and Tonbridge, near my home, were invested in Wolsey's Cardinal College (or Christ Church), Oxford.[15] The real situation is reflected in the 1547 *Act for the Dissolution of the Chantries*. Although the proceeds of the dissolution were ideally intended for conversion 'to good and godly uses, as in erecting grammar schools to the education of youth in virtue and godliness, the further augmenting of the Universities, and better provision for the poor and needy', this could not 'nor ought to any other manner person be committed than to the King's Highness, whose Majesty with and by the advice of his Highness's most prudent Council can and will most wisely and beneficially, both for the honour of God and the weal of this his Majesty's realm, order, alter, convert, and disperse the same'.[16] Owen Chadwick reflects: 'The gravamen is not that the Church suffered a crippling loss of endowment, but that Protestant sovereigns of Europe, in their need for money, missed a unique opportunity of converting these charitable resources to truly charitable ends like education, hospitals, or the relief of the poor.'[17]

There are certainly disadvantages, private and public, in the church's large endowments. Adam Smith's condemnation of ecclesiastical wealth (see p.99) reads like an endorsement of Henry VIII's policy; and a remark he makes on schools might be applied to other endowed institutions: 'The endowments of schools and colleges have necessarily diminished more or less the necessity of application in the teachers.'[18] That is one problem. Another is that the endowment may preserve the institution after the time it has ceased to serve needs adequately or relevantly, or may provide more resources than it requires. Towards the end of the fourteenth century the Lollards' *Twelve Conclusions* complained, not only that the almshouses were centres of superstition, but also that they maintained a body of people in unnecessary idleness and that they diverted funds from more properly charitable ends.[19] Finally, the endowment might alienate the priest from his people. The commutation of tithes to land which was general in the late eighteenth and early nineteenth centuries gave many of the established clergy an essential qualification for social advancement: the ownership of a significant, rural property holding. This made the 'squarson' financially independent of his parishioners, and also made him disinclined to take the part of his poorer parishioners, when their well-being was threatened by enclosures. One good rector lamented: 'Reverence for my office they had none; consideration for me as a gentleman and landlord, and occupant of a large glebe, they had ...'[20]

The transplantation of methods for endowing the established church to the colonies clarifies the issues. It illuminates the financial relations between established church and state as well as the problems created where there is a strong dissenting presence, as in colonial Upper and Lower Canada. Lower Canada, or Quebec, was predominantly French and Roman Catholic. In Upper Canada, Ontario, there was a strong Church of Scotland presence with a significant proportion of Methodists and Roman Catholics. The anglican Church was not numerically predominant, and failed to achieve full establishment. Nonetheless, under the 1791 Constitutional Act, while the right to collect tithes was denied, provision was made for the support of 'Protestant clergy', a phrase which was initially interpreted as 'Anglican' or 'Episcopal'. In Upper Canada, one seventh of the land was to be set aside as a reserve to generate income for church and clergy; in Lower Canada, land unoccupied by the French was to be set aside in the same proportion (in this region, the roman church held endowments valued at £4,500,000 in 1840). The 'Clergy Reserves' totalled some 675,000 acres in Quebec; some 2,400,000 acres in Ontario. As an historian of the S.P.G. put it: 'While these lands remained mere waste tracts the exclusive right of the Church of England to them was not questioned, but when it was seen that they were becoming valuable other claimants arose in the Presbyterians of the Church of Scotland and various Dissenters.' The argument whether and how these resources should be apportioned between the sects continued from 1818 till 1854, with a series of proposals being blocked in the legislative council. There was also continuing criticism because the lands were mismanaged. An imperial Act of 1840 allowed for the gradual sale of the lands, two sixths of the proceeds being allocated to the Church of England (20% of the population), one sixth to the Church of Scotland (20% of the population), the balance to be applied by the Governor and his Executive Council 'for purposes of public worship and religious instruction in Canada'. In this way, the roman and methodist churches were to benefit to some degree. Meanwhile, canny Sir John Colborne had at the last minute created 44 anglican rectories, endowed with 400 acres apiece. The 1840 settlement was successfully resisted, and in 1853 the imperial parliament surrendered the Clergy Reserves to the Canadian legislature. Under the final arrangement, in an Act dated December 18th 1854, the lifetime interest of the clergy who depended on the Reserves was preserved, while the balance was 'alienated from the sacred purposes to which it had hitherto been devoted and transferred to the several municipalities within the boundaries of which the lands were situated'; in this way, 'All semblance of connexion between Church and State' was removed. Sir John's rectories escaped unscathed, and the clergy committed their life interest to a lump, capital sum, valued at a total of £381,971; but, in the long term, these measures meant that in Canada, 'All churches would have to rely on voluntary support to continue their ministries effectively.'[21]

Fundraising

The history of voluntary fundraising is long and complex; it also evokes theological and social controversy. Analysis of its essential elements reveals four points of emphasis: the needs or cause for which funds are sought and the capital or recurring funds required; the people to whom the appeal is directed, with regard for their means, awareness, beliefs and attitudes; the methods selected for fundraising, allowing for the costs and likely yields and the necessary manpower; the results, in terms of the amounts raised, the goodwill and affection evoked and the organization's improved capacity for future fundraising. Here, the church and its institutions are the cause; those concerned with the work of the church are the targets. The methods and results are my main theme in this chapter, since I have considered both donors and recipients earlier in this study.

It is easy but wrong to suppose that the kinds of fundraising with which we are familiar today are all recent inventions. In fact, many of the principles and techniques were fully developed in the Middle Ages. To take one example, while the charity fair, bazaar (a fair in oriental style) or sale became a specially potent and popular fundraising technique in the early years of the nineteenth century in England,[22] the method was not new. In the drive to raise funds for the building of the *Duomo* in Milan in the years following 1386, jumble sales were a regular feature. In Edmund Bishop's essay on this appeal, published in 1893, the 'jumble' listed comprises: 'A lady's houppelande and hood *(oppellanda a domina)* of dark violet cloth braided around the neck and sleeves; a man's loose cloak *drapi misgii;* two silver pins with a pearl at the head; a knife case with four knives, the handles of ivory, old, mended blades; three daggers; four helmets; three pairs of gauntlets; a checked banker; a copper mortar; two head mufflers; a string of amber beads; a little cross of copper, gilt; a lady's cote-hardie or riding-habit of light blue with 104 buttons of silver gilt, and another white, with 199 round gilt buttons on the hood and sleeves; one jerkin with stuff buttons; one gown of scarlet cloth with Venice braid around the sleeves and throat, without buttons; one gown with 56 buttons of silver enamelled, and gold embroidery around the neck; one set of furs, minever; one blue velvet gown; one green velvet gown, offered by Rugirina, widow of the deceased lord Alberto Visconti; one jacket of black fustian; two pairs of boots; one long towel, offered by a miller's wife; and so on, and so on.'[23] There were also medieval fairs to support hospitals and leper-houses, which would typically last three days. The May-Fair in London is one example and those for St. Bartholomew's, Newbury (Chartered in 1215) and the Cambridge leper-house still survive.[24]

Similarly, the fundraising letter was an ancient invention. The monastery of St. Evurtius was outside Orléans' walls, and consequently vulnerable. After it had been sacked and reduced to a ruin by the Normans, the bishop Stephan in 1174 mounted a major appeal. Here are two of the letters he sent out, the first being to the Dean of St. Martin's church in Tours: 'We are forced to make demands on our friends and our need forces us to mount an appeal. We are rebuilding the church of Father Evurtius, which has been burnt down; and because we lack sufficient means, we are asking for funds from outside. We are going out to the public, with some embarrassment setting embarrassment aside, stirring up what devotion we can in the people through the highways and byways. This is why we have sent these brothers of ours to you with the saints' relics; and I sincerely ask you to use your authority to support our appeal for alms from the good people in St. Martin's church ... We ask for much, but our need forces us to do this, and your kindness encourages us to do so.' The second letter was to a friend, on the same occasion: '(Standing) in the middle of the smoking ashes of our church, and the scorched timber of its re-arrising walls, distressed and shocked, we are forced to approach the general public, and shamelessly to ask for support from outside gifts. The new building in honour of the confessor Evurtius has been started but, because of the costs we must meet, is unfinished; this is why we seek the support of strangers to complete it. We have sent these brothers of ours with the saints' relics so that, through the good intentions of the congregations in a few churches, there may at least be a modest collection which will add to the merit of the donors, and be a comfort to those who receive it. We are asking a great deal; but our need forces us to do this, and your kindness encourages us.'[25]

These letters raise a number of issues, and fit firmly within the medieval tradition. The travels of merit-earning relics are a very common feature. If there was nowhere for pilgrims to come with their money and devotions, as in this case, the relics were to be carried, sometimes from country to country, to the faithful. The very miraculous relics of St. Firmin refused in 1137 to be taken on a fundraising trip beyond the Amiens city limits, stirring greater generosity in the local people. Similar trips are recorded of relics of the Virgin, Cuthbert and many others, borne around the countryside, each in its feretory.[26] The pious and profitable cult of the saints, it has been demonstrated, influenced the design of the great medieval churches, which, like modern cult churches at Lourdes or St. Anne d'Auray or Walsingham, had to accommodate crowds of pilgrims as well as providing space for rich benefactors to be buried near the resident saints.[27]

Another, very interesting feature in these letters is their authorisation of official fundraisers. We have seen there were some official fundraisers in the early christian church; in medieval times, they were common, and at least in England a license to beg was required. Some fundraisers were priests or members of religious orders, most conspicuously the Friars; others, like the canons appointed by Bishop Stephan, were deacons and others in minor orders; many were semi-official, lay fundraisers, who vaunted and abused their odd status, and are familiar to us from Chaucer and Langland. Chaucer's Pardoner was one of the *Quaestores Eleemosynarii* ('Fund raisers') who were active in campaigns for hospitals, churches and other good works in pre-Reformation Europe. He was a fundraiser for a hospital near Charing Cross. The merit-earning veneration of relics and the sale of indulgences were the *Quaestors'* fundraising wares; the occasion was their fund-raising address or sermon. Langland gives a vivid picture of their practice:

> There was a pardoner preached as though he were a priest
> and brought out a Bull with a bishop's seals
> and said he could absolve them all
> of failures in fasting and of vows broken.
> Common men accepted him, welcomed his canting
> and came and knelt and kissed his bulls;
> and he biffed them with his bulls and bleared their eyes,
> and with that screed, raked in their rings and trinkets.

Chaucer's picture is as hostile. His Pardoner used preaching and begging for a clear purpose:

> I will have money, wool and cheese and wheat,
> Even if given by the poorest page,
> Or the poorest widow in the village,
> Even if her children die from hunger.[28]

These men operated under license. A typical document would ask the local clergy to allow the fundraiser to explain to the congregation the indulgences and privileges which he could offer on behalf of the cause he represented, although, where this would be advantageous, the local priest would make the appeal. Bishop Grandisson of Exeter found that the arch-deacon and his officials were making a profit through licensing a squad of fraudulent fundraisers to raise money on their behalf. In a document dated 1359, Bishop Grandisson required that no *quaestor* should be accommodated unless he could show a letter signed and sealed by the bishop himself, with the impression of the bishop's ring on the reverse; and the fundraiser was to limit himself to the exact terms of the letter. Bishop Grandisson was angry with these frauds who were diverting money from his cathedral and the Exe bridge, but he was gentle in comparison with Archbishop Thoresby of York. Thoresby in 1363 cursed the fraudulent *quaestors* who had invaded his territory to be blotted from the book of life, unless they handed in their takings.[29]

Corrupt officers like these, as well as the mendicant clergy, were very natural objects for criticism and ridicule. In 1210 a chronicler mocked at the temporary discomfiture of the Cistercians: 'An unheard of thing happened this year, in that Cistercian monks and Jews ... begged for food in competition with each other.' The friars John and Alexander, licensed by the king in 1247 to raise funds in England on the pope's behalf, secured 11,000 marks, with high-handed authority and perhaps some deception, according to the chronicler Matthew Paris. There were even quarrels between Friars over their fundraising territories.[30] There was a line of criticism which culminated with the arrival of the arch medieval fundraiser, the Dominican John Tetzel, to sell indulgences near Wittenburg in 1517.

The details of this incident are important. There was a double reason for Tetzel's presence: through the sale of indulgences, he was to raise money for the building of the new St. Peter's in Rome; but a proportion of the funds raised was to be used for paying off the huge debt of the prince bishop Albert of Brandenburg to the great bankers or usurers, the Fuggers of Augsburg (see pp.92 & 109). Frederick the Wise of Saxony, in whose city of Wittenburg Luther was professor of Holy Scripture, had banned Tetzel from his territory, but according to E. G. Rupp: 'Frederick's motive was a blunt determination to keep Saxon money at home and to cut out competition with his local shrine', which would by 1518 have accumulated 17,443 revenue-earning relics. Frederick's Saxons evaded the ban by crossing the border to hear Tetzel preach and to purchase his pardons and remissions. It was this that caused Luther to publish his 95 Theses as a protest, largely on theological grounds, but also because he saw it as an injustice that money should be extracted from the poor to build a rich pope's basilica.[31] On similar grounds, he would also call for the restraint of the Fuggers.

The fundraising significance of October 31st 1517 is obvious. The teaching of justification by faith denied the reformed churches and their fundraisers some well-used and effective arguments.[32] Indulgences and other such devices were necessarily outlawed.

Indulgences had first been used as a method for mass persuasion in 1095, when Pope Urban II used them as an inducement for men to join the Crusade; those who died on the Crusade having repented of their sins would go straight to heaven, relieved by the plenary indulgence of the purgatorial cleansing they would otherwise have undergone. Ordinary indulgences granted a period of remission, often expressed as being for a period of thirty or forty days. Indulgences were granted for special occasions, for pilgrimages, through saints' relics and devotions on certain religious feasts, and usually some payment was required. The custom developed by which, instead of going on crusade or pilgrimage, a payment could be made instead to secure the remission of penance. By the fourteenth century, the sale of indulgences had become widespread, but they were not the only fundraising device associated with the purchase of paradise, or of swifter, less painful access thither. There were trentals (a sequence of thirty masses for the souls of the dead), masses for the dead and large sums to be paid for burial in privileged churches where the dead would be remembered. There were Jubilee years, when those who made a pilgrimage to Rome or, after the reign of Boniface IX, paid over a sum equivalent to the cost of a return journey to Rome, obtained plenary indulgences. Some methods of raising funds added vanity to the purchase of pardon, as we have seen; a conspicuous memorial window, monument or chantry could achieve this.

These practices drew criticism from within the unreformed church. From the Lollards' *Twelve Conclusions:* 'The seventh conclusion that we mightily affirm is that special prayers for dead mens souls in our church preferring one by name more than another, this is false ground for alms deeds, on which all the alms houses in England are wickedly grounded.' Opposing Luther, but agreeing with his criticism of some abuses,

Thomas More complains in his *Dialogue* (1528): '... And the priest goes a-begging for all his grant of a good living, and the law is deluded, and the order is rebuked by the priest's begging and lewd living, which either is fain to (wander about randomly) and live upon trentals or worse ...'[33]

Compared with the attacks by Luther and Calvin, such words are mild. Mankind, wrote Calvin, 'saw themselves insulted openly, and without disguise, by the Pope and his bull-bearers; they saw the salvation of the soul made the subject of a lucrative traffic, salvation taxed at a few pieces of money ... . Hence we have from the Pope at one time plenary indulgences, at another for certain years; from the cardinals for a hundred days, and from the bishops for forty. These, to describe them truly, are a profanation of the blood of Christ, and a delusion of Satan, by which the Christian people are led away from the grace of God and the life which is in Christ, and turned aside from the true way of salvation.'[34]

Luther attacked all these fundraising abuses. He complained that the Mass had been reduced to 'mere merchandise, a market, and a profit-making business'. He protested against indulgences: 'They often issue an indulgence on the same pretext of fighting the Turks. They think that those half-witted Germans will always be gullible, stupid fools, and will just keep handing over money to them to satisfy their unspeakable greed'; against pilgrimage and money-making cults: 'In fact, where pilgrimages do not catch on, they set to work to canonise saints, not to honour the saints, who would be honoured enough without being canonised, but to draw the crowds and bring in the money. At this point pope and bishops lend their aid. There is a deluge of indulgences. There is always money enough for these'; against Roman Jubilee years, a practice which impoverished foolish pilgrims' families, but 'has brought in money and fortified (the popes') illegitimate authority'.[35]

In protestant Europe, therefore, fund-raising trips with relics and the marketing of forgiveness in all its forms would cease, but a great deal would continue unchanged. There was more to medieval fundraising than the sale of indulgences. We see in fourteenth century Milan that the campaign for the *Duomo* worked at a number of levels. In the Spring of 1386, the

Archbishop sent out a circular stating that the old cathedral was massively decayed and ruined. In October, the Conte de Virtu gave permission for the organization of house-to-house collections throughout his territory. Up to July 1387, the city of Milan depended on the inertia-method of collection boxes, with some special collections in the churches. However, in March an individual had started a special collection in his own quarter of the city, and by July a large volunteer force had been formed to raise money quarter by quarter on successive Sundays. The Conte de Virtu was asked to make a pace-setting gift, and to secure donations from his courtiers; if they gave, wrote the organizers, 'soldiers, and lawyers, and doctors ... will be all ready to offer along with them'. The body of the Count's father would also be given an honourable tomb in the new building. In the event, the Duke's gift was small. Letters were again sent around the diocese in 1387, and trustees were appointed to oversee expenditure of the funds raised. Meanwhile, many gifts in kind (a horse, a bale of cloth, some old tiles) were sold, and increasing numbers of gifts from individuals, workshops, trade groups and schools flowed in. Events such as concerts and jumble sales were held. And the armourers, drapers, shoe-makers, skinners, students and others turned up in groups to provide volunteer labour.[36]

Compare this account with, for example, the fundraising activities for the medieval hospitals, and it is clear that house-to-house collections and other fundraising methods which look familiar to us today were common before the Reformation. There were even instances of sponsored bell-ringing in fifteenth century Rouen and elsewhere.[37] With the charity sermon there was explicit encouragement for continuity. In 1536, the year in which he issued his *Act against Papal Authority*, Henry VIII's *Beggar's Act* enacted that 'every preacher, parson, vicar, curate of this realm' should use sermons and other occasions to 'exhort, move, stir and provoke people to be liberal, and bountifully to extend their good and charitable alms and contributions from time to time for and toward the comfort and relief of the said poor, impotent, decrepit, indigent, and needy people'.[38]

The patterns and methods for supporting christian or other institutions have varied enormously, before and since the

Reformation; I roughly grade my survey from less to more personal methods of fundraising.

Collection boxes were always present. The maligned Brother Elias, within a year of St. Francis of Assisi's death, was being criticized for installing a collection box on the site of the basilica he was building in the saint's honour. The 'poor men's box' was part of local government machinery in sixteenth century England. There was to be a box 'in some conspicuous part of the (poor) house, and likewise in the church', according to Nicholas Toke's 1770 *Regulations*, and collecting boxes shaped as uniformed, begging charity-school children were on the streets of Cork in the early eighteenth century. 'In the kirk also stood the poor's box', writes G. M. Trevelyan, 'which the thrifty Scots constantly replenished with most of the bad copper of the neighbourhood, besides a useful minority of good coins.' Collections of all kinds (of money and of goods) have continued over the centuries.[39]

Various forms of literature have been used. John Eliot's tracts from 1646 onwards on the needs of the Red Indians so stimulated the population at home that 'A Corporation for the Promoting and Propagating of the Gospel of Jesus Christ in New England' was formed in 1649, and a collection ordered by Oliver Cromwell raised £12,000 for this cause. Descriptive letters to Europe from Jesuits in the north american missions had a similar impact, and were circulated to good effect at home. According to the Quaker William Penn, writing about 1694, George Fox made effective use of such tools: 'He was often where the records of the affairs of the church are kept and . where the letters from the many Meetings of God's people over all the world, where settled, come upon occasions; which letters he had read to him, and communicated them to the meeting that is weekly held there for such services; and he would be sure to stir them up to discharge them, especially in suffering cases ... carefully looking into the respective cases, and endeavouring speedy relief, according to the nature of them.'[40]

The Quaker John Bellers, writing his *Proposals for Raising a College of Industry* in 1696, created an early, model grant application or fundraising prospectus. Although the scheme was unsuccessful (it failed to achieve the right mixture of pragmatism with idealism), the document is nonetheless fascinating. One 'college' was built at Clerkenwell, after Bellers' death; this later became the Saffron Walden Boarding School. The proposal is directed 'To the Thinking and Public-Spirited', and gives an address where they 'may enter their subscriptions'. The INTRODUCTION insists: 'It's the interest of the rich to take care of the poor', and goes on: 'However prevalent arguments of charity may be to some, when profit is joined with it, it will raise most money, provide for most people, hold longest, and do most good ...' He claims: 'This College-fellowship will make labour and not money, the standard to value all necessaries by', and that it is 'much more to put the poor in a way to live by honest labour, than to maintain them idle ...'. He summarises the concept thus: 'A Specimen showing how the rich may gain, the poor maintain themselves, and children be educated, by being incorporated as a college of all sorts of useful trades, that shall work one for another, without other relief: Suppose three hundred in a college, to work the usual time or task as abroad, and what any doth more, to be paid for it, to encourage industry.' The document then goes on to detail the division of tasks within the College. Moving to the fundraising targets: 'I propose for every 300 persons the raising of

£10000 To buy an Estate in Land of £500 per annum
£2000 To Stock the Land and
£3000 To prepare Necessaries to Set the Several Trades to Work
£3000 For New-building or Repairing Old
       In all 18000 pound.'

Colleges in Colchester, Taunton, Stroud and Devonshire are proposed. 'An hundred pound a year in such a College, I suppose will maintain ten times as many people as £100 a year in alms-houses, or hospitals ...'[41]

I have already alluded to charity sermons. These were formerly one of the most popular and powerful methods used. For the charity schools in early eighteenth century England: 'Special sermons, advertised in the newspapers, attracted crowded congregations, and swelled the schools' funds; over £100 on these occasions was collected at the church doors.' On Christmas Day 1786, at St. John's, New Brunswick, 'A "Charity Sermon" preached by (Rev. G. Bissett) ... realized £36, besides private donations, and in the next year was instituted "the humane and Charitable Society" "for the relief of the poor", which it was thought might "probably supersede the necessity of Poor rates" '.[42] In the case of the charity schools, the children themselves were likely to be in attendance, dressed in their distinctively coloured uniforms. They added to the impact of the occasion, the uniform serving a number of functions: it was practical, an instrument of discipline, a sumptuary measure; but it was also an effective fundraising device. John Groom's children 'were dressed in a neat uniform, and allotted stands at Hyde Park Corner, Marble Arch, Poets' Corner, and other places' to attract support for the homes. Massed for a Charity Sermon, neat and clean, the children were a major attraction and motive for giving. It was this that gave force, from 1704 onwards, to the annual Anniversary of Charity Schools, which after 1782 was held in the new St. Paul's, London. Thousands of children, dressed in their uniforms, went in procession through the streets, great crowds looking on.[43] Blake wrote in the 1789-1794 *Songs of Innocence:*

> T'was on a Holy Thursday, their innocent faces clean,
> The children walking two and two, in red and blue and green,
> Grey-headed beadles walk'd before, with wands as white as
>   snow
> Till into the high dome of St. Paul's they like Thames waters
>   flow.
> .....
> Beneath them sit the aged men, wise guardians of the poor;
> Then cherish pity, lest you drive an angel from your door.[44]

Another extension of the regular, fundraising sermon in church was the Sunday Hospital Fund. After 1850, in Birmingham, some churches were persuaded to give up one collection to the local hospitals, a practice which was adopted nationally from 1873. Out of this developed a Saturday Fund, to collect money in factories, at soccer matches and in the streets from those who might not be reached in church. This practice was later adopted by such groups as the Royal National Lifeboat Institution, which in 1891 launched its first Lifeboat Saturday Fund in Manchester; in 1896, R.N.L.I. raised £16,367 or 14% of its income this way.[45]

Robert Nelson (see p.87) was a promoter of the Anniversary of Charity Schools, and was also prominent in many worthy subscription lists, which were another important instrument for eighteenth and nineteenth century fundraising. These lists were published, with names and the amounts subscribed, for almost any good works of the time, and were commonly used by the S.P.C.K. and S.P.G. They added a significant, extra principle to that of publication; a deliberate attempt to get society's leaders, and more especially the monarch, to set an example, so that a worthy mention would be virtually compulsory, simply because of royalty's presence on the list. William III, Queen Anne, Queen Victoria and the dowager Queen Adelaide all featured on S.P.G. lists.[46]

The monarch might do more. Henry III had written an appeal on behalf of St. Giles' Hospital, Shrewsbury, asking: 'that when the brethren come to you to beg alms, you will favourably admit them, and mercifully impart to them your alms of the goods conferred by God upon you'.[47] George III (in a royal line of fundraisers which included Queen Anne, George I, George II, the Prince Regent, William IV and Queen Victoria) issued his letters of appeal on a more organized basis, commending the S.P.G. to his subjects, and requiring that his letter of May 1779 should be published throughout the country: 'and that, upon this occasion, the Ministers in each parish do effectually excite their parishioners to a liberal contribution, whose benevolence towards carrying on the said charitable work shall be collected the week following at their respective dwellings by the Church-wardens and Overseers of the poor in each parish'. This time, £19,372 was collected, compared with £45,747 on the next occasion, under the Prince Regent in 1819.[48] Similarly, in the 1830s, 'The Queen's blessing was the final accolade' for a profitable, charity bazaar'.[49]

These are all aspects of the techniques which became common, at least after the eighteenth century, for harnessing numbers of gifts from the moderately wealthy for charitable institutions, sometimes on a regular basis. S.P.C.K. and others had demonstrated how, with a strong, central organizing body, federal fundraising drives could be mounted on a semi-autonomous basis around the country. All this implies an understanding of motivations and of the demand for effective organization which abide as features of modern fundraising. In the 1820s, the quaker Charles Dudley was applying rigorous organizational principles to his fundraising work for the Bible Society.[50] The Jews had long before applied personal targets and a detailed assignation of tasks to their programmes. The S.P.C.K., the charity schools and the voluntary hospitals were amongst those who had introduced a new discipline to the art. Even the principle of fundraising blackmail was crudely stated in the late nineteenth century *Press Bazaar News:* 'Find a Duchess, flatter her, and get £500.'[51]

One vehicle for more highly organized fundraising of this kind was the supporters' association. This had a precedent in the Fraternities of the Fabric, which were formed to raise money for building the great medieval churches. The S.P.C.K. was a later pioneer, creating a distinction between 'residing' or 'subscribing' members, who lived in or near London and were allowed to vote at meetings, and 'corresponding' members, who lived further away, could attend meetings if they found themselves in London, but were not allowed to vote. In 1712, there were 80 residing members, subscribing £2 to £10 annually, and 370 corresponding members, paying subscriptions between £1 and £3/3/0. These were active members as well as supporters.[52]

In other situations the subscribers' involvement could develop more balefully. Thus, during the nineteenth century, some institutions gave their subscribers the right to cast votes, the number of votes being proportionate to the size of the subscription, to determine which candidates should be admitted for care. The Royal Hospital and Home for Incurables was an example of such a 'voting charity'. The reason for offering this invidious privilege was to strengthen the agency's fundraising appeal; memberships and associations did not necessarily go this far.[53]

Also during the nineteenth century, there was a strong movement for the formation of support organizations harnessing women and children to charities' fundraising efforts. The N.S.P.C.C.'s League of Pity (1894), Waif's and Strays' Children's Union (1888), the Band of Hope and Band of Mercy (1875) are examples of this.[54] While these organizations aimed to edify their supporters, they were largely removed from the agencies' caring activities. This was necessarily the case with the groups formed to support the missions, whether protestant or catholic. Analysis of the catholic support groups for the missions formed between 1818 and 1924 in Europe and North America shows accelerating growth. The numbers of catholic associations formed during this period totalled: 1818-1850, 16; 1851-1880, 43; 1881-1910, 115; 1911-1924, 94. It was estimated that the annual income of these principal roman catholic missionary agencies totalled some 52 million francs in 1923.[55] The five principal comparable protestant associations in the U.K. in 1860 raised over £450,000.[56]

Various kinds of fundraisers were involved. Many of those working for hospitals and other institutions during the nineteenth century were remunerated with a percentage (often 5% to 7½%) of the sums raised, a practice now properly outlawed by good professionals. In the eighteenth and nineteenth centuries, fundraising companies such as Robert Hodgson and Byrd, Hall & Stevenson in the UK took a large proportion of the sums they raised.[57] The fully-fledged professional of the kind we know today, however, emerged in the USA about 1883, with Charles Somner Ward's work for the Y.M.C.A. in Kentucky. It was this Ward who, in 1919, formed the first professional fundraising company, *Ward, Hill, Pierce and Wells*, forerunner of the *Wells* company which introduced large-scale planned-giving programmes in UK churches from 1957.[58] We shall briefly consider their techniques in the next chapter. There had been professionalism in fundraising, however, before the emergence of the professionals. In a minor mode, there were manuals on fundraising, published lists of prospects for appeals, and even Mrs. Beeton gave instruction on how to compose an appeal letter. The fundraiser formerly faced serious risks. Until quite late, a license or 'brief' was required to authorize fundraising activity. For example, a brief was issued in 1673 for 'the ransoming of Christians from Turkish slavery'. If no brief could be shown, there was danger of a charge of mendicancy, perhaps maliciously instigated by a competitor or political opponent. When on a Sunday in 1718 a 'little contingent' from St. Anne's, Aldersgate arrived at Chislehurst on an unlicensed fundraising mission to the church there, 'they were hauled before the High Sheriff of the county and two Whig justices, who, after demanding by what right they went strolling and begging through the country without a license, detained one of the trustees in prison'.[59]

Good fundraisers have occurred in every generation, despite the disapprobation and hostility with which they have tended to be received. Even with an occasionally disreputable operator like Barnardo, the very positive results must balance the criticism; he raised some £3,000,000 during his life for children at risk, which for that time is a remarkable achievement.[60] This does not mean, though, that his publicity-dependent techniques were the only ones which were successful. His precursor, George Müller, whose Orphan houses were founded in 1836, had eschewed all publicity and open solicitation in his fundraising. The principles of Müller's Scriptural Knowledge Institution were extended to the homes: 'They would contract no debts, but would act according to the funds at their disposal, which they would seek for by secret prayer to God.' On this basis, Müller successfully founded and ran homes for over 2,000 orphans and, like his contemporary Jean-Marie-Batiste Vianney in France, he did not find the funds were lacking, although he employed no overt fundraising techniques.[61]

Finally, the forms of giving have been very diverse, and also remarkably modern-seeming. I have already mentioned various occasions on which matching or conditional gifts were made, to provide leverage for increased fundraising: 'In 1865 (the S.P.G.) set apart a sum of £1,000 for the purpose of encouraging by proportionate grants-in-aid the gifts of native Christians towards the endowment of native clergymen in South India. By this means the liberality of native Christians was stimulated, and in Tinevelly several native pastorates have been endowed.' When in the late 1950s, the Rockefeller brothers set up their Sealantic Fund, through which they offered two million dollars to finance theological training in deprived countries, provided the missionary societies matched their contributions, it was with the same intention. In a similar manner, the S.P.G. between 1835 and 1850 applied £171,777 (less £598 expenses), £24,463/3/11 from donations, £62,385/1/0 from parliamentary grants and £84,29/9/1 from the General Fund, to missionary work in the West Indies, Guiana and Bermuda: 'The assistance thus rendered drew out a vast amount of local support, it being a condition that at least one-half of the salaries of the Missionaries and lay teachers should from the first be provided from other sources, and that eventually the entire charge should be undertaken by the Colonies.[62] As early as the fourteenth century, John Thoresby staggered his £2,600 gift for the new choir at York Minster, by making payments of £200 annually.[63] There is even evidence of an early payroll-deduction, when in the eighteenth century the 400 to 500 ironworkers of Winlaton, County Durham gave the local school up 3/8 of a penny weekly, to which the employers added their contribution.[64]

The final section of this essay considers what we have learnt defining the problems, meeting them and paying for the solutions.

Part Three

10

Summary, The Present Situation and Conclusions

At the beginning of this essay, I stated that our journey had a purpose, and that this was not to enjoy the views. Evidently, there is no single, coherent christian doctrine on wealth; different christian teachings have at times opposed or contradicted each other. They have also transmitted non-christian thinking. This does not mean that there is no attitude to earning, owning and disposing of wealth which is uniquely, specifically christian, although it may be that the living relevance of Christianity to our business and social activity partly shows itself in the tension between christian teachings on, for example, actual poverty and commercial stewardship. I believe that christian teaching demands a revolution in our economic lives. This is my subject for the last chapter of this essay, and it draws on the material presented and discussed earlier.

Summary and Abstract of Christian Teachings

This material presents a series of sometimes incompatible propositions:

1. (a) People have a right and duty to provide themselves and their dependents with food, shelter, clothing, health facilities, education, rest and pleasure at a level justified by the expectations and resources of the society in which they live. (Today, a definition of 'society' as the state in which one happens to live is too narrow; the economic behaviour of one part of the world's population determines the expectations and the resources available to their more distant neighbours.) At the worst, they are entitled to earn the means to maintain their own and their dependents' lives, self-sufficiency and integrity, even if they must in fact live below the level at which their

expectations might justly be pitched. If their reasonable, economic requirements are not met, Christians may actively pursue political, social and economic change.

(b) However, while self-support through work is morally important for a Christian, and is the normal way to exercise stewardship of talents, to realize personality and to remain harmlessly occupied, it cannot be a Christian's sole or sufficient object. To be distracted by business from love, care, prayer and reflection is an evil.

(c) Wealth created through work does not become a Christian's absolute possession.

(d) In producing wealth, Christians must observe personal justice and kindness, in relation to employees, suppliers, purchasers, and the public generally. It is a fault to pay employees less than their entitlement or need, having regard to their personal circumstances, or to deal unfairly in buying and selling, to misrepresent the product or to produce and sell anything physically, mentally or morally damaging.

(e) The capitalist concept of a wage or salary-earner on the one hand, with a profit-taker on the other, may be antichristian.

2. (a) Some form of property ownership is a right and a necessity, especially if no real distinction can be made between use and ownership of wealth. However, for a Christian, this right is not absolute. Traditional christian teaching accommodates the marxist distinction between individual or personal property, which is a necessity, and private or exclusive property, which is damaging and divisive.

(b) A Christian's property, however received, is held in trust; the title to absolute ownership is weak and probably spurious. God, an absolute provider and owner of everything, is the true Master of all property. In any case, it is argued that a Christian's historical titles to riches are likely to be unjust.

(c) At least what Christians own in excess of their simple requirements should be treated as property common to all.

(d) An ordered, systematic re-distribution of inherited wealth is encouraged.

3. (a) Possessions, property and all forms of wealth are actually perilous. Tradition characterises wealth as the root of evil (for Paul, the problem is the *love* of wealth); Jesus's warn-

ings are stronger: He says 'Woe to you rich', and that it is hard for a rich man to enter heaven. The bias of individuals, institutions and nations towards unjust wealth and the power it brings is a commonplace. Wealth is a manifest, universal, eternally-sought-after evil. It corrupts the usurer in his counting house and the hermit in his cell. It is the cause of injustice in society; is a distraction from prayer, reflection and the study of religion; destroys tranquillity of mind; is a compelling encouragement to self-indulgence, extravagance and immorality.

(b) Enjoyment of the good things in life should be an aspect of a Christian's experience.

4. (a) Some form or degree of poverty is a requirement for Christians. This includes, but is more than, an internal detachment from wealth and indifference at the prospect of impoverishment, which after all were stoic requirements. It also includes a self-liberating despisal of riches, as in the cynic tradition, but without pride or contempt towards others (see Ch. 1). Poverty makes a strong demand on Christians. Christ says that the truly, desolately poor are blessed and that a man must abandon everything to follow him.

(b) Christian poverty requires sumptuary restraints, in the enjoyment and use of goods.

(c) As with the Jews, practical measures such as tithing may be required to wean people from wealth and accustom them to the enjoyment of fewer goods than they can in fact afford.

(d) Christian poverty encourages some degree of voluntary austerity, self-deprivation and asceticism.

(e) Christian teaching explicitly promotes the free election of an extraordinary, necessarily unworldly poverty, which is always likely to go beyond what is regarded as normal or couth by the majority of Christians in any place or period.

(f) Actual poverty may be a pre-requisite for the committed, contemplative life.

5. (a) Christians have a duty to care for the needy, whether friends, strangers or enemies, importunate or mute, as a function of justice and of love.

(b) This is an active rather than a passive duty; it is not enough to make a token reaction to random requests for support. A Christian must respond constructively, sacrificially and inconveniently to need, and intelligently, persistently seek the needy out. This demands very positive responsiveness to new situations in society.

(c) A Christian's charity may embrace animals and other creatures.

(d) Christian (like jewish) charity is a responsibility which requires that the indigent should have access with dignity and confidence to the goods held in trust by a Christian on their behalf. This demands sensitive consideration for the benefit, welfare, position and pride of the needy, and a rejection of any impulse to use charity punitively, as a form of bribery or as an instrument of sectarianism.

(e) It should admit no excuses for witholding kindness and support.

(f) It may make use of institutions for the distribution and application of the resources it provides, but must ensure that these institutions are and remain just and kind and that charity is not depersonalised.

(g) It can choose statutory, governmental measures and agencies to achieve its ends.

(h) It should involve personal relationships; a Christian's door should be open and his table welcoming to the needy.

(i) It should be coterminous with the world and universe of which Christians are aware at any time.

(j) Whatever Christians do to support their indigent neighbours is a function of justice, not of elected benevolence or condescension.

(k) Above all, it is Jesus who acts through a Christian's charity, and it is Jesus who personally receives the charitable act. Charity is the natural and necessary expression of Jesus's presence in a Christian. He stands as benefactor and as beneficiary.

6. A Christian's charity must embrace practical and effective measures to secure the welfare of the needy. Inefficient and disorganized charity, in terms of planning, management or skilled implementation, falls below the standards required by kindness or justice. This means that the selection and treatment of recipients, the forms and style of the relief given, the attitudes, the scale of the relief and the fundraising to make an adequate response possible must all reflect the absolute call on

love, kindness, wealth, intelligence, commitment, time and talent which is imposed by christian charity. It leaves no scope for compromise or complacency.

This is an unsystematic, incomplete series of propositions; and the same series could, in principle, have been deduced from non-christian teaching. Only the argument for poverty might appear in the West as distinctive. I repeat my statement that the point is not the ethical teaching. What characterises and distinguishes a christian life, and therefore christian economic behaviour and charity, is the reality of the Incarnation. It is Christ who lives and works in the individual Christian, and it is Christ whom the Christian encounters in the people and the events of daily life. This is not a fiction or game or charade. The substance of the history of the Incarnation is the substance of history itself. Nothing is left out. Christ is realized in society through its natural, historical, evolutionary, social, political, economic, intellectual and cultural processes. For individual Christians, who must live the life of Christ in their own generation and respond to his presence personally, continually and ubiquitously around them, this imposes inescapable demands. It means that, in earning and handling wealth, in conducting business, in buying and selling, as in all other activities, christian life is led, not by observing a code of behaviour, but by realizing the contemporary life of Christ. Above all, the life of Christ is realized in any age through the living relationships of Christians with all their fellow men, none excepted. This of course includes all categories of the needy, and Christ's teaching gives special priority to the hungry, the thirsty, the naked and others so deprived; but the encounter with Christ is also the conditioning factor and the true substance of all other relationships — with employers, employees, customers, clients, patients, officials, public servants, blood relations, friends and everyone a Christian hears of or meets, no matter how remotely or casually. The propositions I have listed give a framework or discipline and detailed guidelines to assist a Christian's decisions; but it is in living Christ's life in the real world and experiencing his presence there in all other people that Christians express the essential, dangerous and necessarily unpopular reality of their faith and love, and only in the context of this truth can the details of a genuinely christian life (including economic life) be judged or comprehended.

In very practical terms, this means that experiences of economic success, drudgery or calamity must be regarded as opportunities to develop the real life and presence of Christ in the world. This is true with individuals, groups, nations and associations between nations.

The World We Live In

On the basis of this view of the Incarnation, a consideration of the world we live in is the necessary point to start from in a study which aims to assist a re-appraisal of contemporary christian economic behaviour. Events since the late 1950s and early 1960s have very fundamentally changed the context for such a reappraisal. In the West, the assumptions of protestant and roman catholic sects, confidently established over generations, are no longer accepted by a majority of the people; while some christian teachings have become part of the culture (including many christianised aspects of ciceronian and senecan stoicism), the basic assumptions of our civilization are decreasingly religious or theistic. After 1945, measures to improve and extend the state's welfare provisions, which had been strongly promoted by churchmen and utilitarian agnostics since the nineteenth century, were at last being introduced increasingly broadly. One effect was to change the roles and importance of religious and other voluntary institutions. This was an aspect of the levelling or progressive socialisation of western societies; by the end of the sixties at the latest, many privileges and sumptuary distinctions between different social groups in Britain, for example, had been eroded: at least amongst the young, a working-class pub could no longer be identified simply by the clothes worn by its regulars.

Advertising gives a good illustration of the kinds of change which had established themselves by 1960. Although the trends had become evident between the two world wars, tones of the tradesman faded relatively slowly from British advertising: 'Over a century's experience in outfitting gentlemen — soldiers, civilians, and explorers — proceeding to India, the

Colonies, and all countries in the world enables us to provide sportsmen with exactly what is required on big-game hunting expeditions in tropical and sub-tropical climates' runs an advertisement in the *Times* of November 2nd 1909; on January 7th 1916, again in the *Times,* Harrods declared: 'Imperially British — Proud — with reason prouder today than ever before in history — is every Briton of the mighty British Empire and its far-flung flag ... Precisely this (British spirit indomitable) it is which, despite vicissitude, despite the upheaval of almost every normal social condition, has enabled Harrods not only to maintain but to enhance its prestige as the great Imperial Department store.' In the USA, tougher and subtler advertising had arrived earlier; the mass prosperity required to support vigorous consumer markets with the range of branded products first established itself there. November 25th 1959 is identified as the date on which 'The battle hymn of the affluent society' resounded through Britain from the pages of *The Times* and other papers: 'Four bedrooms, three children, two cars' ran the Ford headline on that day, launching the two-car (a big Ford and an Anglia), prosperous family with a detached house on a modern estate, as the newborn consumer society's ideal.

In terms of marketing, the exploitation of press and television responded to unprecedented increases in disposable income for the majority of the population and in the availability of goods for purchase. If consumers express and partly realize their personalities through the clothes they wear and the products they buy, strong brand advertising might avert a universal personality crisis. Formerly, sumptuary regulations, poverty and convention defined the clothes, the goods, the styles and therefore the *personae* the humbler orders might adopt. Now, quite suddenly, an almost infinite variety of products and *personae* could be acquired, without any strong religious or social sanctions to regulate the new world of opportunity, and the orders were no longer humble; chaos threatened. In addition to its other roles, advertising could limit the choices and define the desirable, available *personae*. Mythology was as important an ingredient in an advertisement as the skilful description of unique brand advantages. The themes were often conventional, traditional: cloud-chariot, sword, happy-ever-after, brave and handsome hunter-husband-protector, devoted all-providing wife, good mother, secure home, secret mountain fastness, universally popular hero, disguised and enchanted prince, trickster-transformer, wily peasant. In this, advertising showed a continuity with *märchen*, ballad and fairytale, perpetuating a popular gospel of wealth with tales of sudden riches and the enduring happy life. Advertising did something that had to be done; it fed on and fostered cupidity and greed, but it also helped to contain and control their effects.

The point I am making concerns the potency of wealth and consumer opportunity in a world without effective social or moral restraints for the enjoyment of wealth. My idiosyncratic description of advertising is intended to stress this point; of course, advertising is neither the sufficient cause of consumer greed nor its effective regulator. Greed which is overwhelmingly vicious and immoral is a characteristic of our society. It is seen in the powerful commercial lobbies which prevent effective legislation to reduce lethal hazards in the asbestos industry. It is seen where companies ignore or exploit evil social and labour conditions, at home or in South Africa and the Soviet Union, in their commercial dealings. It is seen wherever profits and the rewards for labour are unjustly disparate. It appears where trade unionists, for the sake of a pay increase required neither for health nor livelihood, mount a strike endangering others' health and lives.

Whatever the motivations of the former British Labour minister who, in February 1982, supported legislation to limit trade union powers, his stated reason was impeccable: 'He would never have believed that trade unionists (in the Winter of 1978-'79) would refuse to sand roads at a risk to life or would prevent people from entering hospital or would refuse to bury the dead' (an extraordinary contradiction of the judaeo-christian works of mercy; see p.113). It was disturbing to hear a 'christian trade unionist', on the religious *Sunday* programme, explain his life-endangering strike action by saying: 'It's not the money; it's because they've gone back on their agreement.' The concept that the standard of living, still in England pitched at a level which is not modest but prosperous, should be at worst preserved and more usually improved, even if lives are

risked, may have roots in a misreading of christian stewardship, but has no foundation in Christianity. However, to drain
this paragraph of priggishness, the context for christian economic behaviour today is convinced envy and greed; this must
inevitably affect all living Christians.

Again to take a random illustration, there was an apotheosis
of the cult of wealth in the offshore-fund boom during the
decade from the early 1960s to the early 1970s. I.O.S.,
Gramco, REFA and the rest were the companies; Bernie Cornfeld was the archetypal star. He selected and trained his salesmen within the explicit discipline: 'Do you sincerely want to
be rich?' He challenged his trainees: 'Do you want to be used
by the capitalist system? Or do you want to use it?' A photo-
graph promoting the image of the ideal I.O.S. salesman shows
a trim, confident, well-suited young man, portable typewriter
on his knee, with ghastly leather baggage, desk-set, clock-
with-calendar, chess-board, portable roulette-wheel and Jet
Sell game around him: 'Let your success and confidence
show', reads the caption, 'Be the complete I.O.S. man.' The
customers, with their often fugitive money, were greedy to
preserve their old wealth or to enjoy wealth for the first time.
Greed motivated the salesmen and court surrounding Bernie
Cornfeld at I.O.S. and Rafael Navarro and Keith Barish at
Gramco. They were the apostles and uninhibited, cynical
exploiters of the re-invigorated capitalist system. When Lou
Ellenport, a relatively unsuccessful I.O.S. salesman, had accumulated $250,000, he told a younger salesman what he was
worth. ' "But is that enough", the young man asked sympathetically, "for people like us?" '[1] The style they flaunted lives
on as a popular ideal in magazines, television commercials,
films and best-sellers today. If this is society's model and
aspiration, my christian trade-unionist's response looks less
unreasonable. What I have just outlined is the context for a
contemporary Christian's work, decisions and elected actions.

The outline evidently does not contain the total reality. This
same, greedy, prosperous society has been made aware by
cheap travel, press, television and books that other societies
are poor, sick, homeless and starving. The West has yielded
notional assent to the idea that distant poverty is its concern;
real assent is still withheld. The Brandt Commission Report

reaffirmed the danger and injustice of the situation in which a large minority of the world's population can thrive, while sections of the majority ail, starve and suffer in enforced economic and political impotence: 'The poor and illiterate are usually and conveniently silent'. Despite the modern communications which daily force the alien, destitute, inconvenient fallers-among-thieves on our consciousness, Brandt's statement is valid: 'Few people in the North have any detailed conception of the extent of poverty in the Third World or of the forms it takes. Many hundreds of millions of people in the poorer countries are preoccupied solely with survival and elementary needs. ... In the North, ordinary men and women face genuine economic problems — uncertainty, inflation, the fear if not the reality of unemployment. But they rarely face anything resembling the total deprivation found in the South. Ordinary people in the South would not find it credible that the societies of the North regard themselves as anything other than wealthy'.[2] Three years later, the Commission reported further decline and a threat of worldwide anarchy, again urging the need for effective statutory and voluntary remedies.[3]

In Britain, we even find it difficult to acknowledge and cope with poverty within our own society. There are categories and areas of indigence which are instinctively disregarded. The mad; returned convicts, addicts and alcoholics; coloured people with social and employment problems; single-parent families and teenage mothers and the old are amongst the groups who particularly suffer. Because we can be simultaneously asked to attend to poverty in our family and neighbourhood, in our country and its existing and former dependencies, amongst nations which have commercial and cultural dealings with us and in countries we may scarcely be able to locate and certainly cannot describe, it is very easy to react to nothing at all, despite the fact that there is a real crisis of poverty even amongst our most immediate neighbours.

Where there are societies as affluent as ours the defining of 'poverty' is a problem. There are absolute, physical levels below which survival, let alone any self-preserving protest, may be impossible; there are also in every society limits to the relative degrees of poverty which can be tolerated. This implies that, across the world, there may be poverties in conflict, as the interests of the starving clash with the interests of those who fall below the minimum, current economic expectations of the prosperous society in which they live. Peter Townsend: 'Poverty, I will argue, is the lack of the resources necessary to permit participation in the activities, customs and diets commonly approved by society.'[4]

In still prosperous Britain, there are areas and groups within the community which are, by Townsend's definition, poor. Every society seems to contain a few who evade or are missed by almost every welfare provision — the tramps or travellers, helpless addicts, the simple and insane and the proud, immobile old are included in this category. There are those who live in areas where the houses are primitive and decrepit, where there is a high incidence of chronic unemployment and wages are low, or where there are other, sometimes established, degrading traditions and influences, who suffer real, imposed poverty, often perceived by the sufferers as irremediable.

Qualitative and quantitative methods must combine in the description of poverty; while there are objective criteria, subjective perception may be as important in the experience of such poverty. Thus, for Northern Ireland, one can detail the depressing statistics which place the province amongst the poorest regions in Europe, but the sum of facts does not equal the impact of deprivation there. In Northern Ireland, there is a higher incidence of infant deaths and of general sickness, average incomes are £13 less, more households fall below the official poverty line, costs for fuel and clothes and food are higher, the housing stock is more decayed, unemployment is worse, than anywhere else in the UK. 50% of children there are brought up in poverty. These are some of the quantifiable facts.[5] Peter Townsend: 'The summary of comparative statistics cannot convey the impact upon any observer of the poverty to be found in these areas. In my first visit to Belfast in 1968 ... I was struck not only by the evident poverty in Catholic and Protestant areas alike, but by scenes which seemed to belong more to the 1930s — of red-haired boys using scales on a cart drawn by an emaciated pony to sell coal by the pound, teenage girls in a second-hand clothing shop buying underslips and skirts, and some of the smallest 'joints' of meat in

butchers' windows that I have ever seen. Here, as in other
areas, working conditions, housing and the immediate
environment of the home were often harsh. ... by various of
our measures, the deprivation in these areas was undeniable.'[6]
The economic situation in Northern Ireland, in terms of statistics and of observation, has not improved; it has been disas-
trously exacerbated since 1968 by violence, with christian
sectarianism as an aggravating cause and a huge demoralisation of its communities as a result. Yet Northern Ireland is
relatively neglected by British charity; there is an instinct to
dissociate from the terrible, neighbourly reality of its crisis.

What I have just been saying touches a recent problem, in
charity and justice. The people of Northern Ireland, Glasgow,
South Wales, Toxteth, Brixton, Liskeard are physical neighbours; but few of the avoidable tragedies of indigence in these
areas compare with the tragedies in Somalia, India, El Salvador
and Indo-China. Implicit is a very recent problem of judgement, forced on us by television, which has made these remote
neighbours visible to us. My account may also undervalue the
response that has been made to distant needs. Moving back a
little, the first impact of the new wealth, of the mass consumer
market and of the revolution in communications coincided
and made possible other world-changing events: 'The emergence into prominence of the third world agencies during the
late fifties and early sixties was so conclusive and conspicuous
an event, they may easily be taken for granted. Historically, it
was the achievement of independence by the North African
countries, famine in the Congo and Biafra, the impact of World
Refugee Year, the wide and shocking distribution of hunger
photographs, which projected Oxfam, War on Want, Save the
Children Fund and other such agencies into the consciousness
and consciences of people in the prosperous capitalist west.'
The same shift in the distribution of wealth which inaugurated
a new age of marketing, advertising and consumption also
'made it possible for the third world agencies to conduct the
kind of mass appeals for funds through which they originally
prospered'.[7] What I stated in this article and is clear from the
evidence I have offered earlier (see p.115), is that this development of large-scale, generally disinterested, distant relief was a
revolution in philanthropy, and it was inaugurated by the

same societies I have just been criticizing for their greed. In terms of third-world needs, however, it has also been absolutely inadequate. Voluntary funds, at least on their historical scale, are unlikely ever to suffice, either in principle or in relation to the needs.

There has been no decline in philanthropy in the West; improved fundraising techniques have probably effected an increase. Such research as there is suggests that, at least in the anglo-saxon countries, most of the population give something to charity during any year, that the average amounts given are small, that a few give relatively generously, and that disasters can boost the normal levels. The scale of philanthropy is in some ways impressive: in the USA it is moving towards 50 billion dollars annually, compared with an estimated one thousand million pounds for the UK.[8] Within these figures, it is difficult to estimate the scale of general giving which has religion as a cause, and figures for members' contributions to their own churches are incomplete and uncertain, at least for the UK. The Churches of England and of Scotland publish regular figures, even if fear of the *quota* or other, internal ecclesiastical taxes on parish incomes may deflate the figures submitted. The roman catholic church, on the other hand, has tended to be reluctant, or possibly unable, to produce sound figures; there may be an unworldliness in the clergy which prevents them from keeping useful accounts.

Within the area of general charitable giving, specifically religious or religiously-inspired charitable organizations, christian and jewish, take some 41% of the total income of the 200 largest, grant-seeking agencies in the UK. Amongst the 200 largest jewish and christian grant-making trusts, those with an explicitly, religiously-inspired origin take some 27% of the total income.[9] Of course, the percentages would be higher if I included charities and trusts which originated and were nourished within christian and jewish cultures, but whose specific origins and purposes were less clear. Direct giving to religious purposes obviously makes up a very significant proportion of total giving in these same areas; almost 59% in the USA, and an improbably low 20% in the UK.[10] Beyond these threadbare fabrications of fact, it is reasonable to propose that regular church-goers are also regular donors, and that their weekly outreach makes their contributions proportionately significant within the total of giving. I think it may also be assumed that the bulk of Christians' charity is instinctive rather than reflective; that it marks conventional rather than revolutionary behaviour in relation to a Christian's wealth.

There is no observable consistency of behaviour amongst the specifically religiously inspired organizations which are active today. A number of groups have, for explicit religious reasons, remained commitedly sectarian. The reasons for this are very clear with the Salvation and Church Armies, and understandable with CAFOD, where the Director must be a loyal catholic, prepared to accept the authority of the catholic bishops who govern the organization. Others, like John Grooms, look for senior staff who are in sympathy with their religious outlook; this limits the intake less sectarianly. At the other pole are organizations as different as the R.S.P.C.A. and Dr. Barnardo's, which originated in an explicitly religious impulse, but which are today secular institutions.

There are also divergences amongst various groups of donors or philanthropists. The committed, religious philanthropist remains: in the UK, one could fairly randomly select the Laings, the Wates, the Breninkmeyers, the Sieffs and less familiar names like William Leech, Julian Hodge and Philip Henman. In an extraordinary manner, the late Ernest Bader also belongs within the tradition. He gave his successful company to its workers, endowing it with a tradition of corporate philanthropy. Ernest Bader's handling of wealth was based on highly developed views of christian stewardship and of the evils of capitalism; and his christian idealism created problems, very relevant to the discussion in this chapter. The Scott Bader Commonwealth was founded on christian principles, and the vision was shared, at least to an extent, by its members. Ted Nichols, Secretary of the Commonwealth: 'When we first drew up the Constitution the amount that we were going to give to charity was based on a percentage of the profit (c 5% to 10%) ... We'd been working at it for about two years when one of the Community Council chaps .. he said quietly at one meeting, ''Don't you think, Mr. Bader, that if we really believe in what we're doing we should give an equal amount to charities as we take in bonus (c 20%)? ... We did, and it's been that ever since" .' The principle, primarily inspired by Christianity, was not exclusively christian; it was encouraged by Robert Owen (p.101) and Gandhi. It therefore appealed to non-christians. Since the foundation was christian, its christian continuity was important to such men as the baptist minister Ron Munday, who discussed the issue with Bader, saying: 'If (the Commonwealth's) going to keep on as we hope, then the majority have got to be committed Christians otherwise it's going to go over'. Bader hoped to convert the uncommitted to his outlook, but: 'Today Ron Munday says sadly, "This has happened. There are very few committed Christians up there now. As I understand it, you can have a co-ownership on different foundations: some are on purely death duties, that's all; others are on humanitarian lines, others on social. But this was a unique one. It was on christian principles." '[11]

In this way, Scott Bader shares a problem with other companies whose christian and jewish founders built philanthropy into their corporate policies. With some, the religious interest and motivation have remained; but with others, sometimes because of mergers and takeovers, sometimes because of growth, sometimes because the religious motivation has simply vanished, there has been a secularisation of philanthropy, and a shift of focus intended to make philanthropy more purposefully serve the interests of employees, local communities, and corporate image and self-interest in their various forms. The executives responsible for philanthropy at Cummins Engine, Levi Strauss, I.B.M. and Marks and Spencer have brought planning and professionalism and secular idealism to their companies' practice of giving, so that it may be more effective and responsible. The Cadbury, Rowntree and Marble Arch trusts, all still committedly christian, have applied comparable, secular disciplines to their practice. Although the religious motive may have faded with some, I have argued that the effects of such professionalism can be regarded as benign: 'There are companies striving to improve the quality of their philanthropy, not merely to enhance image or internal communications, but also because they want to make a positive contribution to the world's welfare. It is as though they have entered a third age of maturity, having long ago lost their philanthropic founder and having sustained his benevolence almost unconsciously, they have suddenly embraced corporate altruism because they see it as valuable in itself rather than because it is a quaint and self-flattering custom'. Perhaps the extreme instance of this trend is the adoption of corporate philanthropy by Japanese companies. Without tradition or fiscal incentives to encourage them, they have developed policies for company giving because, from observation of major US corporations, this seems to be an honourable requirement in a company of international standing.[12] Such random behaviour may justify David Sheppard's comment: 'Firms which accept that they have moral responsibilities to the community face questions much nearer the heart of the enterprise than questions about how much money should go to charities in the area.'[13]

The majority of new charities registered in the UK year by year are now wholly secular by origin and character. In recent reports from the Charity Commissioners, the new registrations are predominantly characterized as being small, mutual-support, self-help groups. The difference between now and a hundred years ago is not that benevolent initiative is less frequent, but that the presence of clergy and churchgoing laity cannot be presupposed, and the form and intention of the new institutions is mainly a-religious.

Indeed, there is a more radical trend in thought and practice, which opposes the use of voluntary funds or agencies for the relief of need and the provision of welfare services in the community. Earlier we saw that revolutionary legislation in France, inspired by Rousseau, outlawed voluntary institutions and associations (see p.144). The theory behind this is clear and not unreasonable. It is implicit in the arguments produced by the department of economics at York that tax concessions to charities should be regulated by the welfare policies of government prevailing at any time, so that the creation of alternatives or challenges would lack positive, official, fiscal encouragement.[14] The argument further to the left has run like this: that a tory government's encouragement of an independent, voluntary sector can be seen for what it is 'when we consider the State in its context as part of the framework that maintains the exploitative economic and social relations of capitalism'. The State is the prime provider, in the funding of welfare agencies as in all else, especially since 'funding is fundamentally about negotiating the manner in which part of the community's wealth is committed.' Support from business and industry and the adoption of their methods are repugnant: 'Commerce and industry, conventionally organized, in ideology and in daily practice, have nothing to offer to a socialist analysis of the issues that concern us.' Further: 'Widespread appeal to individuals necessarily dilutes information and analysis to a lowest common denominator', and is equally repugnant.[15] The consequences of such thinking are seen where local authorities withold support from voluntary agencies; or where, as in Sweden, an initiative to use lonely old people to visit lonely hospital inmates is prevented because, if a welfare task should be done, it should use people properly paid and supported by public funds. It scarcely needs to be added that voluntary agencies of the kind I have described here are little known in the Soviet bloc, although volunteers are used for public works and in Poland voluntary relief has been organized for dissident prisoners. Before moving on, I must note that socialist objections to conventional charity can be consistent with christian idealism; if justice rather than benignity is the point, the object must be to find the most equitable, kind and effective channel to meet a community's needs, and that channel should frequently (or, it is argued by the left, invariably) be statutory rather than voluntary.

There are issues here which must be left till the conclusion of this chapter, but a few comments are necessary to preserve its perspective. Considering the scale of the worldwide needs of which we have now been made conscious, the potential, material impact of voluntary, charitable initiatives as now established is wholly inadequate, though definitely not irrelevant. In parts of the third world, there is a preference for voluntary above governmental agencies, because they are more efficient, more expert and politically neutral. It may be argued, whether from a radical christian or socialist viewpoint, that the concept and practice of charity obstruct a just response to needs. There is a christian ancestry for the statutory, socialist solution to problems of poverty, sickness, and general welfare needs. Antony Wedgwood Benn, in *The Inheritance of the Labour Movement*, places himself within the tradition of the Lollards, Diggers and Levellers (see p.54). He goes on to say, with some misunderstanding of his sources: 'But some Levellers went beyond the authority of the Bible and began to develop out of it ... a humanist buttress for their social philosophy without losing its moral force. They were, in a special sense, bridge-builders; constructing a bridge that connects Christian teaching with humanism and democratic socialism. ... That bridge is still there for anyone who wants to cross it in either direction. Some use it to go back to trace one of the paths leading to the Bible. Others like the modern pilgrims — for example the Catholic priests and others in Latin America — whose experience of modern world poverty, persecution and oppression has spurred them on to cross that same bridge from Christianity to social action and democratic socialism, have based it on their Christian faith and the inspiration of saintly Christians who have pioneered along the same path.'[16] This implies a gulf between 'Bible', 'Christianity' on one hand and 'humanism and democratic socialism' and 'social action' on the other, which would be alien to many of the ancient and modern pilgrims to whom he refers, but it very clearly declares the christian origins of some contemporary socialist thinking.

Charitable Activity and Fundraising Today

Leaving aside, for the time being, the principle of voluntary, charitable relief and initiative, I want to complete this survey by looking at two aspects of present-day charity: the quality of its works, and the ways these are funded. As far as possible, I shall avoid covering matters discussed by me in other books, but some repetition is necessary.[17]

Even on a secular basis, the responsibilities of any charity are severe, and increase in proportion to the urgency of the needs it serves. I have defined a 'charity' as 'an independent, not-for-profit organization existing solely to make an adequate and relevant response to need within the community'.[18] The only justification for the presence of a charity's board, volunteers, staff and supporters is such a response to well defined needs, and all four groups I have just mentioned — donors with the rest — have achievement of the ideal as their responsibility. This should strip their involvement of self-indulgence and complacency. Concentrating here on the donors, since this is the role of most members of christian congregations, we must agree that the responsibility at least requires a little, accurate information about the agency being supported, the quality of its service and the priority that should be given to the needs it serves. It cannot be assumed that an established charity with distinguished patrons will therefore be efficient, effective or relevant; and the fame and popularity of its cause will not in themselves guarantee that its work merits preference above the work of some less known, less well patronised, less popular agencies. The annual statistics show, for example, that cancer research is if anything over-supported, while causes involving mental health are relatively starved.[19] To take another example, there is a tendency for support to be given to agencies, ecumenical, catholic, or evangelical, purely on the basis of sectarian affiliations, but these are not the agencies which necessarily deliver the most effective or least harmful service in all parts of the third world where they operate. Yet, in this fairly new field of voluntary, distant relief, the evidence of the damage that can be done and of the mis-direction of aid is overwhelming. 'At its most conspicuously damaging, such charity may deliver senna into a dysentery epidemic, may dispatch ancient surplus drugs simply because they are available, may refuse to dig latrines where cholera threatens because that is not the charity committee's policy. It may even become sinister, where charity is used to achieve a foreign government's political ends, as perhaps with the Kurds after the Lice earthquake in 1975.'[20] During 1981, unrequired relief poured into the Gambia, at a time when there was terrible famine in Ethiopia. In 1982, churches gave a priority to Poland and the families of one group of lifeboat victims which their relative needs did not justify. Although the work of the International Disaster Institute, the International Institute for Environment and Development (which in New York in February 1980 secured a declaration from the seven principal aid agencies that they would conserve rather than deplete the natural resources of the third world) and greater co-operation between agencies signal improvements in this new art, donors themselves are responsible for the works they fund, and information is required to ensure that those works measure up to the standards imposed by christian love and by secular justice. Yet uptake by churches and congregations of the available sources of information is minimal.

The methods now used to raise funds across the range of charitable causes are as diverse as in former ages, and many of the techniques are the same: there are collecting boxes, door-to-door and street collections, jumble sales and other events, regular subscriptions, membership lists, letters and brochures, public meetings and the flaunting of patronage (see p.156ff.). However, improved marketing techniques, the impact of film, television, telephone and radio combined with a widespread increase in disposable income have increased the potency of the old fundraising methods, even if they have not altered their principles. Some church groups have, for their own, proper reasons, excluded certain techniques — lotteries, wine-and-cheese parties, bottle stalls and the like — from their fundraising arsenals. Most, in the UK, have weakened or ignored more significant methods, and it is on this I concentrate here.

As we have seen, powerful personal leadership in fundraising and the establishment of individual targets are familiar to jewish and christian communities. From the end of the last century, in the USA, these two elements were developed to form one of the most potent fundraising tools that has ever existed. I am not going to describe the history of this development, but the main features of the method must be outlined. In essence, it requires a series of steps. First, a case needs to be made out, describing the cause for the appeal and justifying its financial targets. Research will identify the possible donors, assess the gifts they could make and set individual targets for them. A few of the major potential donors identified by this research will be involved at an early stage, and those of them who make pace-setting gifts will provide leadership for the appeal. It is the donors themselves who do the real fundraising. A critical point is that the sizes of gifts committed by the leaders in such an appeal should be known to the individuals or groups whom they approach for funds. In any appeal, prospects are necessarily uncertain what gifts are expected of them, even after they have decided that they should give. They therefore need to be given targets; and if those leading the appeal have pitched their gifts below the target levels appropriate to them, there will be no reason why those who follow should do better. This is not theory. It is the technique which has generated at least £100m of new money in the UK since 1960, has raised billions of dollars for US institutions and has been a major factor in lifting the annual income of United Way (the principal community chest organization in the USA) beyond $1.68 billion annually.[21]

This technique therefore has a solid, secular basis, which of course does not mean it is inappropriate for churches and church groups. If the church of the Incarnation is by definition in the world, the opposite is true; and the principles I have been describing were indeed applied to church fundraising in the USA, Canada, Australia and New Zealand and after that, in the late 1950s, in the UK. During the 1960s, planned giving or stewardship campaigns became familiar here. Inevitably, there was resistance to the use of outside professionals, particularly if the company's management and style were perceived to be american. It was often felt that the consultants were too tough and insensitive for parish sensibilities, and there was particular resistance to what remains, in the secular field, a key to the method: a donor's personal, public statement of the gift he has made. In time, the churches appointed their own, often untrained and underqualified specialists, and many uncomfortable elements were dropped — for example, the real fundraising leadership which can be achieved only when there is awareness amongst prospective donors of what those first involved have given. Even allowing for the novelty of the early campaigns, the effect now is a fairly widespread under-achievement in church giving, if results today are compared with those of fifteen years ago.[22] While recently the Church of England has done a certain amount to improve its stewardship resources, attainment parish by parish is below the real potential. Direct giving to the Church of England is still a poor 77p weekly per member.

The emasculation both of secular technique and of community principle can be seen by comparing the Church of England's advice to its parish fundraising visitors with that given by George F. Regan, a priest of the Episcopal Church in Pasadena, USA. The anglican *Do's and Don'ts for Visitors* says to the lay people who will visit parish families during a campaign: 'If you think it will help *and if asked,* you can state the amount of your own pledge.' More weakly still, in *Explaining Christian Stewardship:* 'Even if they ask him (the visitor) for guidance ... he will do no more than tell them how he arrived at his own pledge.'[23] George Regan: 'The best way to do both stewardship and fund raising is through a personal witness in the home. With candor a layperson shares what's happening to him or her: '"This is what I'm giving; this is why I am giving it; this is what it has meant to my life"'. ... there was a time when you would put a pledge in an envelope and seal it ... Everything was secret. ... We have brought a new candor to our church which is absolutely refreshing. The vestry talks openly about income and the percentage of income the pledge represents. They talk about where they are in giving and where they hope to go — and why. The personal witness is crucially important, for it combines stewardship and fund raising by asking a person to join you at a certain level of pledging'.[24] The principle is not invalidated by english temperament or tradition; where it has been applied properly here, it has worked, and left the parishes stronger than they had been before.

This is not a fundraising guide, but I have a reason for pausing here which will appear presently. Poor fundraising technique and communications, which are also faults of many secular charities, are symptoms of something more serious than incompetence in the church, and their consequences are graver than financial under-achievement. It must therefore be said that some individual churches or groups of churches have taught and achieved far more. In the Diocese of Owerri, in Nigeria, the proportions of annual yield farmers are recommended to 'set apart for God' are: one in seven baskets of yams, two in twenty baskets of cassavas, two in twelve baskets of maize, two in twelve tins of oil, one in eight sheep or goats, two in twenty chickens, five in fifty eggs, one in ten bananas or plantains and four in twenty bundles of vegetables. A student is invited to set apart 2/- for each £1 of pocket money; the wine tapper to 'give 2d to the Lord each day he sells his calabash of wine'.[25] In the Church of Jesus Christ of Latter-Day Saints, the

Mormons, members make two voluntary but obligatory contributions: the tithe, which takes first priority and is paid either on the gross wage or salary or on the take home pay; and the fast offering, the proceeds of a family's abstinence from two meals on the first Sunday of each month. The tithe goes into the general church fund, the proceeds of the fast into the bishop's fund for the needs of the poor in the ward, and both are regarded as commandments of God. Beyond them, voluntary but strongly encouraged, are the 1% of income given for maintenance of buildings and of church programmes in the ward and once-off contributions towards capital projects, 30% of such costs usually being found by ward members. Finally, there may be contributions towards the costs of the 30,000 young missionaries sent out from Salt Lake City, and Mormons support non-mormon charitable causes. This enables them to maintain elaborate and careful welfare services, which they say are 'not a program, but the essence of the gospel. *It is the gospel in action.*' The giving and the caring are expressions of a Mormon's self-reliance, stewardship and love for his fellow man.[26]

I believe the main point is that regular giving is not the end but a means. It is only a preparation for what is important in a Christian's economic behaviour. Like the tithe in Maimonides' teaching (see p.27), planned giving and other forms of regular giving are preliminaries only. They are the habits which discipline a Christian's enjoyment of wealth and create the detachment and predisposition required if christian justice and charity are to permeate and govern a Christian's life. The kind of giving I have been discussing is neither the end nor the main process; it is one condition which makes the real process possible. The reasons why the churches have failed to create a radical, christian revolution in economic systems and behaviour is partly attributable to their failure in the kind of elementary re-education just considered, which is a precondition for such a revolution. The following paragraphs are intended to expose the patterns of giving I have first described, which may amount to no more than a distribution of spare pennies, as inadequate and jejune.

A Revolution in Thinking

It is a platitude that Marx has been more radical in his analysis, more influential and effective through his works than any christian teacher on wealth of our time. The capitalist system he analyzes was created by Christians in the name of Christianity, as an exercise of stewardship (see p.103). However, Marx presents capitalism as a stage of historical evolution which obeys scientific laws, by which capitalism generates its own contradiction. This is not a view which diminishes man: 'To be radical is to grasp things by the root. But for man the root is man himself.' Marx's teaching is centrally concerned with man's complete self-realization; but man operates within history: 'Men make their own history, but they do not make it just as they please; they do not make it under circumstances chosen by themselves, but under circumstances directly encountered, given and transmitted from the past. The tradition of all the dead generations weighs like a nightmare on the brain of the living.'[27]

The effects of the capitalist system on man are central to Marx's discussion of the nature of capitalist wealth and production. In the *Grundrisse,* he presents, on the one hand, 'the exchange originally found in production — which is an exchange not of exchange values but of activities determined by communal needs and communal aims — (which) would from the start imply the participation of individuals in the collective world of products. ... Instead of a division of labour necessarily engendered by the exchange of values, there is an organization of labour, which has as its consequence the participation of the individual in collective consumption. ... If we suppose communal production, the determination of time remains, of course, essential. The less time society requires in order to produce wheat, cattle, etc., the more time it gains for other forms of production, material or intellectual. As with a single individual, the universality of its development, its enjoyment and its activity depend on saving time.' What happens in capitalist societies is that they 'turn individual labour directly into money': 'While the worker sells his labour to the capitalists, he retains a right only to the price of labour, not to the product of his labour, nor to the value that labour had added to the product.' Thus labour 'becomes productive only for capital ... work for wages, as such, presupposes the existence of capital, so that considered from this aspect, it, too, is part of this transubstantiation; this being the necessary process in which its own forces are made alien to the worker'.[28] What is in excess of the wage, labour's surplus production, is appropriated by capital.

This was the general pattern fostered by godly, industrious, enterprising capitalists at home and in the colonies. Marx writes: 'In *The Times* of November 1857 there appeared a delightful yell of rage from a West Indian planter. With great moral indignation this advocate, in support of his plea for the re-establishment of Negro slavery, described how the Quashees [the free negroes of Jamaica] were content to produce what was strictly necessary for their own consumption, and looked upon laziness itself ("indulgence and idleness") as the real luxury article alongside this "use value." ... Capital, as capital, had no existence in opposition to them, because objectified wealth exists only through either direct forced labour and slavery, or intermediary forced labour, that is, wage-earning labour.'[29]

The alienation of labour from its own product is crucial to the argument. Labour is not an incidental demand nor, as Adam Smith suggests, a mere curse on man; it is through labour that he realizes himself and relates to society. 'It seems to be far from A. Smith's thought that the individual ... might ... require a normal portion of work, and of cessation from rest. It is true that the quantity of labour to be provided seems to be conditioned by external circumstances, by the purpose to be achieved, and the obstacles to its achievement that have to be overcome by labour. But neither does it occur to A. Smith that the overcoming of such obstacles may itself constitute an exercise in liberty, and that these external purposes lose their character of mere natural necessities and are established as purposes which the individual himself fixes. The result is the self-realization and objectification of the subject, therefore real freedom, whose activity is precisely labour.'[30] This is paralleled in *Das Kapital:* labour 'is the everlasting Nature imposed condition of human existence, and therefore is independent of every social phase of that existence, or rather, is common to every such phase'.[31]

It is for these reasons a catastrophe demanding remedy when value takes on 'independent and autonomous existence ... as against living labour power', when 'the objective, self-centred indifference, the alien nature of objective conditions of labour as against living labour power' reach a point in the confrontation of classes where 'these conditions face the worker, as a person, in the person of the capitalist', and the content of work becomes alien to the worker himself. In this passage, Marx 'makes it clear how the objective world of wealth progressively extends through labour itself as a force alien to it, and achieves an ever wider and fuller existence, so that relatively, in relation to the values created or the real conditions of the creation of value, the indigent subjective world of living labour power forms an ever more glaring contrast'.[32]

It is self-realizing labour which fulfils the labourer; free competition within the capitalist system, far from being 'the final development of human liberty', is its contradiction. Wealth in our society depends on the 'theft of others' labour time'. Yet it is the nature of a capitalist society progressively to intensify these conditions of alienation, and Marx anticipated that mechanisation in factories would accelerate and exacerbate the process. The capitalist system would generate its own destruction. Marx writes: 'When the worker recognizes the products as being his own and condemns the separation of the conditions of his realization as an intolerable imposition, it will be an enormous progress in consciousness, itself the product of the method of production based on capital, and a death-knell of capital in the same way that once the slaves became aware that they were persons ...'; And: 'Thus the last form of enslavement taken on by human activity — wage-labour on one side and capital on the other — is thus sloughed off and this process is in itself the result of the capitalist mode of production.'[33]

Marx envisaged a society in which machines would be 'agents of social production' and would become 'the property of associated workers'.[34] He despised current views on ownership: 'Private property has made us so stupid and partial that an object is *ours* when we have it, when it exists for us as capital or when it is directly eaten, drunk, worn, inhabited, etc., in short *utilized* in some way ...'. The route ahead he summarized 'in the single sentence: Abolition of private property'. Consequently, Ernst Fischer writes: 'Individual ownership of objects of luxury, of clothing, housing, furnishings, of articles of comfort rendered possible by technology, can be secured on the basis of co-operation and common ownership of the land and of the means of production created by labour itself'. Half-measures, as promoted by socialist bourgeois 'economists, philanthropists, humanitarians, improvers of the conditions of the working class, organizers of charity, members of societies for the prevention of cruelty to animals, temperance fanatics, hole-and-corner reformers of every imaginable kind' are condemned in *The Communist Manifesto* because they 'want all the advantages of modern social conditions without the struggles and dangers necessarily resulting therefrom. They desire the existing state of society minus its revolutionary and disintegrating elements. They wish for a bourgeoisie without a proletariat.' They require 'that the proletariat should remain within the bounds of existing society, but should cast away all its hateful ideas concerning the bourgeoisie.' I must repeat, however, that Marx's concern is for the fulfilment of the whole man, not for the creation of a differently stunting, frustrating, divided structure for society.[35]

It may seem perverse that I present this nineteenth-century teaching in a twentieth-century context, but it is only now that Marx is achieving adequate understanding and impact amongst christian thinkers. The reasons for this are mixed. The churches' sympathies, loyalties, relationships were very much with the established, capitalist order, even when they criticized its excesses and called for adjustment and superficial reforms. Marx characterized religion as a form of alienation, and Marxism was from the beginning atheistic and usually hostile to the churches. In any case, Marxism tended from an early stage to take on ruthless, violent, coercive forms, cruder than Marx in their analyses, threatening and ultimately triumphant in their manifestations. It is not surprising that churchmen initially reacted with alarm and total rejection. In any case, such a fundamental work as the *Grundrisse* was not published in Moscow until 1939, and became available in the West only in 1953; the first English translation was published in 1973. For these reasons (after a period roughly equivalent to that separating the Crucifixion from the *Didache*) Marx should be given current authority.

Certainly, Pope Leo XIII's reaction to communist socialism in *Rerum Novarum* (1891) was one of incomprehension and hostility: 'To remedy these wrongs the Socialists, working on the poor man's envy of the rich, are striving to do away with private property, and contend that individual possessions should become the common property of all, to be administered by the State or by municipal bodies.' This would be 'emphatically unjust, for they would rob the lawful possessor, distort the functions of the State, and create utter confusion in the community.' The pope concedes 'that it is only by the labour of working-men that States grow rich', but maintains the principle: 'Every man has by nature the right to possess property as his own', and, with Locke, sees 'the duty of safeguarding private property by legal enactment and protection' as a prime responsibility of the State. 'The law ... should favour ownership, and its policy should be to induce as many as possible of the people to become owners.' Since 'Capital cannot do without Labour, nor Labour without Capital', the interests of both are to be preserved. For labour, this means that there is an entitlement to a living wage: 'Each one has a natural right to procure what is required in order to live; and the poor can procure that in no other way than by what they can earn through their work'. 'Wages ought not to be insufficient to support a frugal well-behaved wage-earner', and (in the spirit of Samuel Smiles) should be sufficient to allow the worker 'to put by some little savings and thus secure a modest source of income'. Workers also have a right to form Unions and Associations, to protect their common interests and serve their mutual needs. In general, the encyclical promotes the preservation of the existing social order, and sees charity as the method for meeting the needs of those who fall into poverty. It is traditional, in an eighteenth and nineteenth century sense (cf. p.85), even in its teaching that 'Christian morality, when adequately and completely practised, leads of itself to temporal prosperity.'[36] If *Rerum Novarum* is essentially an argument for the preservation of existing patterns of property ownership and capitalism, it was progressive (and unselfconsciously subversive of the old order it favoured) in its advocacy of free if controlled associations of labour.

Forty years on, in *Quadragesimo Anno* (1931), Pius XI reaffirmed most of his predecessor's principles. He even praises *Rerum Novarum* for its ready acceptability to the capitalist states in their labour legislation following the 1914-1918 war. He condemns religious socialism and christian socialism as contradictions in terms, because socialism 'conceives human society in a way utterly alien to Christian truth'. He too praises the existing social order, looking to the situation in which the workers will 'cease to feel discontent at the position assigned to them by divine Providence in human society; they will become proud of it, well aware that they are working usefully and honourably for the common good, each according to his office and function ...'; meanwhile, the 'many young men, destined soon by reason of their talents or their wealth to hold distinguished places in the foremost ranks of society, are studying social problems with growing earnestness. These youths encourage the fairest hopes that they will devote themselves wholly to social reconstruction.' There is some balance in the statement of property rights: 'On the one hand, if the social and public aspect of ownership be denied or minimized, one falls into "individualism", as it is called, or at least comes near to it; on the other hand, the rejection or dimunition of its private and individual character necessarily leads to "collectivism" or to something approaching it.' The pope asserts that it is 'entirely false to ascribe the results of their combined efforts to either capital or labour alone; and it is flagrantly unjust that either should deny the efficacy of the other, and claim all the product'; but he goes on to condemn 'those of the proletariat who demand for themselves all the fruits of production, as being the work of their hands'. He seeks a society inspired by social charity, and one in which rights to private property are preserved but not abused. Whatever the situation, 'a wide field will always remain open for charity', although the pope condemns societies organized 'as though it were the task of charity to make amends for the open violation of justice, a violation not merely tolerated, but sometimes even ratified, by the legislators'.[37]

I have selected these papal texts to illustrate an established, christian reaction to socialism because they form a continuity, and have extended to today. What is remarkable in the two encyclicals I have quoted is that they are prepared to palliate the capitalist and private property systems, but not intentionally and radically to question whether they are still humanly and christianly right or expedient. They treat Marx's analysis, if not marxists and marxisms, frivolously. They even appear to spurn the christian radicalism which has its origins in the gospel and has been transmitted in a continuous line from Hermas, Chrysostom and Pelagius through Langland and the Lollards and the seventeenth century puritans to the present day. Perhaps, at this point, Richard Niebuhr can help us keep focus: 'Not Tertullian, but Origen, Clement of Alexandria, Ambrose, and Augustine initiated the reformation of Roman culture. Not Benedict, but Francis, Dominic and Bernard of Clairvaux accomplished the reform of medieval society often credited to Benedict. Not George Fox, but William Penn and John Woolman, changed social institutions in England and America. And in every case the followers did not so much compromise the teachings of the radicals as follow another inspiration than the one deriving from an exclusive loyalty to an exclusive Christ.

'Yet the radically Christian answer to the problem of culture needed to be given in the past, and doubtless needs to be given now.'[38]

Niebuhr reaffirms the role of the extreme christian views which create fruitful, christian tensions. With this in mind, it is interesting to look at John Paul II's *Laborem Exercens* (1981), which marked the fiftieth anniversary of *Rerum Novarum*.

In *Laborem Exercens,* as in the texts from Marx considered above, man has primacy and man is central to the pope's theme: progress 'must be made through man and for man and it must produce its fruit in man'. Man has primacy over things and he is the proper subject of work. It is 'through work man *not only transforms nature,* adapting it to his own needs, but he also *achieves fulfilment* as a human being and indeed, in a sense, becomes "more a human being" '. There is 'a reversal of the order laid down from the beginning by the words of the Book of Genesis' whenever *'man is treated as an instrument of production,* whereas he ... ought to be treated as the effective subject of work and its true maker and creator.' 'At the beginning of man's work is the mystery of creation.' Having considered the necessary, class opposition of labour to capital postulated by Marx and Engels, the encyclical goes on: 'A labour system can be right, in the sense of being in conformity with the very essence of the issue, and in the sense of being intrinsically true and morally legitimate, if in its very basis *it overcomes the opposition between labour and capital* through an effort at being shaped in accordance with the principle put forward above: the principle of the substantial and real priority of labour, of the subjectivity of human labour and its effective participation in the whole production process, independently of the nature of the services provided by the worker.' The means of production may not be *possessed against labour* or *for possession's sake* 'because the only legitimate title to their possession — whether in the form of private ownership or in the form of public or collective ownership — is *that they should serve labour'*. This leads to acknowledgement of the legitimacy of *'proposals* for *joint ownership of the means of work'* or at least 'demands various adaptations in the sphere of the right to ownership of the means of production'. This requires revision of 'rigid' capitalism, but does not sanction *'a priori elimination of private ownership of the means of production.'* 'Merely converting the means of production into State property in the collectivist system is by no means equivalent to "socializing" that property.' As far as the Unions are concerned, their 'demands cannot be turned into a kind of *group or class "egoism"*, although they can and should also aim at converting — with a view to the common good of the whole of society — everything defective in the system of ownership of the means of production or in the way these are managed', presumably in socialist or capitalist states. Finally, in place of the charity so conspicuously praised as a remedy for ills in *Rerum Novarum* and *Quadragesimo Anno,* John Paul II puts the claim to unemployment benefits on the same basis as the right to proper remuneration of work: *'the principle of the common use of goods.'*[39]

Here there is continuity with the earlier encyclicals, but also remarkable change. There appears to be some assimilation of Marx's thinking. There is a different emphasis on the role of man as worker, there is explicit acknowledgement that man fulfils himself through work, there is at least an implicit challenge to established views of production, there is a suggestion that the distribution of the products of labour should be guided by the ancient but difficult principle that goods should be common to all. This principle has been made more difficult in its application since the two earlier encyclicals appeared, as John Paul points out: 'If one studies the development of the question of social justice, one cannot fail to note that, whereas during the period between *Rerum Novarum* and Pius XI's *Quadragesimo Anno* the church's teaching concentrates mainly on the just solution of the ''labour question'' within individual nations, in the next period the church's teaching widens its horizon to take in the whole world. The disproportionate distribution of wealth and poverty and the existence of some countries and continents that are developed and of others that are not call for a levelling out and for a search for ways to ensure just development for all.'[40] Having said all this, it is unclear how the pope would have his comparatively radical doctrines applied.

Concentration on the practice of an equitable capitalism rather than a fundamental questioning of the historical development and contemporary character of wealth has not been a feature only of the catholic church leadership. Archbishop William Temple was one of the first senior anglican bishops to speak out radically on social issues, although in his *Christianity and Social Order* (1941) he cautioned: 'The Church is committed to the everlasting Gospel and to the Creeds which formulate it; it must never commit itself to an ephemeral programme of detailed action.' He wrote: 'The method of the Church's impact upon Society at large should be two-fold. The Church must announce Christian principles and point out where the existing social order at any time is in conflict with them. It must then pass on to Christian citizens, acting in their civic capacity, the task of reshaping the existing order in closer conformity to the principles.' He reflected sympathetically on economic and industrial man: 'They ceased to ask what was the purpose of this vast mass of production. It tended to be an end in itself. It was no longer subordinated to the general scheme of a complete human life in which it should be a part.' He reaffirmed the Foundations of Peace formula laid down by the four religious leaders in *The Times* of December 21st 1940: 'The resources of the earth should be used as God's gifts to the whole human race, and used with due consideration for the needs of the present and future generations'; he summed up his policy in a phrase: *'The aim of a Christian social order is the fullest possible development of individual personality in the widest and deepest possible fellowship.'* He detailed six-fold objectives towards attainment of this policy. *Christianity and Social Order* advocates a considerable degree of state intervention and the nationalization of urban land, and admits that a labourer's wages will usually be too little 'to bring up a large family in proper decency and comfort'.[41] In spite of all this, Archbishop Temple leaves the foundations of capitalism and the system of private ownership intact. Like Jeremy Taylor (see p.100) he invokes standards of christian justice to modify the existing order rather than to overthrow it.

Christian Radicalism

Since 1941, there have been more radical, christian voices. Ivan Illich, who worked as a priest with irish and puerto rican poor in New York during the early nineteen-fifties, has called for 'convivial reconstruction'. By 'conviviality' he designates 'the opposite of industrial productivity. I intend it to mean autonomous and creative intercourse among persons, and the intercourse of persons with their environment ...'. He argues: 'The transition to socialism cannot be effected without an inversion of our present institutions and the substitution of convivial for industrial tools.' People need new tools to work with rather than tools that 'work for them'.[42] This harmonizes with the analysis by Fritz Schumacher and George McRobie of 'the damage done to men and women and their families by the growth of large-scale industries and the lifestyles they impose on society ...'.[43] Schumacher saw damaging intellectual confusion in the way 'we preach the virtues of hard work and restraint while painting utopian pictures of unlimited consumption without either work or restraint. We complain when an appeal for greater effort meets with the ungracious reply: "I couldn't care less", while promoting dreams about automation to do away with work, and about the computer relieving men from the burden of using their brains.' He approved of the private property of the working proprietor as 'something natural and healthy', but not of 'the private property of the passive owner who lives parasitically on the work of others'. His most famous concern was with the growth of manufacturing enterprise, which too often reaches a scale at which 'the connection between ownership and work ... becomes attenuated'.[44] This has implications for the kinds of technology appropriate for people generally, and especially for the poor in the third world. On September 3rd 1977, the day before he died, Fritz Schumacher said in a lecture that the technology required for rural India or Latin America needed to 'be really much more intelligent, scientific if you like, than the very low level of technology employed there, which kept them very poor. But it should be very, very much simpler, very much cheaper, very much easier to maintain, than the highly sophisticated technology of the modern West. In other words it would be an *intermediate technology,* somewhere in between.'[45]

Both Illich and Schumacher demand revolutions in attitudes, prejudices, practices relating to work and in the form of property ownership, and both assume that the revolution is attainable. 'We call you to join man's race to maturity, to work with us in inventing the future', writes Illich;[46] Schumacher: '... we are quite competent enough to produce sufficient supplies of necessities so that no one need live in misery. Above all, we shall then see that the economic problem ... has been solved already: we know how to provide enough, and do not require any violent, inhuman, aggressive technologies to do so.'[47] As evidence that change can be attained, George McRobie lists experiments in alternative forms of community living in the UK and USA, estimating that some 3 million people have joined 'the growing movement towards voluntary simplicity in the USA. ... deliberately going for a low-consumption, more socially co-operative, life style'.[48] Here also there is a mixture of christian, religious and secular initiatives, with the latter in the majority. John V. Taylor, Bishop of Winchester, sees 'the growth of specifically christian cells and communes' as highly significant 'for anyone concerned about the relevance of the church to the human condition in our day. Moreover, because the christian minority in this movement has its roots in the long tradition of Western monasticism, it has some well proved insights to contribute to strengthen the movement as a whole.' He cites Taize, the Iona community and L'Arche among his list of examples.[49]

Bishop Taylor's argument for a change of lifestyle seems timid, however, when compared with some bolder, contemporary, christian voices. Liberation theology has been described as '... probably the first non-imitative theology to have sprung from the Third World nations; indeed, the first creative theological thought to have arisen outside of Europe or North America since the earliest years of the Church'.[50] It bases itself firmly on practical issues of social and economic justice, assimilating Marx to the Bible. Liberation Theology declares, according to Jose Miranda, that 'the Gospel is war to the death against the motive of acquisition.'[51] Positively, in the words of Gustavo Gutierrez, it is concerned with 'the struggle to construct a just and fraternal society, where people can live with dignity and be the agents of their own destiny'. He develops the theme: 'Man is saved if he opens himself to God and to others', to his neighbour; but relationship with the neighbour is not passive. 'The neighbour was the Samaritan who *approached* the wounded man and *made him his neighbour.* The neighbour, as has been said, is not he whom I find in my path, but rather he in whose path I place myself, he whom I approach and actively seek.' 'A spirituality of liberation will center on a *conversion* to the neighbour, the oppressed person, the exploited social class, the despised race, the dominated country. Our conversion to the Lord implies this conversion to the neighbour.'[52] Miranda also argues for conversion, and gives a special role in this process to Marx, whose theses must be studied, he says, with great dedication: 'But institutions have always demonstrated a conspicuous inability to repent, to recognize errors and injustices and remedy them. Thus we must realize that it is not enough merely to take seriously today the Marx whom we scorned yesterday ... If we are to abandon yesterday's position, we must also revise the whole system of ideas and values which made such a position necessary. Real conversion is needed, not lukewarm concealment of changes which are made underhandedly.'[53]

The argument is radical and revolutionary. Gutierrez: 'Attempts to bring about changes within the existing order have proven futile. ... Only a radical break from the status quo, that is, a profound transformation of the private property system, access to power of the exploited classes, and a social revolution that would break this dependence would allow for the change to a new society, a socialist society — or at least allow that such a society might be possible.' The concern, in a Christianity of and for the poor, must be for the deprived, at home and, possibly more critically, in the third world. Gutierrez again: 'Universal love comes down from the level of abstractions and becomes concrete and effective by becoming incarnate in the struggle for the liberation of the oppressed. It is a question of loving all people, not in some vague, general way, but rather in the exploited person, in the concrete person who is struggling to live humanly. ... our love is not authentic if it does not take the path of class solidarity and social struggle. To participate in class struggle not only is not opposed to universal love; this commitment is today the necessary and inescapable means of making this love concrete. For this participation is what leads to a classless society without owners and dispossessed, without oppressors and oppressed. In dialectical thinking, reconciliation is the overcoming of conflict. The commission of paschal joy passes through confrontation and the cross.'[54]

It will not be surprising that Liberation Theology returns very positively to hebrew concepts of *justice* as against our traditional views of benevolence or charity: '*Mishpat* consists in doing justice to the poor, neither more nor less' (see p.126). Miranda very bluntly expresses this fundamental view: 'The fact that differentiating wealth is unacquirable without violence and spoliation is presupposed by the Bible in its pointed anathemas against the rich; therefore almsgiving is nothing more than restitution of what has been stolen, and thus the Bible calls it justice. ... We have said that when the Bible calls 'justice' what Western culture calls 'almsgiving', it is because the private ownership which differentiates the rich from the poor is considered unacquirable without violence and spoliation; the Fathers of the Church also understood this very clearly'.[55]

Gutierrez makes a point to which I shall return presently: 'Once the autonomy of the world is asserted, the layman acquires a proper function which has not been recognized as his before.' In a situation in which 'the Church must allow itself to be inhabited and evangelized by the world' — a situation which 'puts us on the track of a new way of conceiving the relationship between the historical church and the world' and is wholly consistent with my argument on the present meaning of the Incarnation — this should prepare Christians to be selectively receptive, not only to Marx, but to other, pertinent secular teaching.[56]

Miranda goes further in his approximation of Marx to the Bible, and affirms the brotherhood of Marx with St. Paul.[57] There are, as Andrew Kirk argues, good reasons for giving Marx a place in the pre-understanding of biblical interpretation: at least 'Marxism used as an ideological 'suspicion' has a positive role to play in helping to overcome the identification between empirical Christianity and biblical faith; thus helping to deter the former from being able to suppress the subversive nature of the latter.'[58] Miranda is far bolder than this. With the Jesuit Pierre Bigo, he assents to Marx's analysis, for example of the wage system: 'The antagonism of individuals ... is transformed by the salary system into an antagonism of class, which rests on a fundamental inequality among men and on a disguised form of slavery. The confiscation of surplus value is the direct consequence of this state of affairs. Capitalism is at the same time the elimination of men's freedom, of some men's freedom with respect to others, and of their equality. It means that man is no longer a man for man.' Miranda also argues that 'in both Marx and the Bible the possibility of ... definitive liberation is absolutely the basis of all the thinking. ... we believe that man can cease being selfish and merciless and self-serving and can find his greatest fulness in loving his neighbour. ... If the West calls Marx utopian, it must first give up its pretence and call the Gospel utopian. ... There is nothing in strict exegesis which authorizes us to postpone (the elimination of acquisitiveness) to another world or another life. The ridiculing of hope which is made by qualifying it as "utopian" constitutes, in the first place, ignorance of reality and history and, in the second place, a mordic defense of the status quo, ideological in the strongest sense of the word.'[59] Through this very marxist application of dialectical, materialist historical theory and of 'ideology' in its negative, technical sense (contrast Kirk's usage, above), Miranda argues the case for the perfectability of temporal, human society.

This is a concept which I find wholly unacceptable; to me, it is impossible to conceive of any human society, regime or institution which would not be necessarily limited, flawed and almost certainly self-corrupting. My criticism is concerned only with the idea that the *eschaton* may be in this world, not with the argument for a christian radicalism which admits the force of Marx's analysis. I would extend Jurgen Moltmann's statement: 'There will be no *Christian*, that is, no *liberating theology* without the life-giving memory of the suffering of God on the cross'[60] to an affirmation of the continuing, hopeful reality of that suffering in the life and experience of the churches and their members, and in the institutions and societies they create.

It is worth noting Nicholas Lash's comment, in his theologians's reflections on the thought of Karl Marx: 'There is no doubt ... but that Christianity is ... compatible with commitment to revolutionary struggle. For a number of reasons, however, christian participation in that struggle will, or should be, ambiguous. In the first place, the christian community will, or should, always include elements which insist on "standing aside" from the struggle to bear witness both to the partial and provisional nature of all historically realizable transformations of social reality, and to the antithetical relationship between divine power and human force. In the second place, christian participation should include the reminder ... that no political movement is lacking in "particular interest", that the use of force is always ambiguous and infected with impurity ... and that not all means are appropriate in pursuit of even the most admirable of ends.'[61]

Before reaching the conclusions to this study, I cite one more, contemporary authority, who also insists on Christ's revolutionary role. Karl Barth asserts: 'Jesus was not in any sense a reformer championing new orders against the old ones'; his 'passive conservatism' 'was certainly not an invitation to maintain and augment our financial possessions as cleverly as possible — a process which later came to be regarded almost as a specific Christian virtue in certain parts of the Calvinist world — but it is obviously not a summons to socialism'. But Barth argues that 'the crisis which broke on all human order in the man Jesus' is both 'radical and comprehensive.' The new cloth rends the old, the new wine bursts the old bottles: 'It was the new thing ... of the royal man Jesus penetrating to the very foundations of economic life in defiance of every reasonable and to that extent honourable objection.' He goes on: 'In so far as [the final and supreme menace of this royal man] has been present as such for the world ... the confrontation of the old order with the incommensurable factor of the new has been inescapable in this respect too. From the very outset and continually — cost what it may — the presence of this man has meant always that the world must wrestle with this incommensurable factor.

'In all these dimensions the world is concretely violated by God Himself in the fact that the man Jesus came into it and is now within it'; and 'We do not really know Jesus ... if we do not know him as this poor man, as this ... partisan of the poor, and finally as this revolutionary.'[62]

As one would expect, the realization of liberation theology's principles has caused conflict in the churches. From the description I have just given, the roots of the following declaration by Father Pedro Arrupe, retiring General of the jesuit order, are clear. Speaking in Bangkok in August 1981, he said to some fellow Jesuits there: 'Should we help spiritually the guerillas in Latin America? No? Well, I cannot say no. Perhaps I have said it, but they are men, souls suffering.

'If you have a wounded person, even if he were a guerilla, you have to help him. That is the meaning of being a Good Samaritan. Is that political? People say so. No.

'Now I am a priest. I am helping this poor man here. I don't care if he were a guerilla, a religious or a non-Catholic. He is a poor man. He is a poor man who is suffering'.[63]

For such attitudes, and because of their positive promotion of political, even revolutionary, measures to secure justice for the people in El Salvador and elsewhere in Latin America, the pope disgraced Father Arrupe and reprimanded the jesuit order. On 27th February 1982, he warned the order against 'progressivism' — 'the identification of the Church with a political struggle to improve the lot of the poor and oppressed by pulling down the mighty from their seats, even when that struggle involves violence and is carried out under the leadership of atheists'; and 'integralism — 'which emphasizes the authority of the Church and the necessity of accepting its traditional teaching as a seamless whole, including its identification in many Christian or nominally Christian countries with the political status quo — from which it is a short step to justifying the violence of the oppressor who seeks to defend the status quo against the challenge of the oppressed'.[64] At this point, I only want to comment that the pope's rebuke was directed to the Jesuits *as priests.* None the less, it touches an issue which can only grow in importance in the coming years.

Working for Change

In one sense, the churches are, accidentally if not necessarily, at an apparent disadvantage today. For the most part, they must operate in societies at best nominally christian and in almost all cases effectively pagan; yet the churches are culturally, socially and actively in sympathy with the dominant establishments in these societies, and in many cases form part of their establishments. The time is by no means past when to be a social or political non-conformist is to be imputed as probably godless. In another sense, though, the churches have a freedom and opportunity which they have scarcely enjoyed in the West since the reign of Constantine, when they began to be drawn into the working structures of the state (see p.66). As active Christians become a minority in societies with whose morals, practice and even laws they may need to be in conflict, there is an opportunity for the churches and their members to rediscover their christian independence and integrity. Certainly, at present, the remarkable thing about most Christians' lives is that they are so conformist; that, by implication, they are based, not on the gospel of Christ, but on scriptures of acquisition and wealth. If Christianity is to have its desperately-required impact on society, it must be after the restoration or reformation of its ideals.

As in the primitive churches, Christians must be open to the philosophy, political theory and economic analysis of the time; we have seen how openness to Marx can reinforce articulation of the christian view that, in justice, there should be changes in patterns of work and in the distribution of resources and in the balance of wealth between nations. However, the teachings that emerge and the action they engender must be authentic expressions of Christ's living presence, not a compromise between modern radicalism and christian conservatism. In saying this, two points of faith and hope are implied: that a vividly, specifically christian teaching can emerge, relevant and applicable to our present situation; and that, as in the time of the early church, Christianity can rediscover the force, vitality and relevance to have a revolutionary impact on events. At present, the choice for Christians is limited to capitalism in its various forms, to atheistic communism (whose embodiments rapidly became at least as unjust and evil as those of capitalism) or to withdrawal from society, an option with sound precedents in Egypt, Vivarium, Monte Cassino and New England, but which cannot be the necessary choice for most Christians. A viable, genuinely christian choice is lacking.

There are many problems with urging Christians through their churches to work towards a radical, christian programme for change. I have touched on one difficulty: the identification of the churches with conservative policies and with the established order of society. Further, when church leaders have uttered pleas for economic reform, as in the Bishop of Winchester's *Enough is Enough,* they have most frequently been marked by a failure to understand the nature or dynamic of the economic systems they seek to change, to grasp the real values, priorities and pressures in the lives of working people, or to express themselves in a way that might inspire appropriate action. The leaders of the churches have not been effective leaders of church members in their economic lives.

Probably, they should not be; as the pope, perhaps, implied in his strictures on the Jesuits, the pastoral role of the modern clergy may preclude effective thought and action in the economic sphere, and in any case our clergy in the West seldom have the experience, temperament or aptitude to provide the confident leadership required. Indeed, there is a paradox: serving within a church as institution, the clergy are committed to a body necessarily self-corrupting; seeking to reform it, they will be deemed to have placed themselves heretically outside it. Although a revolutionary lead must be given, I would be amazed to see it given by clergy here. But who else is paying attention? what informed lay-people are prepared to think radically, christianly, constructively, and to act on their conclusions?

There is another problem, by no means peculiar to churches and clergy. Christians must inhabit the real, historical world, not some idealistic and safe hinterland between baptism and eternity; they must therefore work on or through its real structures, or replace them, to achieve their christian aims. It is here that conventional 'charity' may get in the way of christian attainment. Christians are concerned with providing realistic help and support for the most needy and indigent in society; this is not a free option, but a qualifying requirement for all those who declare themselves Christians; therefore christian preoccupation should not be with gratuitous favours and benevolent doles, however generous, but with justice, with the aptest and most comprehensive possible remedies. This must usually require statutory, institutional intervention, involving public officials and bureaucracies. It is also likely to demand the transformation of the official institutions and bureaucracies and of the individuals within them. Christian charity demands this, wherever the spontaneous 'charity' of Christians can produce only a palliative, a salving of conscience or of social expectation, but no just or adequate response. It is here that 'charity' can prevent the realization of christian charity, because it is easier to be benevolent than to achieve justice. However, if human institutions and bureaucracies are involved, their inadequacy, self-contradiction and corruption must be presupposed, or they will grow to exacerbate the ills for which they were the intended remedies. The association of any institution with the churches does not prevent its affliction from these universal ailments of human institutions, so that there is no excuse for any relaxation in vigilance, critical appraisal or the search for the most just solution to the human problems perceived at any time.

It is only in this sense that I admit a permanent role for the more traditional forms and concepts of 'charity'. If it is a Christian's responsibility to meet the personal needs of the indigent in any society, and if statutory provisions will always be inadequate and uncomprehensive, private initiative and organized, group responses will always be necessary. Even if, for a time, the state finds financial and personal resources to meet the major needs of its members and neighbours, it will not provide the variety of resources required by the diverse demands of the needy or by new needs as they emerge. Official provision also tends to become oppressive. For these reasons, there will always be a requirement for voluntary initiatives and organizations, to challenge or offer alternatives to existing provisions, to give scope to individual choice within a possibly restrictive statutory system, and to pioneer new methods and responses to need.[65] Nor is it frivolous to claim that there should be room for at least marginally sacrificial, inconvenient acts of mutual kindness, even amongst the poorest in society, because charity of this kind is a protection from greed, and consequently from the evil and divisive effects of wealth.

Rabbi Nachum L. Rabinovitch, in a letter to the author, raised a fundamental question about the relation between statutory and voluntary observance of the law, which should affect christian thinking and attitudes: 'In Judaism, the boundary line between statutory (or legal) obligations and moral ones is very much farther on than in other cultures. Most of the obligations for combating poverty and general welfare are legally-binding ones. Yet, on the other hand, while the community does possess some few powers to impose sanctions to back up the law, in the main, observance of the law is voluntary, paradoxical as that may sound. In fact, during all the centuries of the Diaspora, the very existence of Jewish communities was an expression of a voluntary choice since there were always powerful forces and real attractions both pushing and pulling Jews to adopt the faiths of the host countries. This characteristic blend of voluntarism with legal obligation is a feature of Jewish society which needs to be analyzed and understood, for it may hold the key to the practical implementation of the other aspects. It is this issue of voluntarism versus state authority which is at the core of many of our current problems.'

There is, in this and similar ways, a demand on Christians to stand apart from the societies in which they live. Several times in this essay I have suggested that, while there is no single, sufficient christian teaching on wealth, certain teachings create a tension which may be the condition for authentically christian practice. Opposed to the doctrine of stewardship, which encourages ordered, christian industriousness and commercial prosperity, is the doctrine of poverty, which urges a repudiation of commercial values, and at least a spiritual detachment in the pursuit of a living (see chapter 5). There is no doubt that in our society, which is daftly, perilously, obsessively preoccupied with profits, the trappings of economic success and an endlessly improving standard of living, the christian prejudice needs to be strongly in the direction of poverty, austerity and self denial. Christians should be conspicuous for their odd behaviour in their theoretical and practical rejection of the prevailing, financial ideals.

This is one point at which the churches could help, but still generally fail. Judaism has noted that routine, standard habits of giving, like the tithe, are a preparation for just, economic practice (see p.7). People whose conventional practice requires regular, noticeable financial sacrifice, beyond the demands of the state tax systems, whether as a condition of church membership or an expected work of supererogation, are better prepared for justice than their fellows. Like disciplined athletes, their endurance and capabilities are greater. This is why the inadequacy of the churches' disciplines for regular giving is a grave matter. It is not that the churches should prosper; their members' offerings should take routes and reach destinations apart from any church; but it is a responsibility on the churches, in justice and charity, to promote programmes for giving that take account of prevailing greed in our society, counter it and offer effective persuasions and methods for their members' routine disciplines of giving.

As I have already implied, the excessive prominence of the clergy and absence of effective lay people in the counsels of most christian churches are causes of failure here. More frequently in recent years, there has been a token involvement of lay people in parish affairs; but those involved — often by appointment rather than election — have tended to be sympathetic, even complacent, spokesmen for the clergy, rather than strong, articulate representatives of independent christian views, which may be less timid and accommodating than those of the clergy, and consequently disquieting to them. I believe that it will be the force and authenticity of lay opinion and leadership which will effect the christian, economic revolution which must come; and the plan for this revolution will have been formulated as a direct response to the teaching of Christ. The mediation of clergy between laity and gospel can be an overwhelming hindrance to this process.

My concluding emphasis rests here. There can be no doubt that Christians must work for a radical transformation of our economic and political systems, even to overturn and replace them. The clergy will not achieve this, and the churches today display themselves as hesitant, spasmodic, unconvincing revolutionaries. The process must start with lay individuals. It is through the encounters of individuals with each other, not through organizational, statutory or institutional strategies, that the life of Christ works itself out in every age. In each individual's life, this demands assent to the totally exacting, present fact of the Incarnation: that every experience of events, and above all every human relationship, without exception, is a realization of the life of Christ in this time, not as a simulation or exercise, but as a living achievement. This is the reality of every relationship of employer with staff and of staff with employer; of company with customer or client; of competitor with competitor; of friend with friend; of stranger with stranger; of Christian with the poor, distant, inconvenient stranger, glimpsed in the newspaper report or on the television screen. It is a terrifying but simple reality, because it leaves nothing out, and is the condition for every form of relationship. As Jesus made clear, each daily encounter with him is the individual's responsibility, even when the encounters are made unawares: 'When saw we thee an hungred and fed thee? or thirsty, and gave thee drink? when saw we thee a stranger, and took thee in? or naked, and clothed thee? or when saw we thee sick, or in prison, and came unto thee?' (Mt. 25:37-39).

The responsibility is dire and thrilling. To realize the Incarnation in the manner I have just described is to contradict social and economic injustice and shut out greed or anxiety about the economic future. It demands total alertness and commitment to the fact of the Incarnation; it therefore also requires the dedication of any Christian's whole experience, talents and energy to the service of Jesus actually present in every person and event encountered in this life.

The same truth has been described in other terms by Teilhard de Chardin: 'If ... Omega (the aim-point of evolution, the *eschaton*) is ... *already in existence* and operative at the core of the thinking mass, then it would seem inevitable that its existence should be manifested here and now through some traces. ... The christian fact stands before us. It has its place among the other realities of the world. ... In the centre, so glaring as to be disconcerting, is the uncompromising affirmation of a personal God: God as providence, directing the universe with loving, watchful care; and God the revealer, communicating himself to man on the level of and through the ways of intelligence. ... Led astray by a false evangelism, people often think they are honouring Christianity when they reduce it to a sort of gentle philanthropism. Those who fail to see in it the most realistic and at the same time the most cosmic of beliefs and hopes, completely fail to understand its "mysteries". Is the Kingdom of God a big family? Yes, in a sense it is. But in another sense it is a prodigious biological operation — that of the Redeeming Incarnation'.[66]

The resolution rests with the individual, and will be a work of grace. It must be sustained through honest and continuing prayer. Here again, I am not talking of an abstract and impersonal process, but of a personal encounter in which the individual Christian exposes his motive, his purpose and his deed to the human individual Christ, whose Incarnation each Christian is fulfilling and whom he is meeting in every experience. Since I am concentrating on economic activity, the humdrum issues to be exposed in this way include the amount to be earned, the amount to be spent on necessities, the amount committed to pleasures, the sums dedicated to others, the time to be spent at work or with family, friends, the needy and others, the treatment of an inefficient employee or unjust employer, positive action to achieve social and political change, participation or abstention during an official strike. For a Christian, this cannot be a mechanical process, since personal relations with a living Christ and with living, mortal fellows are involved. It cannot leave economic behaviour unchanged, unless that behaviour is already perfect. Nothing short of conversion can suffice.

I am using the term 'conversion' here in a strong sense. Although 'a dramatic change in external behaviour is not the principal, or even necessary, result of conversion, but on the contrary a new relationship with Christ, however expressed, is the very definition of Christian conversion'; yet 'implicit in the idea of conversion is that of forsaking the past unconditionally and accepting in its place a future of which the one certain fact is that it will never allow the previous pattern of life to be the same again'.[67] This is one frightening aspect of the process I am describing; although we cannot be certain where it will lead, what it will demand, we can be sure that it will upset comfortable, secure and prosperous ways. It will radically alter private lives and force the replacement of Christians' economic goals, practices and institutions. It will demand at least a measure of hurtful poverty.

This does not mean that conversion will be disembodied, taking place regardless of its historic context. At this time we are, I would argue, at the end of the self-destructive cycle which was powered by doctrines of stewardship developed in the protestant Reformation (see p.96). This is one way to interpret Marx's teaching; but the christian conclusion cannot be achieved by tinkering either with capitalist or with marxist doctrines, although it must be aware of both. The conclusion cannot further the compartmentalization and division of human life. The nineteenth century prejudice that christian and economic morals and behaviour should not impinge on each other, or a view that minor benevolence could somehow counterbalance massive injustice, are absolutely repugnant. The charity we are considering is an expression of unity with Christ which permeates and informs all of life. This entails practical, intelligent judgement of the action to be taken, and bold will to perform it, whether the required action must take a political form, or would be more effectively pursued through some non-political channel. On occasion, all that may be required will be a private act of greeting, help or hospitality between individuals. All these actions, for a converted Christian, should form a whole, because they are the manifold expressions of the single Incarnation of Christ.

Because, fairly evidently, few Christians have reached this point and because the existing leadership from the churches is most unlikely to inspire the conversion or institute the change, the ways forward appear lonely and dangerous and arduous. The route, to adapt a chinese proverb, must move outwards from an individual's mind and heart to the family to the neighbourhood to the town to the province and so to the whole state. This requires the initiative of, probably lay, individuals and the formation of, probably lay-governed, groups or movements, of organizations, which will appear ridiculous and be unpopular amongst clergy and other fellow Christians, and which will also suffer the flaws and the tendency towards self-corruption to which all human organizations and institutions are subject. I am talking about individuals acting together — against or away from society — through the action of grace. This has to imply an assertion that the action is right and just, and that it is the expression of hope in Christ's kingdom, whose effects are not to be postponed to eternity, but are to be realized, however imperfectly, now and here. The affirmation must be that a new, christian Reformation can overturn and replace the evil economic order and morals of both capitalist and socialist societies. There is no way in which Christians, even if they live in a morally alien society, can justly abstain from any required, pragmatic action to effect change, although they have no privileged foresight into the likely outcome. All they can be certain about is that, eventually, the consequences of their actions will themselves require correction.

The temporal end of the process and the detail of the process itself are both obscure. It is difficult to see how action, initiated on a small scale, can have an effect on worldwide justice. We know there has to be folly, because that is a condition of the imitation of Christ; but there has also to be a total commitment of ordinary human intelligence, judgement, kindness and courage, because that is the condition of the Incarnation. The obscurity cannot be an excuse for inaction. A genuinely christian change of economic attitudes and systems is not an option but an imperative. As with human love and christian faith, a risky leap into the dark is demanded, humanly perilous but confident in grace. The one certainty in this case will be that, if the conversion or reformation leave economic attitudes, behaviour and expectations fundamentally unchanged, there has been no conversion. That will be more than a petty failure in benevolence; it will be assent to the continuation of injustice, voluntarily placing you and me under Satan's standard in that great plain of Babylon (see p.72). It will be a vote for Barabbas and against Jesus Christ.

Bibliography

Allen, Hope Emily, ed. *English Writings of Richard Rolle*. Oxford University Press, 1931.

Ambrose. *De Officiis Ministrorum*, P.L. 16, 25–183.

Aquinas, Thomas. *Summa Theologica* (Summa).

Arens, Bernard. *Manuel des Missions Catholiques*. Editions du Museum Lessianum, 1925.

Aristotle. *Nicomachean Ethics* (N.E.). Translated by J. A. K. Thompson. Penguin, 1963.

Augustine. *City of God*. Translated by Henry Bettenson. Penguin, 1972.

Backstrom, Philip N. *Christian Socialism and Co-operation in Victorian England*. London: Croom Helm, 1974.

Bakal, Carl. *Charity U.S.A.* New York: New York Times Books, 1979

Barbour, Hugh, and Arthur O. Roberts, eds. *Early Quaker Writings, 1650–1700* (E.Q.W.) Grand Rapids: Eerdmans, 1973.

Barlow, Frank, ed. *Vita Edwardi Regis*. Sunbury-on-Thames, Middlesex: Nelson, 1962.

Barnum, Priscilla Heath, ed. *Dives and Pauper* I. Early English Text Society, 1976.

Barth, Karl. *Church Dogmatics*. Translated by G. W. Bromiley. Edinburgh: T. & T. Clark, 1961.

Basil, St. *Collected Letters*. Translated by Roy J. Deferrari. Loeb, 1928

Bede. *Ecclesiastical History of the English People*. Edited by Bertram Colgrave and R. A. B. Mynors. Oxford University Press, 1969.

Belloc, Hilaire. *Essays of a Catholic*. London: Sheed and Ward, 1931.

Benedict, St. *The Rule*. Translated by Owen Chadwick in *Western Asceticism*. London: S.C.M., 1958.

Benn, Tony. *Arguments for Socialism* . Edited by Chris Mullin. Penguin, 1980.

Bernard, St. *In Annunciatione*.

Bishop, Edmund. *Liturgica Historica: Papers on the Liturgy and Religious Life of the Western Church*. Oxford at the Clarendon Press, 1918, Philadelphia: Fortress Press, 1970,

Blake, N. F. *Middle English Religious Prose*. York: York Medieval Texts, 1972.

Blake, William. *Complete Poetry and Prose*. Nonesuch Library. London: Bodley Head, 1975.

Boethius. *De Consolatione Philosophiae*. In Irwin Edman, comp., *The Consolation of Philosophy*.

Browne, Sir Thomas. *Religio Medici*. In Edman, *The Consolation of Philosophy*.

Bunyan, John. *The Life and Death of Mr. Badman*. Everyman Library. London: Dent, 1956.

Caesarius. *The Dialogue on Miracles*. Translated by H. von E. Scott and C. S. Swinton Bland. London: Routledge, 1929.

Calvin, John. *Institutes of the Christian Religion* (1559). Translated by Henry Beveridge. Grand Rapids: Eerdmans, 1957.

Carr Oscar C., Jr. *Jesus, Dollars and Sense: An Effective Stewardship Guide for Clergy and Lay Leaders*. New York, Seabury: 1976.

Carrington, Philip. *The Early Christian Church*. 2 vols. Cambridge University Press, 1957.

Cassian, John. *Conferences*. In Owen Chadwick, *Western Asceticism*.

Center for Medieval Renaissance Studys. *Dawn of Modern Banking*. Yale University Press, 1979.

Chadwick, Henry. *The Early Christian Church*. Penguin, 1967.

Chadwick, Owen. *The Reformation*. Penguin, 1972.

———. *The Victorian Church*. London: Adam and Charles Black, 1966.

———, ed. *Western Asceticism*. London: S.C.M., 1958, Philadelphia: Westminster, 1979.

Charity Commissioners, *Report of the Charity Commissioners for England and Wales*. H.M.S.O., 1975.

Charity Statistics 1977/78, 1980/81. Charities Aid Foundation.

Charles, R. H., ed. *The Testaments of the Twelve Patriarchs*. London: S.P.C.K., 1917.

Cheney, C.R. *Medieval Texts and Studies*. Oxford University Press, 1973.

Chesterman, Michael. *Charities, Trusts and Social Welfare*. London: Weidenfeld & Nichelson, 1979.

Child, Francis James. *The English and Scottish Popular Ballads*. New York: Dover, 1965.

Christian Stewardship. Diocese of Owerri, Nigeria.

Cicero. *De Officiis*. Loeb, 1921.

Cipolla, Carlo M. *Christofano and the Plague*. London: Collins, 1973.

Clark, W. K. Lowther. *A History of the S.P.C.K.* London: S.P.C.K., 1959.

Clement of Alexandria. *Quis Dives Salvetur*. Translated by G. W. Butterworth, Loeb, 1919.

Cohen, A. *Everyman's Talmud*. New York: Schocken, 1975.

Cohn, Norman. *The Pursuit of the Millennium*. Paladin Books. St. Albans, Herts.: Granada, 1970.

Common Crisis North South: Co-operation for World Recovery. London: Pan, 1983.

Copleston, Frederick, S.J. *A History of Philosophy*, Vol. III, *Ockham to Suarez*. London: Burns, Oates & Washbourne, 1953.

Cornuelle, Richard. *Brief Interpretative History of America's Voluntary Sector*. United Way, 1978

Cowper, William. *Poetical Works*. Sunbury-on-Thames, Middlesex: Nelson, 1867.

Cragg, Gerald R. *The Church and the Age of Reason, 1648–1789*. Penguin, 1970.

Cray, Rotha Mary. *The Mediaeval Hospitals of England*. London: Cass, 1966.

Cyprian. *Epistles*. P.L. 4. *Corpus Christianorum*, Series Latina III, pp. 206–226.

Daniélou, Jean. In *The Christian Centuries*.

Dante, *The Divine Comedy*. Translated by C. H. Sisson. Chicago: Regnery Gateway, 1981.

Defoe, Daniel. "Giving Alms no Charity" (London 1704). In *Works*. Edited by John S. Keltie. Edinburgh: Nimmo, 1972.

Defrasse, A., and H. Lechat. *Restauration et Description des Principaux Monuments du Sanctuaire D'Asclepios*. Paris, 1895.

Dickens, A. G. *The English Reformation*. Fontana Books. London: Collins, 1964.

Diogenes Laertius (D.L.). Translated by R. D. Hicks. Loeb.

Downside Review. July 1893.

Eadmer. *The Life of St. Anselm, Archbishop of Canterbury*. Translated and edited by R. W. Southern. Oxford at the Clarendon Press, 1962 and New York: Oxford University Press, 1963.

Early Christian Writings: The Apostolic Fathers. Translated by Maxwell Staniforth. Penguin, 1968.

Ebeling, Gerhard. *Luther*. Fontana Books. London: Collins, 1975.

Edman, Irwin, comp. *The Consolation of Philosophy*. New York: Modern Library, 1943.

Eliot. T. S. *Four Quartets*. London: Faber and Faber, 1950.

Elton, G. R. *The Reformation, 1520–1559*. Cambridge University Press, 1975.

Eusebius. *Ecclesiastical History*. Translated by Kirsopp Lake. Loeb, 1975.

Evans, Eric J. *The Contentious Tithe: The Tithe Problem and English Agriculture 1750 to 1850*. London: Routledge & Kegan Paul, 1976.

Evason, Eileen. *Ends That Won't Meet*, 1980.

Family Expenditure Survey. H.M.S.O., 1978.

Farmer, David Hugh. *The Oxford Dictionary of Saints*. Oxford University Press, 1978.

Feldman, Hilary. "Some Aspects of the Christian Reaction to the Tradition of Classical Munificence with Particular Reference to the Works of John Chrysostom and Libanius." Oxford M. Litt thesis, 1980.

Felix, Minucius. *Octavius*. Loeb, 1977.

Finnegan, Frances. *Poverty and Prostitution: A Study of Victorian Prostitutes in York*. Cambridge University Press, 1979.

Fischer, Ernst. *Marx in His Own Words*. Translated by Anna Bostock. Penguin, 1970.

Furnivall, Frederick J. *The Fifty Earliest English Wills*. Early English Text Society reprint, 1964.

Garton, Nancy. *George Müller and His Orphans*. Sevenoaks, Kent: Hodder & Stoughton, 1963.

Gildas. *De Excidio Britonum*. Philimore, 1978.

Giving U.S.A. American Association of Fund-Raising Counsel.

Gough, Richard. *The History of Myddle* (1834). Penguin, 1981.

Grant, Robert M. *Early Christianity and Society: Seven Studies*. New York: Harper & Row, 1977.

Gregory of Tours. *History of the Franks*. Translated by Lewis Thorpe. Penguin, 1974.

Groom, John A. *The Romance of the John Groom's Crippleage and Flower Girls' Mission*, 1866–1919.

Gutiérrez, Gustavo. *A Theology of Liberation*. Maryknoll, N.Y.: Orbis Books, 1973.

Hands, A. R. *Charities and Social Aid in Greece and Rome*. London: Thames and Hudson, 1968.

Handy, Robert T. *A History of the Churches in the United States and Canada*. Oxford University Press, 1976.

"Hávamál" in *Edda, Die Lieder des Codex Regius*. Edited by Hans Kuhn. Heidelberg, 1962.

Heasman, Kathleen. *Evangelicals in Action*. London, Bles: 1962.

Hengel, Martin. *Property and Riches in the Early Church*. London: S.C.M. and Philadelphia: Fortress Press, 1974.

Hill, Christopher. *The World Turned Upside Down*. New York: Viking, 1972.

Hilton, Walter. *The Scale of Perfection*. Edited by Evelyn Underhill. Dulverton, Somerset: Watkins, 1923.

Hoe, Susanna. *The Man Who Gave His Company Away*. London: Heinemann, 1978.

Hudson, Anne, ed. *Selections from English Wycliffite Writings* (E.W.W.). Cambridge University Press, 1978.

Iamblicus. *De vita Pythagorica*.

Illich, Ivan. *Celebration of Awareness*. Penguin, 1973.

———. *Tools for Conviviality*. London: Calder & Boyars, 1973.

Jakobovits, Immanuel. *Journal of a Rabbi*. New York: Living Books, 1966.

Jerome. *Epistles*.

Jewell, Helen M. *English Local Administration in the Middle Ages*. Newton Abbey, Devon: David & Charles, 1972.

John of the Cross. *Oeuvres spirituelles de saint Jean de la Croix*. Paris: Editions du Seuil, 1947.

John Chrysostom. *Homilies on the First Epistle of St. Paul to Timothy*. Oxford University Press, 1848.

———. *Homilies on the Second Epistle of St. Paul to the Corinthians*. Oxford University Press, 1848.

John Paul II. *Laborem exercens*. Boston: St. Paul Editions, 1981.

Johnson, John. *A Collection of the Laws and Canons of the Church of England*. Parker, 1950.

Jones, M. G. *The Charity School Movement*. London: Cass, 1964.

Josephus. *Antiquities*.

———. *The Jewish War*. Translated by G. A. Williamson. Penguin, 1959.

Julian. *Epistola*.

Justin. *Apology*.

Kirk, J. Andrew. *Liberation Theology: An Evangelical View from the Third World*. Atlanta: John Knox Press, 1979.

Knowles, Dom David. *The Monastic Order in England*. 2 vols. (M.O.E.). Cambridge University Press, 1976.

———. *The Religious Orders in England*. 2 vols.(R.O.E.). Cambridge University Press, 1976.

Koran, The. Translated by J. M. Rodwell. Everyman, 1950.

Krailsheimer, J. *Conversion*. London: S.C.M., 1980.

Kraus, Henry. *Gold Was the Mortar: The Economics of Cathedral Building*. London: Routledge & Kegan Paul, 1979.

Küng, Hans. *The Christian Challenge*. London: Collins, 1979. A shortened form of *On Being a Christian*, Garden City, N.Y.: Doubleday, 1978.

Lactantius. *The Works of Lactantius*. Translated by William Fletcher. Edinburgh: T. & T. Clark, 1909.

Ladurie, Emmanuel le Roy. *Montaillou: The Promised Land of Error*. New York: Braziller, 1978.

Langland, William. *Piers Plowman*. Edited by Derek Pearsall. London: Arnold, 1978.

Lash, Nicholas. *A Matter of Hope: A Theologian's Relections on the Thought of Karl Marx*. London: Darton, Longman & Todd, 1981.

Latin Poems Commonly Attributed to Walter Mapes. Camden Society, 1841.

Lecky, William Edward Hartpole. *History of European Morals from Augustus to Charlemagne*. London: Longmans Green, 1894.

Leo XIII. *Rerum novarum*. New York: Paulist Press.

Life of Frederick Denison Maurice, Chiefly Told in His Own Letters. Edited by his son Frederick Maurice. London: Macmillan, 1884.

Lightfoot, Bishop. *The Apostolic Fathers*. London: Macmillan, 1912.

Lipomanus, Aloysius, ed. *St. Bonaventure, St. Francis*. Douay 1610. Menston: Scolar Press, 1972.

Lucian. *The Passing of Peregrinus*. Loeb Lucian V. Translated by A. M. Harmon. Loeb, 1955.

Lucretius. *De rerum natura*.

Luther, Martin. *Table Talk*. Edited by Thomas S. Kepler. Grand Rapids: Baker Book House, 1979.

———. *Theologia Germanica*. Translated by Bengt Hoffman. London: S.P.C.K., 1980.

———. *On Trading and Usury*, Works IV.

———. *Three Treatises*. Translated by Charles M. Jacobs and James Atkinson. Philadelphia: Fortress Press, 1970.

McRobie, George. *Small is Possible*. London: Jonathan Cape, 1981.

Maimonides, Moses. *The Commandments* I: *Positive Commandments*. Translated by Charles B. Chavel. Soncino Press, 1967.

———. *The Guide for the Perplexed*. Translated by M. Friedlander. New York: Dover, 1956.

Maitland, F. W. *Equity*. Cambridge University Press, 1932.

Malthus, Thomas Robert. *An Essay on the Principle of Population* and *A Summary View of the Principle of Population*. Edited by Anthony Flew. Penguin, 1970.

Marcus, Jacob R. *The Jew in the Medieval World, 315–1791*. New York: Atheneum, 1969.

Marrou, Henri. In *The Christian Centuries* I, Edited by Louis J. Rogier et al. New York: McGraw-Hill, 1964 and Paulist Press, 1978.

Marx, Karl. *The Grundisse*. Translated and edited by David McLellan. New York: Harper & Row, 1971.

———, and Frederick Engels. *The Communist Manifesto*. Translated by Samuel Moore. Penguin, 1967.

Maycock, A. L. *Nicholas Ferrar of Little Gidding*. Grand Rapids: Eerdmans, 1980.

Melling, Elizabeth, ed. *The Poor*. Kentish Sources IV, Kent County Council, 1964.

Miranda, José P. *Marx and the Bible: A Critique of the Philosophy of Oppression*. Maryknoll, N.Y.: Orbis Books, 1974.

The Mishnah (M). Translated by Herbert Danby. Oxford University Press, 1933.

Mollat, Michael, ed. *Études sur l'Histoire de la Pauvreté (Moyen Age–XVIᵉ siecle)*. Paris: Publications de la Sorbonne, Michel Rouche.

Moltmann, Jürgen. *The Experiment Hope*. London: S.C.M., and Philadelphia: Fortress Press, 1975.

Montefiore, C. G. and H. Loewe, *A Rabbinic Anthology*. New York: Schocken, 1974.

Moore, G. Foot. *Judaism in the First Centries of the Christian Era* (F.M.). New York: Schocken, 1971.

More, Thomas. *Utopia*. Translated by Paul Turner. Penguin, 1965.

Mullin, Redmond. "The Evidence for Miracles." In *Mysteries of the World*. Lyric, 1979.

———. *The Fundraising Handbook*. Oxford: Mowbray, 1976.

———. *Miracles and Magic*. Oxford: Mowbray, 1978.

———. *Present Alms, on the Corruption of Philanthropy*. Phlogiston, 1980.

———. "The Roles of Private Funding in the Context of International Voluntary Activity." In *Associations Transnationales* 4, 1980.

Mynors, R. A. B., ed. *Cassiodori Senitoris Institutiones*. Oxford University Press, 1937.

Neill, Stephen. *A History of the Christian Missions*. Penguin, 1964.

Nelson, Robert. *An Address to Persons of Quality* (1715).

Nickalls, John L., ed. *The Journal of George Fox*. Religious Society of Friends, 1975.

Niebuhr, H. Richard. *Christ and Culture*. New York: Harper & Row, 1951; reprint Gloucester, Mass.: Peter Smith, 1965.

Nightingale, Benedict. *Charities*. Penguin, 1973.

Norman, E. R. *Church and Society in England 1770–1970*. Oxford University Press, 1976.

North-South, a Programme for Survival. London: Pan, 1980

Opie, Iona and Peter. *Oxford Dictionary of Nursery Rhymes*. Oxford University Press, 1951.

Origen. *Contra Celsum*. Translated by Henry Chadwick. Cambridge University Press, 1980.

Outler, Albert C., ed. *John Wesley: A Representative Collection of His Writings.* New York: Oxford University Press, 1964.

Owen, David. *English Philanthropy 1660-1960.* Harvard University Press, 1964.

Owst, G. R. *Preaching in Medieval England c.1350-1450.* New York: Russell & Russell, 1965.

Oxenedes, Johannis de. *Chronica.*

Parenti, Giovanni de. *Sacrum Commercium.* Edited by Canon Rawnsley. London: Dent, 1934.

Paris, Matthew. *Historia Anglorum* (1247).

Parkes, James. *The Jew in the Medieval Community.* Soncino, 1938.

Pascoe, C. F. *Two Hundred Years of the S.P.G., 1701-1900* (S.P.G.). London: S.P.G., 1901.

Patrologiae Latinae. Migne (P.L.).

Pelagius. *Tractatus de Divitiis,* P.L. Suppl. Vol. 5, 1379-1418.

Pétré, Hélène. *Caritas, Étude sur le Vocabulaire Latin de la Charité Chrétienne.* Louvain University Press, 1948.

Philo. *Quad omnis probus liber sit,* Vol. IX of Philo's collected works. Loeb, 1941.

———. *De Vita Contemplativa: Hypothetica.* Translated by F. H. Colson. Ibid.

Picarda, Hubert. *The Law and Practice Relating to Charities.* Sevenoaks, Kent: Butterworth, 1977.

Pierson, A. T. *George Müller of Bristol.* Glasgow: Pickering & Inglis, 1972.

Pirke Aboth (P.A.), *The Ethics of the Talmud, Sayings of the Fathers.* Edited by R. Travers Herford. New York: Schocken, 1962.

Pius XI. *Quadragesimo anno* (1931). New York: America Press.

Plato. *The Republic.* Translated by Desmond Lee. Penguin.

Pliny. *Epistola.*

Polano. H. *The Talmud.* London: Frederick Warne, 1978.

Pomey, Michel, *Traité des Fondations d'Utilité Publique.* Paris: Presses Universitaires de France, 1980.

Pool, P. A. S. *The History of the Town and Borough of Penzance.* Corporation of Penzance, 1974.

Pope, Alexander. *Poems.* London: Methuen, 1963.

Porphyry. *On Abstinence from Animal Food.* Translated by Thomas Taylor. Arundel, Sussex: Centaur Press, 1965.

Pound, Ezra. *The Cantos.* London: Faber and Faber, 1968.

Poverty. London: S.P.C.K., 1961.

Prochaska, F. K. *Women and Philanthropy in 19th Century England.* Oxford University Press, 1980.

Raven, Charles E. *Christian Socialism 1848-1854.* London: Cass, 1968.

Raw, Charles, Bruce Page, and Godfrey Hodgson. *Do You Sincerely Want to Be Rich?* Penguin, 1972.

Richards, Thomas. *The Puritan Movement in Wales, 1639 to 1635.* National Eisteddfod Association, 1970.

Robertson, D. W., Jr. *Essays in Medieval Culture.* Princeton University Press, 1980.

Robinson, F. N., ed. *The Works of Geoffrey Chaucer.* Oxford University Press, 1957.

Rogier, Louis J. et al. *The Christian Centuries: A New History of the Catholic Church.* 5 vols. New York: McGraw-Hill, 1964- and Paulist Press, 1978-.

Rosenthall, Joel T. *The Purchase of Paradise: The Social Function of Aristocratic Benevolence 1307-1485.* London: Routledge & Kegan Paul, 1972.

Rowntree, B. S. *Poverty, a Study of Town Life* (1901). New York: Garland, 1980.

The Sayings of the Desert Fathers (Sayings). Translated by Benedicta Ward. Glasgow: Mowbray, 1975.

Schappes, Morris U., ed. *A Documentary History of the Jews in the United States 1654-1875*. New York: Schocken, 1971.

Schumacher, E. F. *A Guide for the Perplexed*. New York: Harper & Row, 1959.

——. *Small Is Beautiful: Economics as if People Mattered*. New York: Harper & Row, 1973.

Schürer, Emil. *The Jewish People in the Time of Jesus*. New York: Schocken Paperback, 1961.

Seneca. *De Beneficiis*. Loeb, 1935.

——. *Letters*. Translated by Robin Campbell. Penguin,1969.

Severus, Sulpicius. *Vie de Saint Martin*. Translated by Jacques Fontaine. Paris: Editions du Cerf, 1967.

Seymour, Harold J. *Designs for Fund-Raising*. New York: McGraw-Hill, 1966.

Sheppard, David. *Bias to the Poor*. Sevenoaks, Kent: Hodder & Stoughton, 1983.

Sieff, Israel. *Memoirs*. London: Weidenfeld & Nicholson, 1970.

Sir Gawain and the Green Knight and Pearl and Sir Orfeo. Unwin Paperbacks, 1979.

Smiles, Samuel. *Self-Help* (1859). Centenary edition. London: John Murray, 1958.

Smith, Adam. *An Enquiry into the Nature and Causes of the Wealth of Nations* (1776). New York: Collier, 1909; Chicago: Encyclopedia Britannica, 1955.

Smith, Toulmin, and Lujo Brentano. *English Gilds*. Early English Text Society reprint, 1963.

Social and Economic Trends in Northern Ireland, No. 6. H.M.S.O., 1980.

Southern, R. W. *Western Society and the Church in the Middle Ages*. Penguin, 1970.

Sozomen. *Ecclesiastical History*. Translated by Edward Walford. Bohn, 1825.

Tanner, J. R. *Tudor Constitutional Documents A.D. 1485-1603*. Cambridge University Press, 1930.

Tate, W. E. *The Parish Chest*. Cambridge University Press, 1979.

Tawney, R. H. *Religion and the Rise of Capitalism*. New York: Harcourt, Brace, 1926; Penguin 1938.

Taylor, Jeremy. *Holy Living* (1650). *The Rule and Exercise of Holy Living*. Abridged. New York: Harper & Row, 1970.

Teilhard de Chardin, Pierre. *The Phenomenon of Man*. New York: Harper & Row, 1959.

Temple, William. *Christianity and Social Order*. London: S.P.C.K., 1976.

Tertullian. *Apologeticus*. Loeb, 1977.

Teresa of Avila, St. *The Way of Perfection*. Translated by E. Allison Peers. Garden City, N.Y.: Doubleday, Image Books, 1964.

Thesaurus Spiritualis Societatis Jesu. Roehampton, 1929.

Thomas à Kempis. *The Imitation of Christ*. In Edman, *The Consolation of Philosophy*.

Thomas, Charles. *Christianity in Britain to A.D. 500*. London: Batsford, 1981.

Thousellier, C. "Polemiques autour de la notion de pauvreté spirituelle." In Mollat, *l'Histoire de la Pauvreté*.

Toke, Nicholas, of Godington. *Five Letters on the State of the Poor in the County of Kent* (1770).

Tolkien, J. R. R., trans., *Pearl*. Unwin Paperback, 1979.

Torr, Cecil. *Small Talk at Wreyland* (1918). Oxford University Press, 1979.

Townsend, Peter. *Poverty in the United Kingdom*. Penguin, 1979.

Training Visitors. Church Information Service.

Trevelyan, G. M. *English Social History*. Penguin, 1980.

Twersky, Isadore, ed. *A Maimonides Reader*. New York: Behrman House, 1972.

Underhill, Evelyn, ed. *The Cloud of Unknowing*. Dulverton, Somerset: Watkins, 1956.

Vermes, Geza. *The Dead Sea Scrolls in English*. Penguin, 1975; Philadelphia: Fortress Press, 1978.

————. *Jesus the Jew: A Historian's Reading of the Gospels.* New York: Macmillan, 1974; Philadelphia: Fortress Press, 1978.

Vidler, Alexander R. *The Church in an Age of Revolution: 1788 to the Present Day.* Penguin, 1971.

Viewpoints on Philanthropy. Charities Aid Foundation, 1978.

Vyronis, Speros, Jr. *The Decline of Medieval Hellenism in Asia Minor and the Process of Islamization from the Eleventh through the Fifteenth Century.* Berkeley: University of California Press, 1971.

Wagner, Gillian. *Barnardo.* London: Eyre and Spottiswoode, 1979.

Wallis, E. J. N. *Explaining Christian Stewardship.* Church Information Service.

Ward, Benedict. *Miracles and the Medieval Mind: Theory, Record and Event, 1000–1215* Menston: Scolar Press, 1982.

Welfare Services, Helping Others to Help Themselves, and *Charitable Giving Practices of the Members of the Church of Latter-Day Saints.* Salt Lake City, Utah: Church of Latter-Day Saints.

Whitefield, George. *Select Sermons.* The Banner of Truth Trust, 1958.

Winstanley, Gerrard. *The Law of Freedom and Other Writings.* Penguin, 1973.

Woodroofe, Kathleen. *From Charity to Social Work in England and the United States.* London: Routledge & Kegan Paul, 1974.

Young, G. M. *Portrait of an Age, Victorian England.* Annotated by George Kitson Clark. Oxford University Press, 1977.

Younghusband, Sir F. *Inter-Racial Relations* (1910). Quoted in Donald Reed, *Documents from Edwardian England 1901–1915.* London: Harrap, 1973.

Notes

Chapter One
Greek and Roman Teaching on Wealth, Poverty, and Relief

1. Origen, *Contra Celsum*, trans. Henry Chadwick, Cambridge University Press, 1980, pp. 8 and 37.
2. Tertullian, *Apologeticus*, XLVI, 2–6.
3. Aristotle, *Nicomachean Ethics* (N.E.), trans. J. A. K. Thompson, Penguin, 1963.
4. Cicero, *De Officiis*, I, XX, 68, Loeb, 1921.
5. He was referred to as "Seneca noster."
6. Seneca, *De Beneficiis,* V, XXI 3 and II, XV, 1, Loeb, 1935.
7. Seneca, *Letters*, II, trans. Robin Campbell, Penguin, 1969, p. 34.
8. *Diogenes Laertius* (D.L.), VI, 51, trans. R. D. Hicks, Loeb.
9. Philo, *Quod omnis probus liber sit*, II, 8 and III, 21.
10. D.L., II, 75.
11. Seneca, *Letters*, XC.
12. N.E., IV, I (p. 115); Cicero, *De Off.* XLII, 150.
13. Cicero, *De Off.,* I, XLII.
14. A. R. Hands, *Charities and Social Aid in Greece and Rome*, London: Thames & Hudson, 1968, p. 62, and Ch. V *passim*.
15. N.E., IV, I and *De Off.* II, XVIII.
16. N.E., I, V, and Hands, *Charities in Greece and Rome*, p. 64.
17. Plato, *The Republic*, trans. Desmond Lee, Penguin, IV (p. 188), VIII (p. 369), and Hands, *Charities*, p. 64 and note 65; cf. the view in Thomas More's *Utopia*.
18. Seneca, *De Ben.*, III, XXVIII.
19. Plato, *Rep.,* IX (p. 373).
20. Seneca, *De Ben.*, V, iv, 3; cf. V, vi, I.
21. D.L., VI, 20, 26, 87, 93.
22. D.L., VIII, I *passim*; Iamblicus, *De vita Pythagorica*, 80–81.
23. D.L., X, 130; Lucretius, *De rerum natura*.
24. CF. Hands, *Charities in Greece and Rome*; A. Defrasse and H. Lechat, *Restauration et Description des Principaux Monuments du Sanctuaire D'Asclepios*, Paris, 1895; Robert M. Grant, *Early Christianity and Society*, New York: Harper & Row, 1977, Ch. III.
25. D.L., I, 54.
26. Pliny, *Epistola*, X.
27. Cicero, *De Off.*, II, IV; cf. Alexis de Tocqueville's comments on mutual help and co-operation in North America in 1831.
28. Grant, *Early Christianity*, p. 135.
29. D.L., VI, 49.
30. Hands, *Charities in Greece and Rome*, p. 206.
31. N.E., VIII (p. 256); Cicero, *De Off.*, II, xx; Seneca, *De Ben.*, I, i, 9; III, 1, 1.
32. N.E., IV, 1 (pp. 111 and 114); *De Off.*, I, XIV, 42; *De Ben.*, I, 1 *passim* and I, ii, 1.
33. Cicero, *De Off.*, I, XIV, 43–45.
34. Ibid., I, XVI, 51; Seneca, *De Ben.*, III, xii; D.L., V, 17 and 21.

35. Seneca, *De Ben.*, II, ii, 1; xxxi, 2; I, i, 8; I, iii, 5.

36. Ibid., IV xxxix, 2.

37. Cf. N.E., II, vii (pp. 68–69); IV, ii and iii (p. 119); VIII, xiii (p. 255).

38. Seneca, *De Ben.*, I, vi, 1 and II, xxxi, 2.

39. Cicero, *De Off.*, I, XIV, 44.

40. N.E., IX, 7 (p. 272).

41. Seneca, *De Ben.*, III, xxviii, 2; II, xvii, 7; IV, xi, 1.

42. Ibid., II, x, 1 and 4; cf. the popular story about St. Nicholas.

43. Cf. Martin Hengel, *Property and Riches in the Early Church*, London: S.C.M. and Philadelphia: Fortress Press, 1974, p. 29 and Seneca, *De Ben.*, IV, xxv *passim*.

44. D.L., VI, 46.

45. Ibid., VII, 22.

Chapter Two
Jewish Teaching at the Time of Christ

1. See, for example, Philip Carrington, *The Early Christian Church* I, Cambridge University Press, 1957, p. 323.

2. *Pirke Aboth* (P.A.), *The Ethics of the Talmud, Sayings of the Fathers*, ed. R. Travers Herford, New York: Schocken, 1962, p. 45.

3. Ibid.

4. *The Mishnah* (M.), trans. Herbert Danby, Oxford University Press, 1933, p. xxi, and P.A., pp. 106 and 85.

5. M. Terumoth (M., p. 52); *M. Shekalim,* (M., p. 152); *M. Maaseroth* (M., p. 66, n. 9); Numbers 18:21 (and cf. Maimonides *passim*); Leviticus 18:26; Deuteronomy 14:22, 22:26, 14:28, and 26:12; *M. Maaser Sheni* (M., p. 73); *M. Peah* (M., pp. 10–11).

6. M., pp. 4–15, *M. Peah passim*; *M. Shebiith* (M., p. 39), and cf. Emil Schürer, *The Jewish People in the Time of Jesus*, New York: Schocken Paperback, 1961, p. 37.

7. Josephus, *Antiquities*, xviii, 3, 2; *Wars*, ii, 9; Luke 11:42.

8. Moses Maimonides, *The Guide for the Perplexed*, trans. M. Friedlander, New York: Dover, 1956, p. 341.

9. See note to Ch. 1 of Maimonides' *Mishneh Torah* in Isador Twersky's *A Maimonides Reader*, New York: Behrman House, 1972, p. 135; G. Foot Moore, *Judaism in the First Centuries of the Christian Era*, Vol. II (F.M.), New York: Schocken Paperback, 1971; A. Cohen, *Everyman's Talmud*, New York: Schocken, 1975, p. 219.

10. P.A., I, 2; Cohen, *Everyman's Talmud,* pp. 224f; H. Polano, *The Talmud,* London: Frederick Warne, 1978, pp. 204f.

11. *M. Peah* (M., p. 20).

12. F.M., pp. 174f and 176.

13. Schürer, *Jewish People*, p. 288.

14. Polano, *The Talmud*, p. 243.

15. C. G. Montefiore and H. Loewe, *A Rabbinic Anthology*, New York: Schocken, 1974, p. 415, and F.M., pp 176f.

16. From "By-Paths of Charity," in Immanuel Jakobovits's *Journal of a Rabbi*, New York: Living Books, 1966, pp. 110–117.

17. *M. Gittin* (M., p. 311), and a personal letter to the author.

18. Julian, *Epistola*, 84a.

19. Quoted in Immanuel Jakobovits's contribution to *Viewpoints on Philanthropy*, Charities Aid Foundation, 1978, pp. 5–9.

20. Jakobovits, "By-Paths."

21. Cohen, *Everyman's Talmud*, p. 185; F.M., p. 175; Schürer, *Jewish People*, p. 288.

22. F.M., pp. 176f; *M. Horayoth* (M., p. 466).

23. Cohen, *Everyman's Talmud* , p. 177.

24. F.M., p. 177.

25. *M. Kiddushin* (M., p. 328).

26. Polano, *The Talmud*, p. 298.

27. P.A., p. 41; cf. F.M., p. 177 and Cohen, *Everyman's Talmud*, p. 191.

28. Montefiore and Loewe, *Rabbinic Anthology*, p. 429.

29. Ibid., p. 418.

30. Ibid., p. 422.

31. F.M., p. 166 and note.

32. Polano, *The Talmud*, p. 246; *M. Shekalim* (M., p. 158).

33. Cohen, *Everyman's Talmud*, p. 224; Montefiore and Loewe, *Anthology*, p. 425.

34. Polano, *The Talmud*, p. 198.

35. *M. Gittin* (M., p. 314) and Montefiore and Loewe, *Anthology*, p. 424.

36. *Anthology*, pp. 421f and Polano, *The Talmud*, p. 246.

37. Jakobovits in *Viewpoints on Philanthropy*.

38. F.M., pp. 89f.

39. Cohen, *Everyman's Talmud*, pp. 222 and 220f (cf. D.L., II, 57).

40. F.M., p. 100.

41. Montefiore and Loewe, *Anthology*, p. 429; P.A., pp. 31f; and Polano, *The Talmud*, p. 302.

42. Cohen, *Everyman's Talmud*, pp. 211 and 224; cf. Genesis 3:21, 18:1, 25:11 and Deuteronomy 24:6.

43. Montefiore and Loewe, *Anthology*, p. 272.

44. Polano, *The Talmud*, p. 304 and *M. Shekalim* (M., p. 158).

45. P.A., p. 72; Polano, *The Talmud*, p. 304; Cohen, *Everyman's Talmud*, p. 220.

46. Polano, *The Talmud*, p. 304.

47. Ibid., p. 298 and Montefiore and Loewe, *Anthology*, p. 288.

48. Polano, *The Talmud*, p. 300; Cohen, *Everyman's Talmud*, p. 304; F.M., p. 35.

49. Cohen, *Everyman's Talmud*, p. 230; Montefiore and Loewe, *Anthology*, p. 446.

50. Cohen, *Everyman's Talmud*, p. 195.

51. F.M., p. 142.

52. *M. Baba Metzia* (M., pp. 355f): F.M., pp. 143f; Montefiore, *Anthology*, p. 413.

53. *Anthology*, p. 517.

54. Ibid., pp. 542 and 425.

55. P.A., p. 24.

56. Polano, *The Talmud*, pp. 262 and 213.

57. Josephus, *The Jewish Wars,* II, 7, trans. G. A. Williamson, Penguin, 1959, p. 125.

58. Geza Vermes, *The Dead Sea Scrolls in English,* Penguin, 1975, p. 54.

59. Josephus, *Wars,* II, 7 passim.

60. Philo, *Quod omnis probus,* pp. 83 and 86ff.

61. Vermes, *Dead Sea Scrolls,* pp. 82, 79, and 116.

62. Eusebius, *Ecclesiastical History,* 2 vols., trans. Kirsopp Lake, Loeb, 1975, II, xvii.

63. Philo, *De Vita Contemplativa* I, i; II, 13 and 18; IX *passim; Hypothetica* 11, 11, Vol. IX of Philo's collected works, trans. F. H. Colson, Loeb, 1941.

64. Vermes, *Dead Sea Scrolls,* pp. 73, 88, 109, and 84f.

65. Geza Vermes, *Jesus the Jew: A Historian's View of the Gospels,* Penguin, 1975, Philadelphia: Fortress Press, 1978, p. 224.

66. R. H. Charles, ed., *The Testaments of the Twelve Patriarchs,* London: S.P.C.K., 1917, p. 86.

Chapter Three
New Testament

1. Charles, *Testaments,* p. 86.
2. *M. Shekalim* 1, 3 (M., p. 152).
3. Hans Küng, *The Christian Challenge,* London: Collins, 1979, p. 149 and see p. 115.
4. Montefiore and Loewe, *Rabbinic Anthology,* p. 433.

Chapter Four
Wealth, Poverty, and Relief in the Early Church

1. John Chrysostom, *Homilies on the First Epistle of St. Paul to Timothy,* Hom. XII, Oxford University Press, 1848, pp. 100f; Pelagius, *Tractatus de Divitiis,* Migne, *Patrologiae Latinae* (P.L.), Suppl. Vol. 5, 1387f.
2. *The Shepherd of Hermas,* trans. Bishop Lightfoot, *The Apostolic Fathers,* London: Macmillan, 1912, pp. 411ff.
3. Origen in his commentary on Matthew 15:15.
4. Clement of Alexandria, *Quis Dives Salvetur,* trans. G. W. Butterworth, Loeb, 1919, pp. 273, 281, 291f.
5. Tertullian, *Apologeticus,* XLII, i and 2., Loeb, 1977.
6. *The Sayings of the Desert Fathers (Sayings),* trans. Benedicta Ward, Oxford: Mowbray, 1975, p. 62.
7. Ambrose, *De Officiis Ministrorum,* P.L. 16, 73.
8. Hengel, *Property and Riches,* p. 1 and Polano, *The Talmud,* p. 14.
9. *Shepherd of Hermas,* pp. 441, 458.
10. Pelagius, *Tractatus de Divitiis,* P.L., Suppl. Vol. V, 1396.
11. John Chrysostom, *Homilies on the Second Epistle of St. Paul to the Corinthians,* Hom. VIII, Oxford University Press, 1848, p. 207.
12. John Cassian, *Conferences* I, 6, in *Western Asceticism,* ed. Owen Chadwick, London: S.C.M., 1958, p. 198.
13. Pelagius, *De Divitiis,* P.L., Supp. Vol. V., 1383, 1397, 1401.
14. *Sayings,* p. 190; Cassian, *Conferences* I, 9 (p. 201); Hengel, *Property and Riches,* p. 2.
15. *Sayings,* p. 180, cf. p. 200.
16. Tertullian, *Apologeticus,* XXXIX, 5 and 6.
17. Clement, *Quis Dives,* pp. 301, 297; Augustine, *City of God.,* XII, 8, trans. Henry Bettenson, Penguin, 1972, pp. 480f.
18. Lactantius, *The Divine Institutes,* VI, xii in *The Works of Lactantius,* trans. William Fletcher, Edinburgh, T. & T. Clark, 1909, Vol. I, p. 387; cf. John Chrysostom on 1 Timothy, p. 207.
19. Augustine, *City of God,* XIV, 4; XV, 1 and 5; XXI, 1 (pp. 552ff, 596, 600ff., 964).
20. Chrysostom on 1 Timothy, p. 90; *Early Christian Writings: The Apostolic Fathers,* trans. Maxwell Staniforth, Penguin, 1968, p. 218; Clement, *Quis Dives,* pp. 303 and 337.
21. *Collected Letters of Saint Basil,* Ep. 284 in Loeb edition, 1928.
22. Quoted in Philip Carrington, *The Early Christian Church,* Vol. II, Cambridge University Press, 1957, p. 352.
23. *Sayings,* p. 193, cf. p. 146 (51).

24. Ambrose, *De Officiis Ministrorum,* P.L. 16, 70, 71.

25. Augustine, *City of God,* XVII, 4 and XVIII, 2 (pp. 722 and 762).

26. *Early Christian Writings,* p. 181; cf. Hengel, *Property and Riches,* p. 8; Ambrose, *De Officiis,* P.L. 16, 73; Clement, *Quis Dives,* p. 347.

27. Cf. Hélène Pétré, *Caritas, Étude sur le Vocabulaire Latin de la Charité Chrétienne,* Louvain University Press, 1948, p. 205 and passim; *Early Christian Writings,* p. 80.

28. Minucius Felix, *Octavius,* XXXII, 7, Loeb, 1977.

29. *Early Christian Writings,* pp. 218, 227, 235.

30. Tertullian, *Apologeticus,* XLII, 8 and 9.

31. Clement, *Quis Dives,* p. 341.

32. Lucian, *The Passing of Peregrinus,* Loeb Lucian V, trans. A.M. Harmon, Loeb, 1955, p. 15.

33. Cf. Henry Chadwick, *The Early Christian Church,* Penguin, 1967, p. 157.

34. Origen, *Contra Celsum,* p. 180: "social service" here translates *koinonikon;* cf. also Henri Marrou in *The Christian Centuries* I, ed. Louis Rogier et al., New York: Paulist Press, 1978, pp. 327 ff.

35. *Early Christian Writings,* p. 148 and *Christian Centuries* I, pp. 328, 382.

36. Origen, *Contra Celsum,* pp. 329f; cf. Grant, *Early Christianity,* p. 132.

37. Ambrose, *De Officiis,* P.L. 16, 72.

38. Ibid., P.L. 16, 131 (cf. *Contra Celsum,* p. 60).

39. *Early Christian Writings,* p. 227.

40. Pétré, *Caritas,* p. 249.

41. Lactantius, *Institutes,* VI, XII *passim,* pp. 382ff.

42. Ambrose, *De Officiis,* P.L. 16, 74, 129, 150, 168.

43. Tertullian, *Apologeticus,* xxxix; Marrou, in *Christian Centuries* I, p. 328.

44. Ambrose, *De Officiis,* P.L. 16, 71, 72; Augustine, *City of God,* XIX, 14, pp. 873f.

45. Porphyry, *On Abstinence from Animal Food,* trans. Thomas Taylor, Arundel, Sussex: Centaur Press, 1965, p. 142.

46. Augustine, *City of God,* XIX, 19, p. 880; cf. Carrington, *Early Christian Church,* I, pp. 265, 268, 471, 476; Marrou in *Christian Centuries* I, pp. 328, 442.

47. *Early Christian Writings,* p. 146.

48. Ibid., p. 95; Ambrose, *De Officiis,* P.L. 16, 128, 129.

49. Pétré, *Caritas,* p. 263.

50. Justin, *Apology,* LXVII, 6.

51. *Shepherd of Hermas,* p. 476.

52. Chrysostom, Homily on 1 Timothy, p. 120.

53. Eusebius, *Ecclesiastical History,* IV, XXIII, p. 10, trans. Kirsopp Lake, Loeb, 1975, pp. 381ff.

54. Cyprian, Ep. 62, *Corpus Christianorum,* Series Latina III; cf. Hengel, *Property and Riches,* p. 44.

55. Marrou in *Christian Centuries* I, p. 240 and Grant, *Early Christianity,* p. 134.

56. Basil, *Collected Letters* II, translated by Roy J. Deferrari, Loeb, 1928, Ep. XCIV to Elias, the provincial governor, written in 372; Sozomen, *Ecclesiastical History,* vi, 34, trans. Edward Walford, Bohn, 1825, p. 301.

57. Jerome, *Epistles,* 77, 8.6.

58. *Early Christian Writings,* p. 234.

59. Grant, *Early Christianity,* pp. 139f.

60. Cf. Hilary Feldman, "Some Aspects of the Christian Reaction to the Tradition of Classical Munificence with Particular Reference to the Works of John Chrysostom and Libanius," Oxford M. Litt. thesis, 1980, p. 231.

61. Tertullian, *Apologeticus,* XXIX, 5–10.

62. Justin, *Apology,* LXV and LVIII, and cf. Marrou in *Christian Centuries* I, p. 74.

63. Feldman, "Some Aspects," cites the terms "arca," "gazophylacius," and the Hebrew "corban."

64. Eusebius, *Ecclesiastical History,* V, XVIII, 1 and 2, vol. I, p. 487.

65. *Sayings,* pp. 206ff; Ambrose, *De Officiis,* P.L. 16, 72.

66. *Sayings,* pp. 164f.

67. *Shepherd of Hermas,* p. 445.

68. Cf. Feldman, "Some Aspects," pp. 143f; and Jerome, *Letters,* XXII, 32 and LII, 6.

69. Gregory of Tours, *History of the Franks,* I, 31, trans. Lewis Thorpe, Penguin, 1974, p. 88; and Charles Thomas, *Christianity in Britain to* A.D. 500, London: Batsford, 1981, p. 155.

70. Feldman, "Some Aspects," pp. 270f.

71. Hengel, *Poverty and Riches,* pp. 81f.

72. Cf. Chadwick, *Early Christian Church,* p. 58.

73. Grant, *Early Christianity,* p. 144.

74. Chadwick, *Early Christian Church,* p. 128; Marrou in *Christian Centuries* I, pp. 236, 324f.

75. Tertullian, *Apologeticus,* XLII, 8; Grant, *Early Christianity,* Ch. 7 *passim.*

76. Basil, *Collected Letters* II, CXLII and CXLIII, pp. 347, 349.

77. Cf. Pétré, *Caritas,* p. 64.

78. Ibid., p. 355.

79. Thomas, *Christianity in Britain,* p. 77.

80. Feldman, "Some Aspects," p. 7.

81. Jean Daniélou in *Christian Centuries* I, p. 328.

82. From Michel Mollat, *Études sur L'Histoire de la Pauvreté (Moyen Age–XVIᵉ siècle),* Paris: Publications de la Sorbonne, Michel Rouche, p. 101 and Evelyne Patlangean, p. 81.

83. Boethius, *De Consolatione Philosophiae,* in *The Consolation of Philosophy,* comp. Irwin Edman, New York: Modern Library, 1943, pp. 46f and 62.

84. R. A. B. Mynors, ed., *Cassiodori Senatoris Institutiones,* Oxford University Press, 1937, pp. 79, 82.

85. *The Rule of Saint Benedict,* trans. Owen Chadwick, in *Western Asceticism,* London: S.C.M., 1958, pp. 297, 313, 316, 331, 335.

86. Gildas, *De Excidio Britonum,* LXVI passim, Philimore, 1978.

Chapter Five
Christian Poverty

1. Peter Lombard, P.L. 191, 581.

2. *Thesaurus Spiritualis Societatis Jesu,* Roehampton, 1929, pp. 115ff.

3. Martin Luther, *Table Talk,* ed. Thomas S. Kepler, Grand Rapids: Baker Book House, 1979, p. 135.

4. Dom David Knowles, *The Monastic Order in England* (M.O.E.), Cambridge University Press, 1976, pp. 219, 221.

5. R. W. Southern, *Western Society and the Church in the Middle Ages,* Penguin, 1970, p. 216.

6. *Rule of Saint Benedict,* 33, p. 314.

7. M.O.E., p. 693.

8. Bonaventure, *St. Francis,* Ch. 7, ed. Aloysius Lipomanus, Douay 1610, Menston: Scolar Press, 1972, p. 73.

9. Ibid., p. 83; cf. pp. 77, 74, 67; and cf. M. D. Lambert, *Franciscan Poverty,* London: S.P.C.K., 1961, pp. 40, 50.

10. Lambert, *Franciscan Poverty,* pp. 39, 43.; David Knowles, *The Religious Orders in England* I (R.O.E.), Cambridge University Press, 1979, p. 120.

11. Lambert, *Franciscan Poverty,* p. 127.

12. R.O.E. I, pp. 246f.

13. F. W. Maitland, *Equity,* Cambridge University Press, 1932, pp. 23 and 25, and Lambert, *Franciscan Poverty,* pp. 84, 94, 97f.

14. Ibid., Lambert, pp. 235f, and R.O.E. I, p. 248.

15. Bede, *Ecclesiastical History of the English People,* III, xxvi and IV, iii, ed. Bertram Colgrave and R. A. B. Mynors, Oxford University Press, 1969, pp. 310, 338.

16. Norman Cohn, *The Pursuit of the Millennium,* St. Albans, Herts.: Granada, 1970, p. 100, and David Hugh Farmer, *The Oxford Dictionary of Saints,* Oxford University Press, 1978, p. 295.

17. C. Thousellier, "Polémiques autour de la notion de pauvreté spirituelle," in Mollat, *Histoire de la Pauvreté,* p. 378.

18. Sulpicius Severus, *Vie de Saint Martin,* ed. Jacques Fontaine, Paris: Editions du Cerf, 1967, III, i and ii; and cf. Redmond Mullin, *Miracles and Magic,* Oxford: Mowbray, 1978, pp. 53f.

19. The Latin text is printed in Mollat, *Histoire de la Pauvreté,* pp. 432ff.

20. Cf. Cohn, *Pursuit of the Millennium,* pp. 65ff., and Gregory of Tours, *History of the Franks,* X, 25.

21. Emmanuel le Roy Ladurie, *Montaillou: The Promised Land of Error,* New York: Braziller, 1978, pp. 120, 15, 336f.

22. Walter Hilton, *The Scale of Perfection,* ed. Evelyn Underhill, Dulverton, Somerset: Watkins, 1923, pp. 3, 5.

23. *English Writings of Richard Rolle,* ed. Hope Emily Allen, Oxford University Press, 1931, pp. 94f.

24. Teresa of Avila, *The Way of Perfection,* trans. E. Allison Peers, Garden City, N.Y.: Doubleday, Image Books, 1964, p. 49.

25. *The Cloud of Unknowing,* Ch. 68, adapted from Evelyn Underhill's edition, Watkins, 1956, p. 250.

26. John of the Cross, *Llama de Amor Viva,* III, IX, and collected maxims.

27. T. S. Eliot, *Four Quartets,* Burnt Norton III, London: Faber and Faber, 1950, p. 11.

28. *The Theologia Germanica of Martin Luther,* trans. Bengt Hoffman, London: S.P.C.K., pp. 70, 79, 142.

29. Thomas à Kempis, *The Imitation of Christ,* chs. I, XIII, and LIX, in *The Consolation of Philosophy,* comp. Irwin Edman.

30. *Pearl* 62, trans. J. R. R. Tolkien; *Sir Gawain and the Green Knight, Pearl and Sir Orfeo,* Unwin Paperbacks, 1979, p. 101.

31. Owen Chadwick, *The Reformation,* Penguin, 1972, p. 18.

Chapter Six
Christian Wealth

1. Luther, *Theologia Germanica,* p. 62.

2. M.O.E., pp. 100–102.

3. Ibid., pp. 348–356.

4. Caesarius, *The Dialogue on Miracles,* trans. H. von E. Scott and C. C. Swinton Bland, London: Routledge, 1929, I, p. 264.

5. M.O.E., p. 352.

6. Printed in C. R. Cheney, *Medieval Texts and Studies,* Oxford University Press, 1973, pp. 277–284.

7. Ibid., pp. 314–327.

8. Giovanni de Parenti, *Sacrum Commercium,* 12 *De avaritia,* ed. Canon Rawnsley, London: Dent, 1934.

9. Cf. *The Latin Poems Commonly Attributed to Walter Mapes,* Camden Society, 1841.

10. William Langland, *Piers Plowman,* ed. Derek Pearsall, London: Arnold, 1978, p. 14 of his Introduction.

11. Ibid., *passus* II, 41–68 (pp. 56f); XIV, 19.

12. For discussion, cf.: Cohn, *Pursuit of the Millennium,* p. 217; R. H. Tawney, *Religion and the Rise of Capitalism,* New York: Harcourt, Brace, 1926, Penguin, 1938, p. 112; Christopher Hill, *The World Turned Upside Down,* New York: Viking, 1972, p. 124 and 283f; Gerrard Winstanley, *The Law of Freedom and Other Writings,* Penguin, 1973, pp. 85, 100, 134.

13. Cf. Hill, *World Turned,* pp. 265f., Tawney, *Religion and Capitalism,* p. 98, and E. R. Norman, *Church and Society in England 1770–1970,* Oxford University Press, 1976, p. 33.

14. Daniel Defoe, "Giving Alms no Charity" (London 1704), in *Works,* ed. John S. Keltie, Edinburgh: Nimmo, 1972.

15. Samuel Smiles, *Self-Help* (1859), centenary edition, London: John Murray, 1958, Ch. 10 *passim.*

16. Thomas Aquinas, *Summa Theologica,* II–II, LXVI, art. ii and vii.

17. Tawney, *Religion and Capitalism,* Ch. 1 *passim.*

18. Luther, *Table Talk,* pp. 88 and 101 and *To the Christian Nobility of the German Nation,* in Martin Luther, *Three Treatises,* trans. Charles M. Jacobs and James Atkinson, Philadelphia: Fortress Press, 1970, pp. 81f.

19. John Calvin, *Institutes of the Christian Religion* (1559), III, vii, 8, trans. Henry Beveridge, Grand Rapids: Eerdmans, 1957, II, pp. 13f.

20. Ibid., III, vii, 1 and 5 (II, pp. 7 and 10f).

21. Robert Nelson, *An Address to Persons of Quality* (1715), pp. 19, 125.

22. Quoted in *Early Quaker Writings 1650–1700* (E.Q.W.), ed. Hugh Barbour and Arthur O. Roberts, Grand Rapids: Eerdmans, 1973, p. 431.

23. The Koran, Sura LVII, cf. Sura IV, trans. J. M. Rodwell, Everyman Library, 1950, pp. 407, 416.

24. Thomas Aquinas, *Summa,* II–II, LXXVII, art. i and iv.

25. John Bunyan, *The Life and Death of Mr. Badman,* Everyman Library, 1956, pp. 235f, 245f, and 250f.

26. Jeremy Taylor, *Holy Living* (1650), III, iii 3, 5, 7, and 9. See *The Rule and Exercise of Holy Living,* abridged, New York: Harper & Row, 1970.

27. Martin Luther, *On Trading and Usury, Works* IV, p. 13.

28. For a schematic summary, see *The Dawn of Modern Banking,* Center of Medieval Renaissance Studys, Yale University Press, 1979, pp. 292–310.

29. The Koran, Sura II (p. 369).

30. Cf. E.Q.W., pp. 436, etc.

31. Dante, *Inferno,* Canto XVII.

32. Langland, *Piers Plowman, passus* VI, 306–308.

33. Quoted in Iona and Peter Opie, *Oxford Dictionary of Nursery Rhymes,* Oxford University Press, 1951, p. 49.

34. Hilaire Belloc, *Essays of a Catholic*, London: Sheed and Ward, 1931, "On Usury," p. 29.

35. *The Cantos of Ezra Pound,* Canto XLV, London: Faber and Faber, 1968, p. 239.

36. Cf. *The Dawn of Modern Banking,* p. 33.

37. Thomas Aquinas, *Summa,* II–II, LXXVIII, art i.

38. A. G. Dickens, *The English Reformation,* London: Collins, 1964, p. 431.

39. *Dawn of Modern Banking,* pp. 68f.

40. Ibid., p. 169.

41. Luther, *To the Christian Nobility,* in *Three Treatises,* pp. 106f; cf. Tawney, *Religion and Capitalism,* p. 115.

42. Tawney, p. 115.

43. *Dawn of Religion and Capitalism, Modern Banking,* pp. 1 and 52. The Latin *bancus* translates the Greek *trapeza,* "the bench or table where a professional banker displayed his money and his records."

44. *John Wesley: A Representative Collection of His Writings,* ed. Albert C. Outler, New York: Oxford University Press, 1964, pp. 238–250; cf. Calvin, *Institutes* III, vii, in trans. II, p. 13.

45. Hill, *World Turned,* p. 261.

46. Smiles, *Self-Help,* p. 285.

47. *To the Christian Nobility* in *Three Treatises,* pp. 105f.

48. Jacob R. Marcus, *The Jew in the Medieval World, 315–1791* (1938), New York: Atheneum, 1969, pp. 195, 194.

49. Thomas More, *Utopia* II, trans. Paul Turner, Penguin, 1965, pp. 78f.

50. Richard Rolle, "Ego Dormio," in *English Writings of Richard Rolle,* ed. Hope Emily Allen, Oxford University Press, 1931, p. 67.

51. Luther, *Table Talk,* pp. 67 and 81.

52. A. L. Maycock, *Nicholas Ferrar of Little Gidding,* Grand Rapids: Eerdmans, 1980, pp. 10f.

53. E. Q. W., pp. 438f.

54. Owen Chadwick, *The Victorian Church* II, London: Adam and Charles Black, 1966, p. 422.

55. *The Parson's Tale, De Superbia* in F. N. Robinson, *The Works of Geoffrey Chaucer,* Oxford University Press, 1957, p. 240; cf. *Piers Plowman,* XXII, 143f.

56. Cf. D. W. Robertson, Jr., *Essays in Medieval Culture,* Princeton University Press, 1980, p. 247.

57. Chaucer, *Prologue,* 193 and 262 (Robinson, p. 19); and cf. Dickens, *English Reformation,* p. 83, and Cheney, *Medieval Texts,* p. 199.

58. R.O.E. II, Ch. 5 *passim.*

59. Cf. Frederick Copleston, S.J., *A History of Philosophy,* Vol. III, *Ockham to Suarez,* London: Burns, Oates and Washbourne, 1953, Ch. 11 *passim.*

60. Adam Smith, *An Enquiry into the Nature and Causes of the Wealth of Nations* (1776), Chicago: Encyclopedia Britannica, 1955, V, iii, art 3.

61. Norman, *Church and Society in England,* p. 90, and Alexander R. Vidler, *The Church in an Age of Revolution, 1788 to the Present Day,* Penguin, 1971, p. 46.

62. Teresa of Avila, *The Way of Perfection,* in trans. p. 15.

63. Chadwick, *Victorian Church* I, p. 273.

64. Mollat, *Histoire de la Pauvreté,* p. 375.

65. From *Selection from English Wycliffite Writings* (E.W.W.), ed. Anne Hudson, Cambridge University Press, 1978, pp. 85f.

66. Taylor, *Holy Living* III, iii, 10.

67. Bede, *Ecclesiastical History,* I, xxvii, 1, p. 80; *Piers Plowman, passus* XVI, 42; More, *Utopia* I, p. 64.

68. Maycock, *Nicholas Ferrar,* p. 117.

69. Cf. Robert T. Handy, *A History of the Churches in the United States and Canada,* Oxford University Press, 1976, p. 223.

70. Chadwick, *Victorian Church* I, p. 348; cf. H. Richard Niebuhr, *Christ and Culture,* London: Faber and Faber, 1952 and Norman, *Church and Society,* p. 246.

71. Quoted in Philip N. Backstrom, *Christian Socialism and Co-operation in Victorian England,* London: Croom Helm, 1974, p. 58.

72. From *The Life of Frederick Denison Maurice, Chiefly Told in His Own Words,* ed. by his son Frederick Maurice, London: Macmillan, 1884, Vol. II, p. 35.

73. Ibid., pp. 106f.

74. Backstrom, *Christian Socialism, passim.*

75. Charles E. Raven, *Christian Socialism 1848–1854,* London: Cass, 1968, pp. 10, 14.

76. Backstrom, *Christian Socialism,* pp. 64, 197, 325, 343.

77. Raven, *Christian Socialism 1848–1854,* pp. 325, 343.

78. Karl Marx and Friedrich Engels, *The Communist Manifesto,* trans. Samuel Moore, Penguin, 1967, p. 108.

79. Hill, *World Turned,* pp. 46, 92f, 106f; and Winstanley, *The Law of Freedom,* pp. 43, 120, 133, 137 etc.

80. Cf. Cohn, *Pursuit of the Millennium,* p. 199; E.W.W., p. 117; *Piers Plowman, passus* IV, 114 and 115; Priscilla Heath Barnum, ed., *Dives and Pauper* IV, Early English Text Society, 1976, viii; Niebuhr, *Christ and Culture,* p. 73.

81. Cf. Cohn, *Pursuit of the Millennium,* p. 330.

Chapter Seven
Christian Philanthropy

1. B. S. Rowntree, *Poverty, a Study of Town Life* (1901), New York: Garland, 1980, pp. 167–172.

2. Ladurie, *Montaillou,* p. 123.

3. C. F. Pascoe, *Two Hundred Years of the S.P.G., 1701–1900* (S.P.G.), London: S.P.G., 1901, p. 263.

4. Kathleen Heasman, *Evangelicals in Action,* London: Bles, 1962, p. 33.

5. Cf. F. K. Prochaska, *Women and Philanthropy in 19th Century England,* Oxford University Press, 1980, pp. 42f.

6. Barnum, *Dives and Pauper* I, "Holy Poverty," A, i, p. 51.

7. *Piers Plowman, passus* XIV, 13 and 14.

8. Luther, *Theologia Germanica,* Ch. 56 and Ch. 22, cf. Ch. 19 and Ch. 55, pp. 149, 89, 85, and 147.

9. Cf. Frank Barlow, ed., *Vita Edwardi Regis,* Sunbury-on-Thames, Middlesex: Nelson, 1962, p. 44; Rotha Mary Cray, *The Medieval Hospitals of England,* London: Cass, 1966, Ch. VI.

10. Cf. S.P.G., and W. K. Lowther Clarke, *A History of the S.P.C.K.* (S.P.C.K.) London: S.P.C.K., 1959, *passim.*

11. Joel T. Rosenthall, *The Purchase of Paradise: The Social Function of Aristocratic Benevolence 1307–1485,* London: Routledge & Kegan Paul, 1972, p. 8.

12. Luther, *To the Christian Nobility,* in *Three Treatises,* p. 86.

13. Bede, *Ecclesiastical History* I, xxvii, p. 80; cf. Mollat, *Histoire de la Pauvreté* I, p. 86.

14. From John Johnson, *A Collection of the Laws and Canons of the Church of England* I, Parker, 1950, p. 196; R.O.E. I, pp. 287f. and M.O.E., p. 484.

15. Henry Kraus, *Gold Was the Mortar, The Economics of Cathedral Building,* London: Routledge & Kegan Paul, 1979, p. 147 and *passim.*

16. From Cray, *Mediaeval Hospitals,* p. 82.

17. Cf. Dickens, *The English Reformation,* pp. 106 and 431ff.

18. M. G. Jones, *The Charity School Movement,* London: Cass, 1964, pp. 12f.

19. For a summary account, see Richard Cornuelle, *Brief Interpretative History of America's Voluntary Sector,* United Way, 1978.

20. Owen Chadwick, *The Reformation,* Penguin, 1972, pp. 228f; Gerald R. Cragg, *The Church and the Age of Reason 1648–1789,* Penguin, 1970, pp. 141f; Vidler, *Church in Age of Revolution,* pp. 37 and 39.

21. S.P.G., p. 649; Tawney, *Religion and Capitalism,* p. 89; Mollat, *Histoire de la Pauvreté,* p. 785; and Francis James Child, *The English and Scottish Popular Ballads* III, New York: Dover, 1965, p. 213.

22. Hill, *World Turned,* p. 86.

23. Toulmin Smith and Lujo Brentano, *English Gilds,* Early English Text Society reprint, 1963, p. 50, and P. A. S. Pool, *The History of the Town and Borough of Penzance,* Corporation of Penzance, 1974.

24. *Dawn of Modern Banking,* p. 21, and J. R. Tanner, *Tudor Constitutional Documents* A.D. 1485–1603, Cambridge University Press, 1930, pp. 482f.

25. Cf. Cornuelle, *America's Voluntary Sector,* and Carlo M. Cipolla, *Cristofano and the Plague,* London: Collins, 1973, *passim.*

26. G. R. Owst, *Preaching in Medieval England c. 1350–1450,* New York: Russell and Russell, 1965, pp. 102 and 108.

27. Kraus, *Gold Was the Mortar,* p. 108.

28. E.W.W., p. 88.

29. Eadmer, *The Life of St. Anselm, Archbishop of Canterbury,* trans. and ed. R. W. Southern, Oxford at the Clarendon Press, 1962 and New York: Oxford University Press, 1963, p. 147.

30. Smith and Brentano, *English Gilds,* p. 374 and Tanner, *Tudor Documents,* p. 495.

31. Frederick J. Furnivall, *The Fifty Earliest English Wills,* Early English Text Society reprint, 1964, p. 71.

32. Cf. Helen M. Jewell, *English Local Administration in the Middle Ages,* Newton Abbey, Devon: David & Charles, 1972, p. 189.

33. Richard Gough, *The History of Myddle* (1834), Penguin, 1981, pp. 30–32.

34. Smith and Brentano, *English Gilds,* p. 249.

35. G. M. Trevelyan, *English Social History,* Penguin, 1980, pp. 334f.

36. *Report of the Charity Commissioners for England and Wales,* 1975, p. 18.

37. Hill, *World Turned,* p. 105; and Winstanley, *Law of Freedom,* p. 75, from those "Beginning to Plant and Manure the Waste Land upon George Hill, in the Parish of Walton, in the County of Surrey."

38. Mollat, *Histoire de la Pauvreté,* p. 745.

39. E.W.W., pp. 84–88; Smith and Brentano, *English Gilds,* pp. 166, 169; Furnivall, *Earliest Wills, passim.*

40. Furnivall, *Earliest Wills,* pp. 58f and 98.

41. *Piers Plowman, passus* IX, 21–36, p. 162; Hubert Picarda, *The Law and Practice Relating to Charities,* Sevenoaks, Kent: Butterworths, 1977, p. 8.

42. Printed in N. F. Blake, *Middle English Religious Prose,* York Medieval Texts, 1972, p. 82.

43. Ibid., p. 142.

44. "Hávámal" 2 and 3 in *Edda, Die Lieder des Codex Regius,* ed. Hans Kuhn, Heidelberg, 1962, p. 17.

45. Tanner, *Tudor Documents,* p. 491.

46. Ibid.

47. Smith and Brentano, *English Gilds,* p. 228.

48. E.Q.W., pp. 493 and 88.

49. Calvin, *Institutes* II, viii, 55, in tran. I, p. 359.

50. Hill, *World Turned,* p. 272.

51. Tanner, *Tudor Documents,* p. 489, and Dickens, *English Reformation,* p. 67.

52. *The Journal of George Fox,* ed. John L. Nickalls, Religious Society of Friends, 1975, Ch. XV, pp. 348f; Penn's Preface to the 1694 edition, p. xv.

53. G. R. Elton, ed., *The Reformation 1520–1559,* Cambridge University Press, 1975, p. 603, and S.P.G., *passim.*

54. S.P.G., p. 548, and Vidler, *Church in Age of Revolution,* p. 233.

55. In *A Documentary History of the Jews in the United States 1654–1875,* ed. Morris U. Schappes, New York: Schocken, 1971, pp. 273–277.

56. "Hávámal," in *Edda,* p. 29.

57. Ladurie, *Montaillou,* p. 327.

58. Rosenthall, *Pursuit of Paradise,* pp. 126, 130.

59. Alexander Pope, *Moral Essays: Epistle to Bathurst,* pp. 248–298.

60. From "Charity" by William Cowpar.

61. Cf. Kraus, *Gold Was the Mortar,* pp. 179f.

62. *Piers Plowman, passus* III, 50–54, pp. 67f.

63. Caesarius, *Dialogue on Miracles* I, p. 271.

64. Luther, *Table Talk,* pp. 193f.; cf. Caesarius, *Dialogue on Miracles* I, p. 271.

65. "Hávámal," 41, in *Edda,* p. 23: *vidrgefendr oc endrgefendr erost lengst vinir.*

66. Johnson, *Laws and Canons* I, pp. 255, 341.

67. Caesarius, *Dialogue on Miracles,* I, p. 272.

68. Furnivall, *Earliest Wills,* p. 78.

69. Cf. Rosenthall, *Purchase of Paradise,* p. 101; Kraus, *Gold Was the Mortar,* p. 102; Furnivall, *Earliest Wills,* p. 101.

70. Cray, *Mediaeval Hospitals,* p. 82, and Furnivall, *Earliest Wills,* p. 117.

71. Tawney, *Religion and Capitalism,* p. 61.

72. Bernard, *In Annunciatione* I; Calvin, *Institutes* III, ii, 41, in trans. I, p. 505.

73. Luther, *Three Treatises,* p. 309; *Table Talk,* pp. 93f.; and cf. Gerhard Ebeling, *Luther,* London: Collins, 1975.

74. *Select Sermons of George Whitefield,* The Banner of Truth Trust, 1958, p. 75.

75. Cecil Torr, *Small Talk at Wreyland* (1918), Oxford University Press, 1979, p. 3.

76. Gillian Wagner, *Barnardo,* London: Eyre and Spottiswoode, 1979, pp. 30ff.; John A. Groom, *The Romance of the John Groom's Crippleage and Flower Girls' Mission,* 1866–1919, p. 3.

77. Sir Thomas Browne, *Religio Medici* II, in Edman, *Consolation of Philosophy;* cf. Terence, *homo sum: humani nil a me alienum puto.*

78. Speros Vryonis, Jr., *The Decline of Medieval Hellenism in Asia Minor and the Process of Islamization from the Eleventh through the Fifteenth Century,* Berkeley: University of California Press, 1971, p. 358.

79. Hill, *World Turned,* p. 87; and Michael Chesterman, *Charities, Trusts and Social Welfare,* London: Weidenfeld & Nicholson, 1979, p. 50.

80. S.P.G., pp. 297–299.

81. Luther, *Three Treatises,* pp. 294f.

82. Quoted in Prochaska, *Women and Philanthropy,* p. 201.

83. *Journal of George Fox,* p. 35.

84. Maimonides, *Guide for the Perplexed,* Ch. LIII, pp. 292f.

85. Maimonides, *Mishneh Torah* VII, 10, quoted in *A Maimonides Reader,* ed. Isadore Twersky, New York: Behrman House, 1972, pp. 136f.

86. *Piers Plowman, passus* IX, 63, p. 164.

87. Calvin, *Institutes* III, vii, 6, in trans. II, p. 11.

88. *Journal of George Fox,* p. 111; and cf. Cohn, *Pursuit of the Millennium,* p. 327.

89. *Piers Plowman, passus* VIII, 224, p. 155.

90. Child, *Popular Ballads,* p. 161.

91. More, *Utopia,* p. 61; cf. Hill, *World Turned,* p. 32.

92. Text given in Tanner, *Tudor Documents*, p. 77.

93. Ibid., p. 470; More, *Utopia*, p. 55; Tawney, *Religion and Capitalism*, p. 267.

94. Luther, *Table Talk*, p. 101.

95. William Edward Hartpole Lecky, *History of European Morals from Augustus to Charlemagne* II, London: Longmans, Green, 1894, p. 91.

96. Malthus, *An Essay of the Principle of Population*, Ch. V, and *A Summary View of the Principle of Population*, ed. Anthony Flew, Penguin, 1970, pp. 96, 98, and 270.

97. Cf. Mollat, *Histoire de la Pauvreté*, pp. 110, 768, and Chesterman, *Charities, Trusts*, pp. 14ff.

98. *The Poor*, ed. Elizabeth Melling, Kentish Sources IV, Kent County Council, 1964, p. 71.

99. Gough, *Myddle*, p. 260; Melling, *The Poor*, p. 123; Nicholas Toke of Godington, *Five Letters on the State of the Poor in the County of Kent* (1770), p. 47.

100. Chadwick, *The Victorian Church* I, p. 347.

101. Sir F. Younghusband, *Inter Racial Relations* (1910), quoted in Donald Read, *Documents from Edwardian England 1901-1915*, London: Harrap, 1973, pp. 173f.

102. G. M. Young, *Portrait of an Age, Victorian England*, annotated by George Kitson Clark, Oxford University Press, 1977, p. 30.

103. David Owen, *English Philanthropy 1660-1960*, Harvard University Press, 1964, pp. 215, 221.

104. Heasman, *Evangelicals in Action*, pp. 12, 22; Owen, *English Philanthropy*, p. 219.

105. Cf. Owen, *English Philanthropy*, p. 228.

106. Quoted in Kathleen Woodroofe, *From Charity to Social Work in England and the United States*, London: Routledge & Kegan Paul, 1974, p. 31.

107. *Piers Plowman, passus* XVI, 18 and 19, p. 261; *passus* IV, 105-120, pp. 165f.

Chapter Eight
Christian Charitable Organization

1. Redmond Mullin, *Present Alms, on the Corruption of Philanthropy*, Phlogiston, 1980, p. 3.

2. Smith and Brentano, *English Gilds*, pp. 169, 425.

3. Marcus, *The Jew in the Medieval World*, p. 206.

4. Mollat, *Histoire de la Pauvreté*, pp. 166f.

5. Cf. Moses Maimonides, *The Commandments* I: *Positive Commandments*, trans. Charles B. Chavel, Soncino Press, 1967, p. 195; *Mishneh Torah* IX, 3 quoted in commentary, p. 210.

6. Marcus, *The Jew in the Medieval World*, pp. 206f, 219.

7. Smith and Brentano, *English Gilds*, pp. xiv, xv.

8. There is a fine one in the London Museum, and see W. E. Tate, *The Parish Chest*, Cambridge University Press, 1979, pp. 35-42.

9. Smith and Brentano, *English Gilds*, pp. 271, 319, 137, 319.

10. Cheney, *Medieval Texts*, pp. 359f.

11. Smith and Brentano, *English Gilds*, pp. 164, 181, 8, 23, 29, 156f. and 183.

12. Luther, *Three Treatises*, p. 84; Elton, *Reformation 1520-1559*, p. 166; Dickens, *The English Reformation*, pp. 285f, 295.

13. Tanner, *Tudor Documents*, pp. 480f.

14. Mollat, *Histoire de la Pauvreté*, pp. 788ff.

15. Ibid., Michel Rouche on the *matricula pauperum* and pp. 224f.

16. R. W. Southern, *Western Society and the Church in the Middle Ages*, Penguin, 1970, pp. 224, 228; M.O.E., p. 175; Cragg, *Church and Age of Reason*, p. 568.

17. M.O.E., p. 85; Dickens, *English Reformation*, p. 84.

18. Redmond Mullin, "The Evidence for Miracles," in *Mysteries of the World*, Lyric, 1979, pp. 75ff.; Mollat, *Histoire de la Pauvreté*, p. 590 etc.; Kraus, *Gold Was the Mortar*, p. 57.

19. Dickens, *English Reformation*, p. 294; Cray, *Mediaeval Hospitals*, p. 236.

20. Cray, *Mediaeval Hospitals*, p. 237.

21. Dickens, *English Reformation*, pp. 341f.; Hill, *World Turned*, p. 240; Cipollo, *Cristofano*, pp. 45f., where Cipolla states that the pay for a community doctor in Prato about 1630 was 700 lira; additionally, they could earn from private practice, and were given 126 lira annually as a housing allowance.

22. Quoted in Heasman, *Evangelicals in Action*, p. 294.

23. Young, *Portrait of an Age*, p. 24.

24. Some general references: Israel Sieff, *Memoirs*, London: Weidenfeld & Nicholson, 1970; Benedict Nightingale, *Charities*, Penguin, 1973; Carl Bakal, *Charity U.S.A.*, New York: New York Times Books, 1979; Owen, *English Philanthropy*, *passim*

25. Woodroofe, *From Charity to Social Work*, p. 143.

26. Norman, *Church and Society in England*, pp. 42, 123.

27. Cf. Michel Pomey, *Traité des Fondations d'Utilité Publique*, Paris: Presses Universitaires de France, 1980. p. 35.

28. Frances Finnegan, *Poverty and Prostitution, A Study of Victorian Prostitutes in York*, Cambridge University Press, 1979, pp. 173f., 210f.

29. Wagner, *Barnardo*, p. 267.

30. *People and Events, A History of United Way*, United Way of America, 1977, pp. 21f.

31. Chadwick, *The Victorian Church* I, p. 97.

32. Melling, *The Poor*, pp. 91, 97, 101; Toke, *The Poor in Kent*, passim.

33. Toke, *The Poor in Kent*, pp. 46f.

34. Wagner, *Barnardo*, p. 84.

35. S.P.G., pp. x, 195.

36. Handy, *Churches in U.S. and Canada*, pp. 278f.

37. Jones, *Charity School Movement*, p. 9.

38. Elton, *The Reformation 1520–1559*, pp. 211, 229f., 296f.

39. Hill, *World Turned*, pp. 241ff.

40. See Jones, *Charity School Movement*.

41. Chadwick, *Victorian Church* I, pp. 338f.; Heasman, *Evangelicals in Action*, p. 294.

Chapter Nine
Finance and Fundraising

1. Cheney, *Medieval Texts,* p. 196; Johnson's *Canons* for A.D. 1064, p. 524; Eric J. Evans, *The Contentious Tithe, The Tithe Problem and English Agriculture 1750 to 1850*, London, Routledge & Kegan Paul, 1976, *passim*.

2. E.W.W., p. 19.

3. Cf. Elton, *Reformation 1520–1559*, pp. 137, 226f.

4. Cragg, *Church and Age of Reason*, p. 62.

5. *Journal of George Fox*, p. 394.

6. E.Q.W., p. 553.

7. Thomas Richards, *The Puritan Movement in Wales, 1639 to 1653*, National Eisteddfod Asssociation, 1970, p. 164.

8. Cowper's dedication: "Verses addressed to a country Clergyman, complaining of the disagreeableness of the day annually appointed for receiving the dues at the parsonage"; cf. Trevelyan, *English Social History*, p. 527.

9. In Tanner, *Tudor Documents*, p. 77.

10. Dickens, *The English Reformation*, p. 421; Evans, *Contentious Tithe*, pp. 18, 144, 84f, 164, 166.

11. Vidler, *Church in Age of Revolution*, pp. 174, 177.

12. *Edinburgh Review* 26 (1861): 276–81, quoted in Evans, *Contentious Tithe*, p. 87; and E.Q.W., p. 271; Mollat, *Histoire de la Pauvreté*, p. 113.

13. Kraus, *Gold Was the Mortar*, p. 43; James Parkes, *The Jew in the Medieval Community*, Soncino, 1938, pp. 111, 116, 233f.

14. *Dawn of Modern Banking*, p. 146.

15. R.O.E. III, p. 162.

16. Tanner, *Tudor Documents*, p. 104.

17. Chadwick, *The Reformation*, p. 109.

18. Smith, *Wealth of Nations*, V, iii, art. 12.

19. E.Q.W., p. 26.

20. Quoted in Evans, *Contentious Tithe*, p. 106, cf. p. 97.

21. Cf. S.P.G., p. 161ff; Handy, *Churches in U.S. and Canada*, pp. 123f, 240, 245ff.

22. Cf. Prochashka, *Women and Philanthropy*, pp. 45ff.

23. "How a Cathedral Was Built in the Fourteenth Century," *Downside Review*, July 1893, pp, 145ff, and Edmund Bishop, *Liturgica Historica* (1918), trans. Charles M. Jacobs amd James Atkinson, Philadelphia: Fortress Press, 1970, pp. 411–421.

24. Cray, *Mediaeval Hospitals*, pp. 182f.

25. Bishop Stephan (1174), Ep. VIII, IX, P.L. 211, 318, 319.

26. Kraus, *Gold Was the Mortar*, p. 43; and cf. Benedicta Ward, *Miracles and the Medieval Mind: Theory, Record and Event, 1000–1215*, Menston: Scolar, 1982, pp. 134f.

27. Cheney, *Medieval Texts*, p. 350 etc.; Mullin, *Miracles and Magic*, pp. 132ff.

28. *Piers Plowman*, prologue 66–80; *Canterbury Tales*, Pardoner's Prologue, 448–451, in *The Works of Geoffrey Chaucer*, ed. F. N. Robertson, Oxford University Press, 1957, p. 149.

29. Owst, *Preaching in Medieval England*, 103f; Kraus, *Gold Was the Mortar*, p. 142.

30. M.O.E., p. 369, Johannis de Oxenedes, *Chronica*, s.a. 1210; Matthew Paris, *Historia Anglorum*, A.D. 1247, where they are said to have raised funds after many *disceptationes* (arguments or discussions), or *deceptationes* (deceptions); there is a play on words or an ambiguously corrupt text; cf. Owst, *Preaching*, p. 80.

31. See Elton, *Reformation 1520–1559*, pp. 76f; Chadwick, *The Reformation*, pp. 41ff.

32. Dickens, *English Reformation*, p. 94.

33. E.W.W., p. 26, and Tanner, *Tudor Documents*, p. 76; Aquinas had said that there was no simony if payment for indulgences promoted spiritual ends, for example defeating the church's enemies, building churches or bridges, etc. (Supplement to *Summa*, III, q. 25, a.3).

34. Calvin, *Institues,* III, v, 2.

35. Luther, *The Babylonian Captivity of the Church* and *To the Christian Nobility*, in *Three Treatises*, pp. 152, 31, 77, 59.

36. Bishop, *Liturgica Historica*.

37. Cray, *Mediaeval Hospitals*, Ch. III; Kraus, *Gold Was the Mortar*, p. 189.

38. Tanner, *Tudor Documents*, p. 480.

39. Toke, *The Poor in Kent*, p. 28; Jones, *Charity School Movement*, p. 229; Trevelyan, *English Social History*, p. 447.

40. S.P.G., pp. 2f; Stephen Neill, *A History of the Christian Missions*, Penguin, 1964, pp. 399f.; *Journal of George Fox*, p. xlv.

41. E.Q.W., pp. 452-469.

42. Jones, *Charity School Movement*, p. 58; S.P.G., p. 127.

43. *Charity School Movement*, pp. 59f. and John Groom, *Groom's Crippleage*, p. 11.

44. William Blake, *Poetry and Prose*, Nonesuch Library, London: Bodley Head, 1975, p. 59; but contrast the balancing "Song of Experience":

> Is this a holy thing to see
>> In a rich and fruitful land
> Babes reduc'd to misery,
>> Fed with cold usurious hands?

45. Heasman, *Evangelicals in Action*, pp. 225f. and Owen, *English Philanthropy*, p. 178.

46. S.P.G., pp. 53, 783, 649, 742.

47. Cray, *Mediaeval Hospitals*, p. 187.

48. S.P.G., pp. 824f.

49. Prochaska, *Women and Philanthropy*, p. 51.

50. Ibid., p. 25.

51. Ibid., p. 61.

52. Cheney, *Medieval Texts*, pp. 359f; S.P.C.K., pp. 88f.

53. Owen, *English Philanthropy*, pp. 481f.

54. Prochaska, *Women and Philanthropy*, Ch. I and III.

55. Bernard Arens, *Manuel des Missions Catholiques*, Editions du Museum Lessianum, 1925, pp. 272, 228.

56. Owen, *English Philanthropy*, pp. 480f.

57. Pepys was among those who complained against them.

58. Harold J. Seymour, *Designs for Fund-Raising*, New York: McGraw-Hill, 1966, p. 173 and Redmond Mullin, *The Fundraising Handbook*, Glasgow, Mowbray, 1976, p. 96.

59. Owen, *English Philanthropy*, p. 48; Prochaska, *Women and Philanthropy*, pp. 60f; Jones, *Charity School Movement*, pp. 120f; Tate, *Parish Chest*, p. 121.

60. Wagner, *Barnardo*, p. 304.

61. Nancy Garton, *George Müller and His Orphans*, Sevenoaks, Kent: Hodder & Stoughton, 1963, p. 45; cf. A. T. Pierson, *George Müller of Bristol*, Glasgow: Pickering & Inglis, 1972; Mullin, *Miracles and Magic*, pp. 87f.

62. S.P.G., pp. 545, 195; Neill, *Christian Missions*, p. 521.

63. Kraus, *Gold Was the Mortar*, p. 142.

64. S.P.C.K., p. 36.

Chapter Ten
The Present Situation and Conclusions

1. Charles Raw, Bruce Page, and Godfrey Hodgson, *Do You Sincerely Want to Be Rich?*, Penguin, 1972, p. 80.

2. *North-South, a Programme for Survival*, London: Pan, 1980, p. 49.

3. *Common Crisis North South: Co-operation for World Recovery*, London: Pan, 1983, pp. 1, 80f and 152–159.

4. Peter Townsend, *Poverty in the United Kingdom*, Penguin, 1979, p. 88.

5. *Family Expenditure Survey*, H.M.S.O., 1978; Eileen Evason, *Ends That Won't Meet*, 1980; *Social and Economic Trends in Northern Ireland*, No. 6, H.M.S.O., 1980.

6. Townsend, *Poverty in UK*, p. 558.

7. Redmond Mullin, "The Roles of Private Funding in the Context of International Voluntary Activity," *Associations Transnationales* 4 (1980): 176–179.

8. Cf. *Giving U.S.A.*, American Association of Fund-Raising Counsel, and *Charity Statistics*, published by the Charities Aid Foundation.

9. Based on *Charity Statistics* 1980/81.

10. Based on *Giving U.S.A.*, Robert Baird, *Religion in America*, New York: Harper, 1856, and *Charity Statistics* 1978/79.

11. Susanna Hoe, *The Man Who Gave His Company Away*, London: Heinemann, 1978, pp. 123f. and 133.

12. *Associations Transnationales.*

13. David Sheppard, *Bias to the Poor*, Sevenoaks, Kent: Hodder & Stoughton, 1983, p. 140.

14. Cf. the work of John Posnett and Mark Austin from the Institute of Social and Economic Research and Department of Economics, University of York.

15. Notes from Andy Benson's contribution to the South East London Consortium's debate, October 9, 1980 on "The Politics of Funding," opposing views expressed in *Present Alms*.

16. Tony Benn, *Arguments for Socialism*, ed. Chris Mullin, Penguin, 1980, p. 28.

17. See Mullin, *Present Alms* and *The Fundraising Handbook*.

18. *Present Alms*. p. 8.

19. Cf. my commentary in *Charity Statistics* 1977/78, p. 4.

20. *Present Alms*, p. 34 and notes.

21. *Giving U.S.A.*

22. Cf. *The Challenge of Philanthropy*, published by the Wells group.

23. *Training Visitors*, p. 9, and E. J. N. Wallis, *Explaining Christian Stewardship*, p. 18, both from the Church Information Office.

24. In *Jesus, Dollars and Sense: An Effective Stewardship Guide for Clergy and Lay Leaders*, ed. Oscar C. Carr, Jr., New York: Seabury, 1976, p. 58.

25. *Christian Stewardship*, Diocese of Owerri, Nigeria, p. 28.

26. From *Welfare Services, Helping Others to Help Themselves*, and *Charitable Giving Practices of Members of the Church of Latter-Day Saints*, Salt Lake City, Utah, Church of Latter-Day Saints.

27. Ernst Fischer, *Marx in His Own Words*, trans. Anna Bostock, Penguin, 1970, pp. 84, 168.

28. Karl Marx, *The Grundrisse*, trans. and ed. David McLellan, New York: Harper & Row, 1972, Macmillan, 1980, pp. 74f and 85f.

29. Ibid., p. 89.

30. Ibid., p. 133.

31. Fischer, *Marx in His Words*, p. 35.

32. Marx, *The Grundrisse*, pp. 105, 108f.

33. Ibid., pp. 140, 151, 159f., 117, 163.

34. Ibid., p. 161.

35. Fischer, *Marx in His Words*, p. 27; Marx and Engels, *Communist Manifesto*, p. 96; Fischer, p. 82; *Manifesto*, pp. 113f.

36. Leo XIII, *Rerum novarum* (1891), New York: Paulist Press, pp. 4-5, 21, 5, 23, 28, 12, 27, 5, 29, 18.

37. Pius XI, *Quadragesimo anno* (1931), New York: America Press, 1938, pp. 33, 40, 41, 13, 16, 17, 26, 2 (at Downside in the 1950s certain passages conferred a special glow on social studies, which included a critical review of the *Communist Manifesto*): 45; 53; 57; 11 and 136; cf. 51; 137 and 4.

38. Niebuhr, *Christ and Culture*, p. 79.

39. John Paul II, *Laborem exercens* (1981), Boston: St. Paul Editions, pp. 44, 23, 18, 29, 31, 35, 36, 37, 49, 35.

40. Ibid, p. 9.

41. William Temple, *Christianity and Social Order*, London: S.P.C.K., 1976, pp. 41, 88, 85, 97, 112, 102, 197, 101.

42. Ivan Illich, *Tools for Conviviality*, London: Calder & Boyars, 1973, pp. 110, 11,12, 10.

43. George McRobie, *Small is Possible*, London: Jonathan Cape, 1981, p. 77.

44. E.F. Schumacher, *Small Is Beautiful: Economics as if People Mattered*, New York: Harper & Row, 1973, p. 153.

45. McRobie, *Small is Possible*, p. 3.

46. Ivan Illich, *Celebration of Awareness*, Penguin, 1973, p. 18; New York: Harper & Row, 1980.

47. E. F. Schumacher, *A Guide for the Perplexed*, New York: Harper & Row, 1959, London: Jonathan Cape, 1977, p. 153.

48. McRobie, *Small is Possible*, p. 130.

49. John V. Taylor, *Enough is Enough: A Biblical Call for Moderation in a Consumer-Oriented Society*, Minneapolis: Augsburg, 1977, pp. 107f.

50. J. Andrew Kirk, *Liberation Theology, an Evangelical View from the Third World*, Atlanta: John Knox Press, 1979, p. 204.

51. José P. Miranda, *Marx and the Bible: A Critique of the Philosophy of Oppression*, Maryknoll, N.Y., Orbis Books, 1974, p. 255.

52. Gustavo Gutiérrez, *A Theology of Liberation*, Maryknoll, N.Y., Orbis Books, 1973, pp. x, 151, 198, 204f.

53. Miranda, *Marx and the Bible*, p. xv.

54. Gutiérrez, *Theology of Liberation*, pp. 26f, 276.

55. Miranda, *Marx and the Bible*, pp. 127, 19.

56. Gutiérrez, *Theology of Liberation*, pp. 55, 261.

57. Miranda, *Marx and the Bible*, pp. 250, 277, etc.

58. Kirk, *Liberation Theology, an Evangelical View*, p. 165.

59. Miranda, *Marx and the Bible*, pp. 254-255 (he quotes Pierre Bigo, *Marxismo y Humanismo* at pp. 258f).

60. Jürgen Moltmann, *The Experiment Hope*, Philadelphia: Fortress Press, 1975.

61. Nicholas Lash, *A Matter of Hope: A Theologian's Reflections on the Thought of Karl Marx*, London: Darton, Longman & Todd, 1981, pp. 288f.

62. Karl Barth, *Church Dogmatics*, trans. G. W. Bromiley, selected by Helmut Gollwitzer, Edinburgh, T. and T. Clark, 1961, pp. 96-110 (IV, 2, pp. 171-180 of the standard edition).

63. *The Times*, Tuesday, February 23, 1982.

64. Leader, *The Times*, March 1, 1982.

65. My arguments are set out at length in *Present Alms*.

66. Pierre Teilhard de Chardin, *The Phenomenon of Man*, New York: Harper & Row, 1959, pp. 291-293.

67. A. J. Krailsheimer, *Conversion*, London: S.C.M., 1980, pp. 1, 5.

Index